MW00576178

SCREEN SHOTS

Stanford Studies *in* Middle Eastern
and Islamic Societies *and* Cultures

SCREEN SHOTS

State Violence on Camera in Israel and Palestine

Rebecca L. Stein

STANFORD UNIVERSITY PRESS
Stanford, California

Stanford University Press
Stanford, California

© 2021 by the Board of Trustees of the Leland Stanford Junior University.
All rights reserved.

No part of this book may be reproduced or transmitted in any form or by any
means, electronic or mechanical, including photocopying and recording, or
in any information storage or retrieval system without the prior written permission of Stanford University Press.

Printed in the United States of America on acid-free, archival-quality paper

Library of Congress Cataloging-in-Publication Data

Names: Stein, Rebecca L., author.
Title: Screen shots : state violence on camera in Israel and Palestine /
    Rebecca L. Stein.
Other titles: Stanford studies in Middle Eastern and Islamic societies and
    cultures.
Description: Stanford, California : Stanford University Press, 2021. |
    Series: Stanford studies in Middle Eastern and Islamic societies and
    cultures | Includes bibliographical references and index.
Identifiers: LCCN 2020048598 (print) | LCCN 2020048599 (ebook) | ISBN
    9781503614970 (cloth) | ISBN 9781503628021 (paperback) | ISBN
    9781503628038 (ebook)
Subjects: LCSH: Arab-Israeli conflict—1993—Photography. | Arab-Israeli
    conflict—1993—Mass media and the conflict. | Documentary
    photography—Political aspects—Israel. | Documentary
    photography—Political aspects—Palestine. | Video recordings—Political
    aspects—Israel. | Video recordings—Political aspects—Palestine. |
    Political violence—Israel. | Political violence—Palestine.
Classification: LCC DS119.76 .S7985 2021 (print) | LCC DS119.76 (ebook) |
    DDC 956.9405/5—dc23
LC record available at https://lccn.loc.gov/2020048598
LC ebook record available at https://lccn.loc.gov/2020048599

Cover design: Rob Ehle
Cover illustration: Silhouette made from photo of an Israeli soldier blocking
photographers, May 16, 1998. Reuters Pictures.

Contents

Acknowledgments

I DEVELOPED THIS BOOK IN A WIDE RANGE OF LECTURES, WORK-shops, working groups, and classrooms over the last decade, and critical engagement by colleagues and friends in these settings was crucial to its development. Particular thanks to: Diana Allan, Miriyam Aouragh, Ariella Azoulay, Joel Beinin, Robert Blecher, Carlo Caduff, Gabriella Coleman, Hilla Dayan, Maria José A. de Abreu, Donatella della Ratta, Alex Dent, Eitan Diamond, Elle Flanders, Erella Grassiani, Derek Gregory, Inderpal Grewal, Waleed Hazbun, Charles Hirschkind, Gil Hochberg, Amy Kaplan, Caren Kaplan, Chris Kelty, Caroline Libresco, Penny Mitchell, Rosalind Morris, Negar Mottahedeh, Issam Nassar, Sayed Qashou, Shira Robinson, Noa Roei, Rona Sela, Patricia Spyer, Sophia Stamatopoulou-Robbins, Miriam Ticktin, Nancy Updike, Erika Weinthal, Laura Wexner, Annabel Wharton, Nadia Yaqub, and Janine Zacharia. I am especially indebted to Amahl Bishara and Alejandro Paz for their sharp and generous readings; to Zeynep Gürsel for her friendship and feedback through the long life of this project; to Omri Grinberg for years of critical acumen and invaluable research assistance; to Adi Kuntsman for the enriching collaborative work on *Digital Militarism: Israel's Occupation in the Social Media Age* (Stanford University Press, 2015), co-written while *Screen Shots* was being researched. Chapter 3 is particularly indebted to our collaboration.

My thanks to those institutions, communities, and individuals in Israel and Palestine, including many dear friends, who supported this project in numerous ways over the course of this research, many of whom wish to remain anonymous. At B'Tselem, particular thanks are due to Itamar Barak, Yoav Gross, Sarit Michael, Jessica Montell, Ehab Tarabieh, and Helen Yanovsky for their generous engagement with this project. Additional thanks to Ra'anan Aleandrowicz, Guy Butavia, Munir Fakher Eldin, Dror Etkes, Channah Green, Avner Gvaryahu, Rema Hammami, Yariv Horowitz, Rachel Leah Jones, Yaakov Katz, Dina Kraft, Miki Kratsman, Rela Mazali, Allegra Pacheco, David Reeb, David Schulman, Ido Sela, Yehudah Shaul—and to additional colleagues at Breaking the Silence and Activestills.

Special thanks to Kate Wahl at Stanford University Press for editorial skill and care in seeing this manuscript to completion; to Caroline McKusick for enthusiastic guidance; and to two anonymous readers on the book manuscript whose constructive comments proved crucial in revisions. Many thanks to Michelle Woodward whose keen eyes, as photography editor, greatly enriched this book.

I would like to thank my colleagues in the Cultural Anthropology Department at Duke University for fostering such a supportive and collegial environment. Their capacious vision of anthropological scholarship and commitment was instrumental in making this book possible. Particular thanks to Harris Solomon and Anne Allison for friendship, lunch-time advice, and astute interventions. The sharp insights of Duke graduate students proved crucial: Brenna Casey, Anna Dowell, Sophia Goodfriend, Jake Silver, and Alex Strecker. Thanks, as well, to students who provided research assistance: Lama Hamtash, Hannah Kaplon, Yael Lazar, Nir Schnaiderman, and Mackenzie Zapeda.

The research and writing of this book were generously supported by the American Council of Learned Societies Fellowship Program and by a grant from the Wenner-Gren Foundation. Additional support was provided by the Palestinian American Research Center, the Josiah Charles Trent Memorial Foundation, and the John Hope Franklin Humanities Institute at Duke. Earlier versions of this research appeared in *Current Anthropology; Anthropological Quarterly; Middle East Report; The Aesthetics and Politics of the Online Self: A Savage Journey into the Heart of Digital Cultures,* edited by Peter Sarram, Donatella Della Ratta, Geert Lovink, and Teresa Numerico (Palgrave); and *State Machines: Reflections and Actions at the Edge of Digital Citizenship, Finance, and Art,* edited by Yiannis Colakides, Marc Garrett, and Inte Gloerich (Institute of Networked Cultures). My thanks to all these institutions and publications for their intellectual support.

My deepest thanks go to my family for sustaining this research with love and food, humor and patience, over the course of nearly a decade. Particular appreciation to my father, Richard L. Stein, for reading every page and engaging my prose with the persistent care of both a parent and literary scholar; to my mother, Carole Stein, an anthropologist at heart and in deed; to my wonderous sister, Sarah Abrevaya Stein, a powerful model as scholar, parent, and swimmer. My deepest gratitude is always to my partner, Andrew Janiak, for countless acts of care and patience, and endless cups of tea, over the life of this project, and to our two wonderful children, Saul and Isaac, whose exuberance and curiosity kept it all going.

SCREEN SHOTS

IMAGE 1. Israeli soldier blocks the press from photographing the arrest of a Palestinian youth. Jerusalem. 16 May 1998. Source: Reuters.

STATE VIOLENCE AND THE DREAM OF THE PERFECT CAMERA

ON 24 MARCH 2016, A PALESTINIAN WAS LETHALLY SHOT BY AN IS-raeli soldier in downtown Hebron, in the occupied Palestinian territories. The event was captured on camera.[1] The footage was clear, filmed by a Palestinian neighbor from his adjacent roof, and the shot was audible.[2] The soldier could be seen methodically cocking his weapon as he approached his Palestinian target, an assailant who was already lying immobilized on the ground, and firing a single bullet at close range. The footage quickly went viral in Israel, played and replayed on the nightly news, dominating social media. The three-minute video would be committed to Israeli national memory.

Few Israelis knew the name of the slain Palestinian, Abdel Fattah al-Sharif. All knew Elor Azaria, the soldier. Azaria's trial in Israeli military court captivated and polarized the Israeli public, a national media spectacle that many likened to the OJ Simpson case in scale and symbolic import.[3] Military leadership supported the legal process in the name of their "ethical code."[4] In an unprecedented break with their military, most Jewish Israelis disagreed.[5] Thousands demonstrated in solidarity with Azaria in Tel Aviv's Rabin Square, demanding his exoneration in the name of "everyone's child."[6] "If we don't protect our soldiers," their posters read, "who will protect us?" One prominent Israeli magazine named him "man of the year," decorating its cover with his smiling portrait (Image 2).[7] Azaria would

IMAGE 2. *Makor Rishon* magazine names Elor Azaria "man of the year." The photo caption reads: "Sparked the stormiest argument in Israeli society this year." 2016. Source: *Makor Rishon* magazine.

be convicted of manslaughter in Israeli military court in 2017—the first such conviction of an Israeli soldier in more than a decade—but released from prison after serving nine months of his sentence.[8] He was greeted with a hero's welcome.[9] Azaria's celebrity status would grow in months and years hence, coveted for election endorsements, welcomed in Tel Aviv nightclubs and West Bank settlements by cheering crowds.[10] Within the voluminous Israeli national debate that the incident spawned, Israel's status as an occupier was not open for popular discussion. On this, there was no real disagreement.

The case was deemed a landmark for the ways it pitted the Jewish public against their military, the nation's most sacred institution. It was also a milestone in another sense. Although cameras were prolific in the West Bank in 2016, footage of this sort remained a rarity—that is, footage of Israeli state violence that captured both the military perpetrator and Palestinian victim in the same frame: "Azaria was not the first, nor will he be the last, Israeli soldier during the violence of this past year to shoot a Palestinian attacker who no longer posed a threat," wrote one Israeli left-wing commentator. "But he was the only one to find himself caught on film so blatantly. . ."[11] For Palestinian communities living under occupation, the case was yet another incident of military violence with legal impunity, for which there was considerable precedent. Azaria was the occupation's rule, they argued, not its exception. Mainstream Israeli Jews, for their part, read it as a parable of the Jewish state, an illustration of their existential battle against enemies that sought their demise. Through the viral frames, all had told their own story of Israeli military rule.

Screen Shots is a social biography of state violence on camera, studied from the vantage of the Israeli military occupation of the Palestinian territories. My historical context is the first two decades of the twenty-first century, a period when consumer photographic technologies were proliferating globally, chiefly in the form of the cellphone camera, even as communities across the globe were growing increasingly accustomed to life under the watchful eye of cameras. At the core of this study are the various Israeli and Palestinian individuals and institutions who, living and working in the context of the Israeli military occupation, placed an increasing political value on cameras and networked visuals as political tools: Palestinian video-activists, Israeli military and police, Israeli and international human rights workers, Jewish settlers. All trained their lens on the scene of Israeli state violence—some to contest Israeli military rule, others to consolidate it. *Screen Shots* examines this broad field of photographic encounters with Israeli state violence in the occupied Palestinian territories, attentive to political interests they both displayed and disguised, to the political fantasies they both mirrored and mobilized. I am interested in what these encounters reveal about the Israeli and Palestinian colonial present in the digital age and what they suggest about possible futures.[12]

The communities and institutions studied in this book have very different histories behind the lens. Palestinian and Israeli activists and human rights workers would be among the first to adopt cameras and networked visuality as political tools. Israeli military spokespersons would follow, as would (belatedly) Jewish settler communities. Their political aims were radically divergent, as was their access to the technologies, infrastructures, and literacies of the digital age. And yet, across these radical divides, many shared a version of the same camera dream. Many hoped the photographic technologies of the digital age—with the scene of state violence now visible at the scale of the pixel, circulated in real time—could deliver on their respective political dreams. Some, particularly the Israeli state institutions among them, harbored a techno-deterministic fantasy that technological progress (smaller, cheaper, sharper, faster) and political progress were mutually enforcing. All hoped that these new cameras could bear truer witness and thus yield justice as they saw it.

Most would be let down. Israeli human rights workers would painfully learn this lesson: even the most abundant visual evidence of state violence typically failed to persuade the Israeli justice system or Israeli public, as the Azaria case would make spectacularly visible. Palestinian video-activists living under occupation had additional frustrations, rooted in the everyday violence of military rule. Contending with poor internet connectivity and frequent electricity outages, byproducts of the occupation itself, they found that their footage often failed to reach the international or Israeli media for on-time distribution. Or they often faced punitive and violent responses from soldiers at checkpoints, sometimes taking aim at cameras and memory sticks. And even the military grew frustrated. Their footage from the battlefield seemed to be perpetually inadequate and belated, military analysts lamented, always lagging behind their digitally savvy foes. They dreamed of a more perfect public relations camera that would finally redeem their global image. The fantasy was perpetual, the dream always deferred. *Screen Shots* lingers here, on this wide range of broken camera hopes and dreams, born of very different histories and conditions, distributed across the political landscape of Israeli military rule.

Much of this is not new. Photography has been interwoven with the political struggle over Palestine since the late nineteenth and early twentieth century, the early decades of both Zionist settlement and commercial photographic technologies.[13] Nor are the themes of this book unique to this geopolitical case. In the second decade of the twenty-first century, as mobile digital technologies proliferated, political hopes and dreams across the globe were famously attached to the ostensible promise of digital photography. The Arab revolts, the Occupy movement, the Syrian revolution, Black Lives Matter: each depended on the internet-enabled camera as a tool of citizen witnessing.[14] Many of these social movements would

IMAGE 3. Tribute to the citizen journalists of Iran's Green Revolution. 2009. Source: Monte Wolverton.

be represented in the media by photographs of crowds holding their cellphone cameras aloft. The image of digital camera phones held skyward would consolidate as a justice icon, a highly recognizable symbol of popular protest (Image 3).

When these social movements confronted their respective limits—as when livestreams from Syria failed to stem the bloody state crackdown, or when bystander footage of US police shootings failed to produce convictions—digital dreams also faltered. The global rise and spread of surveillance states in these decades, alongside governance-by-data, would further erode the investments of a prior generation of activists and scholars in paradigms of "liberation technology" and "digital democracy."[15] The global Black Lives Matter protests against police violence that erupted in the summer of 2020—ongoing as this book went to press—would reignite popular investments in the radical potential of the bystander camera as a tool of social change.

At the core of this book, as the opening vignette suggests, is the entanglement of consumer photographic technologies and Israeli state violence. By the end of the period chronicled here, this entanglement had become ordinary, both in Palestine and globally. It bears remembering that it wasn't always thus. As recently as two decades ago, the presence of the bystander camera at the site of state violence registered as anomalous and shocking: the Rodney King beating in 1991; the torture at Abu Ghraib prison in 2004; the killing of Neda Agha-Soltan by Iranian paramilitary forces in 2009. In each case, the camera's presence on the scene was part of the ensuing public shock. Media commentators on the King beating by the Los Angeles police stressed the disquieting coupling of police brutality and "home video" technologies ripped from private contexts.[16] In the aftermath of the Abu Ghraib revelations, much would be written about the ways that ordinary "point and shoot" cameras were now proliferating in the hands of the US military, changing the terms of soldiering.[17] Then, these bystander cameras were thought to be jarring: technologies out of place. Much would change in the two decades hence. By 2016, the time of the Azaria shooting with which this book begins, YouTube was functioning as a dense visual repository of Israeli state violence, shot from multiple perspectives and angles, largely by Palestinian activists and bystanders. The eyewitness camera had become an anticipated feature of the landscape of state violence.

Camera technologies have long been tethered to social and political dreams of various kinds—particularly, the historically recurrent fantasy that new photographic innovations will succeed where older ones failed: that is, the dream that they will effectively mediate less, finally ensuring transparency. These hopes and dreams resound with particular frequency and urgency in contexts of war or violent conflict when social demands on witnessing are heightened. Equally recurrent is the lament that follows when these dreams fall short, when these new media fail to stem violence or deliver justice. Taking the Israeli occupation as its case study, *Screen Shots* chronicles the range of political investments that were animated by the new photographic technologies and networked platforms of the early digital age and the conditions under which they faltered. This is a story of camera dreams, and camera dreams undone.

BEHIND THE LENS

Screen Shots begins at the turn of the twenty-first century (2000), amidst both the second Palestinian uprising or intifada (2000–2005) and the early years of consumer digital photography. It concludes amid both smartphone and social media proliferation in Palestine and Israel and a military occupation continuing to expand and normalize (2016). When I began this research in 2010, all of the communities and institutions chronicled in this book—from Palestinian activists to Israeli military spokespersons (Dovrei Tzahal), were still developing their image-making strategies, still experimenting with the potential of viral images as political tools. Five years later, digital image production and circulation had become the sine qua non of all Palestinian and Israeli political claims. All aimed their cameras at the scene of state violence.

The communities and institutions studied in this book have highly varied histories behind the lens of cameras. Israeli and Palestinian anti-occupation activists, working together and separately, were among the first to employ cameras as political instruments, beginning substantively during the early years of the second Palestinian uprising as part of the wave of transnational Palestine solidarity activism that the uprising had catalyzed.[18] The joint Israeli–Palestinian photography collective Activestills (founded in 2005) emerged within this political context, showcasing images of Israeli military repression and its Palestinian victims that had been largely occluded from mainstream Israeli media spheres (and this book includes many of their photographs).[19] Israeli camera-activists worked on the margins of the national political consensus and often under threat of military and settler violence. As years progressed, such activism would be increasingly targeted and constrained by the Israeli state, often violently so.

Video activism and photojournalism were far more encumbered for Palestinians living under occupation. The Israeli military crackdown on Palestinian photographers and journalists was particularly fierce during the second Palestinian uprising, but such assaults and restrictions would continue in its wake.[20] Military beatings and detentions of Palestinian camera operators remained frequent, as did seizures of equipment and targeting of cameras, particularly those in the hands of Palestinian activists, as immortalized in a celebrated film from this period (*5 Broken Cameras*).[21] As late as 2010, despite a boom in mobile telephony in the West Bank and Gaza during the preceding decade, many Palestinian families in the West Bank lacked access to photographic technologies or reliable internet connectivity—the latter a byproduct, in large measure, of the myriad forms of control that Israel exercised over the Palestinian telecommunications sector, constituting what Helga Tawil Souri has called a "digital occupation."[22] The growth of Palestinian camera activism was nonetheless rapid in years that followed, animated by what Rema Hammami has called a "politics of hope" about the political affordances of networked visibility.[23] By 2012, the West Bank's centers of nonviolent popular struggle—for example, Bil'in and Nabi Saleh—had become crowded theaters of competing cameras. Palestinian video-activists were at their helm.[24]

Israeli human rights organizations working in the occupied territories were also at the forefront of camera adoption.[25] Such efforts were led by the NGO

B'Tselem—the Israeli Information Center for Human Rights in the Occupied Territories—an organization that will figure centrally in the chapters that follow. In 2007, before cameras were widely available within the West Bank, B'Tselem launched a camera project that delivered hundreds of hand-held camcorders to Palestinian families living in areas of the occupied territories with elevated state and settler violence. In these years, the integration of digital videographic technologies and human rights institutional practices was still in its nascency for human rights organizations working in the occupied territories and across the globe. Videographic protocols were still being developed, including standards for authentication and models for protecting visual privacy.[26] Video and digital forensics would be gradually integrated into evidence assessment and argumentation, as would discussions of its legal and ethical dimensions ("To function as legal evidence," human rights workers would increasingly ask, "what does the video need?"). The very notion of a human rights violation was changing, increasingly routed through videographic logics of evidence, rights, and humanity itself.

Israeli soldiers have long carried their personal cameras into service, as have soldiers across the globe, often in violation of official regulations. In the late 1990s, they were shooting with analogue cameras and rudimentary cellphone cameras. By the turn of the twenty-first century, pocket-size digital cameras had become a common part of the Israeli military toolkit, carried in vest pockets and employed both for pleasure and ad hoc "operational needs." In Israel, as elsewhere, official policy lagged far behind everyday soldier practice. It would take years for the military to codify rules of engagement where these personal technologies were concerned, and even then, they were selectively enforced.

Official Israeli military photography would also develop markedly in these decades, as the military became "mediatized" in new ways and degrees.[27] In the early twenty-first century, beginning amidst the second intifada, the military would expand its program for combat photographers, aware of the need to respond to its camera-savvy enemies in kind. In the same years, the division of the Israeli military tasked with media and public relations, would enhance their social media presence—struggling, in the early years, with the institutional changes required ("it's just not what armies do," I would be perpetually told). Military spokespersons noted that "the gap between the documentation abilities of the enemy and those of the IDF" had been evident since the first Palestinian uprising (1987 to 1991–93). But it was widening exponentially in the digital age—and, they argued, dangerously so.[28] In the military's estimation, the perceived threat to Israel's global standing was considerable. They longed for "victory images" (*tamunot nitzahon*) from the battlefield with the power to cement a military triumph and combat the "bad images" of their foes.

Jewish settlers and right-wing Israeli nationalists came to camera politics somewhat belatedly, as I have noted. As years progressed, settler raids on neighboring Palestinian villages would increasingly include cameras as tools of terror and documentation, and the resultant footage would be shared on right-wing Israeli media outlets. Israeli populists and their international supporters were increasingly mobilizing online against the digital "incitement" of their Palestinian foes: namely, eyewitness photographs and videos of Israeli state violence.[29] They would gradually embrace the charge of "fake news"—well in advance of its uptake in the US political context—in order to repudiate Palestinian videographic claims.[30] These accusations performed a disappearing act: removing Palestinian victims and Israeli perpetrators from the visual field of Israeli military rule.[31] Or this, anyway, was their fantasy.

Israel's surveillance infrastructure—its history dating to the early years of Zionist settlement in the nineteenth century—would expand considerably in these decades, enabled by new high-tech mechanisms.[32] Now, the Palestinian occupied territories were being controlled by a growing network of electronic sensors, observation towers and CCTV cameras, reconnaissance planes and drones—technological advances lauded by the state in the language of "frictionless" control (see Image 4).[33] By the second decade of the twenty-first century, Israel's surveillance infrastructure was increasingly reliant on biometric systems and remote-sensing technologies.[34] The Israeli security industry was booming, following Israel's successful rebranding as a "homeland security capital" in the aftermath of 9/11. What followed was a sizable growth in demand for Israel's "homegrown technological skills," fed by military technologies and expertise.[35] As a hub for surveillance technologies, and a global leader in the drone market, Israel was exporting these capabilities to governments around the world.[36] Some of these militarized technologies enjoyed a second life on global consumer markets.[37]

Radical inequities crosscut these technological fields at every juncture, structured and sustained by Israel. As Palestinians suffered under the numerous constraints of the "digital occupation," Israelis enjoyed some of the highest rates of internet penetration and technological literacy globally, leading the world in smartphone usage and "social network addiction."[38] The Israeli high-tech sector was booming, fed by technology and expertise from the Israeli military, and

IMAGE 4. Israeli military watchtower covered with surveillance cameras. Road 60, West Bank. 30 January 2006. Courtesy: Keren Manor/Activestills.

proudly celebrated by the Israeli state in the branded language of "Innovation Nation" or "Start-Up Nation" (borrowed from the title of a best-selling book).[39] On the social media accounts of the Israeli state, this branded language—always delivered in English, intended for export—was deployed to draw global eyes away from the military occupation (see Image 5). The formula was simple and recurrent: you say occupation, we say innovation.

POLITICAL FRAMES

Screen Shots is also an anthropological chronicle of the changing Israeli political landscape at the turn of the twenty-first century. Right-wing nationalism was on the rise, having progressively migrated from the margins to the mainstream.[40] If the 1990s had been characterized by widespread Jewish Israeli investment in the possibility of a negotiated settlement with "the Palestinians," however inequitable and illusive, the two decades after the demise of the Oslo Process witnessed a substantial political realignment.[41] Popular interest in a political solution to "the situation" (*hamatzav*)—the euphemism of choice—would all but vanish.[42] Indeed, the very word "occupation"

PM of Israel ☑
@IsraeliPM

PM Benjamin Netanyahu will address #WEF14 in #Davos
today at 14:15 (CET). Watch it live!
weforum.org/sessions/summa...

6:04 AM · Jan 23, 2014 · Twitter Web Client

IMAGE 5. Israeli Prime Minister Benjamin Netanyahu. 2014. Source: Twitter.com/IsraeliPM.

was now missing from national election campaigns, while each successive
Israeli government would be described as "the most right-wing in Israeli history."[43] All the while, the Israeli military regime in the occupied Palestinian
territories grew more entrenched and normalized, despite the legal fiction of
its temporariness.[44] The settlement infrastructure and population expanded markedly during these years even as the settler political agenda gained
ground in the Israeli parliament.[45] The Jewish public granted their military a
mandate to crack down on the Palestinian territories with relative impunity
when national security was deemed at issue, as during three bloody military incursions into the Gaza Strip during this period (2008–2009, 2012, and
2014).[46] Mainstream Jewish attitudes toward Israel's Palestinian citizens also
moved rightward. A majority backed anti-Arab platforms and candidates,
paving the way for the "Jewish nation-state" law in 2018. With its passage

in the Israeli parliament, Palestinians' second-class citizenship was legally enshrined.[47]

Israeli anti-occupation activists continued their political and legal struggles, but under mounting constraints. State crackdowns on free speech, the judicial system, and human rights organizations would intensify.[48] Israeli Jews critical of the occupation found themselves increasingly ostracized, painted as traitors and spies, with many afraid to declare their left-wing allegiances in public.[49] Palestinian citizens of Israel would intensify their legal and political struggles for equality, while the Israeli right employed all possible means to stop them. The language of a human rights claim, made on behalf of a Palestinian living under occupation, was now perceived as a form of injurious speech.[50] In this formulation, the Jewish state was the injured party.

These political trends also took shape in visual terms and ways of seeing. In the same years, images of military occupation were gradually "disappear[ing] from Israeli news," as were Palestinian eyewitness testimonials about Israeli state violence.[51] When present in mainstream outlets, such testimonials tended to be enabled by Israeli lawyers and human rights organizations. On their own, Palestinians were simply not deemed credible witnesses.[52] The built environment of the military occupation, chiefly the separation barrier, fostered other invisibilities. From the Israeli side, at some points along the barrier's path, the view of the occupied Palestinian cities and towns on the other side was simply obscured, blocked by concrete. At other points, the barrier was painted with a pastoral mural from which all human traces had been removed.[53] Taken together, these erasures were part of something larger: an implicit agreement within mainstream Israeli society, fostered by the state, to keep the military occupation out of sight.[54] Good Israeli citizenship, it seemed, depended on it. Of course, not all Jewish Israelis would comply. Anti-occupation activists engaged in the difficult labor of redirecting the national gaze, as did Israeli human rights workers and institutions. But they did so in the face of increasingly difficult political odds.

The Azaria case with which this book began (2016) marked a decisive break in national ways of seeing.[55] In the decade prior, state violence against Palestinians, when caught on camera, had been largely consigned to public invisibility. But in this incident, both the act of killing and the killer were rendered spectacularly visible. Indeed, the military perpetrator was celebrated as a national hero: "Azaria, king of Israel!"—as crowds would chant in Tel Aviv.[56] The Palestinian eyewitness camera, long deemed an enemy agent, became an unwitting abettor in the production of a national icon.

SCHOLARLY ITINERARIES

Scholars have long meditated on the status of cameras at the site of violence, querying "how photography has kept company with death," in Susan Sontag's famous rendering.[57] Several generations of scholarship would follow Sontag's lead, studying (among other things) the ethics of photographic witnessing, the terms of humanitarian spectatorship, and the ways that digital technologies have recalibrated the photographic encounter.[58] Questions of visuality have increasingly occupied scholars in anti-colonial Palestine and Israel studies, fueled by the foundational work of Ariella Azoulay, Gil Hochberg, and Eyal Weizman.[59] While my work draws on these broad scholarly fields, it also parts ways from their predominant methodologies and analytic concerns—in particular, their emphasis on representational politics. *Screen Shots*, by contrast, focuses chiefly on image operations and visual practices, building on a recent wave of anthropological scholarship on the social lives of photography.[60] Turning away from what comes *after* images (representational politics), this book considers what *precedes* their entry into social worlds: namely, the various forms of labor, political and aesthetic assessments, negotiations and contestations, that make images and visual circuits possible. This methodological shift also makes other research questions possible, opening space to consider photographs and circulations that did not happen, whose realization was frustrated at the site of either production or distribution.[61] Or, in a future tense, photographs that will never happen (predicated, as they are, on political and technological fantasies). These impossible images and fantasy cameras are also part of my story.

Periods of media emergence are rich analytic opportunities for scholars, as media historians teach us. These are social moments "before the material means and the conceptual modes of new media have become fixed, when such media are not yet accepted as natural, when their own meanings are in flux."[62] They are times before technologies have acquired social fixity or a sense of ordinariness, before everyday uses and functions have been agreed upon, when they are still subject to debate and negotiation about their functions and meanings. The sense of uncertainty is considerable, and an attendant sense of crisis is frequent, resolved only after uses and conventions have stabilized. Some media emergences result in normalization, as new technologies and associated practices are enfolded into everyday lives and institutional routines. Others never acquire a lasting hold and effectively fail as social forms. These failures, media historians note, are often erased from the historical record in the service of a progressivist notion of media "supercession"—that is, the conviction that each new medium necessarily super-sedes that which came before. What is often lost, in the process, is a sense of the highly uncertain, faltering, and risky ways that new media enter social worlds.

Screen Shots, by contrast, focuses precisely here: on failures and crises, debates and negotiations, that attended the popularization of digital photography as a body of political tools.[63] The associated labor was considerable, and the process gradual. Institutional policies and protocols had to be redrawn, legal processes reconfigured and recalibrated, infrastructures updated. New modes of expertise would emerge, befitting these new tools. Ways of seeing were in flux. The techno-logical innovations of this period literally altered the view of Israel's occupation, a political field that was now visible to the public from the eye of the drone and with the precision of the pixel. These shifts produced changes in everyday practices of witnessing and documenting, assessing and verifying, denying and repudiating. As these photographic tools progressively took hold, the sense of social crisis was abundant. I am particularly interested in the range of breakdowns and glitches, lags and lapses that attended the early uptake of these technologies within the context of the military occupation. At a range of scales and forms, failure crosscut the field of military occupation and its numerous cameras, distributed across political lines.

Screen Shots begins at the turn of the twenty-first century (2000), the relatively early years of consumer digital photography, and concludes in the era of smart-phone and social media proliferation in Palestine and Israel (and globally). The following chapters study Israeli and Palestinian camera politics at varying scales and in varying forms, while threading through some central events in the history of the Israeli military occupation—including the second Palestinian uprising and Israeli military crackdown on the West Bank (2000–2005), the first and third Israeli wars on the Gaza Strip of this period (2008–2009 and 2014), the Israeli attack on the *Mavi Marmara* (2010). Woven through these historical retellings are close studies—indeed, portraits—of the wide range of Israeli and Palestinian individ-uals and institutions employing cameras as political tools. This book frequently engages in a recursive practice, often returning to the same historical episode as refracted through a different camera lens. Such recursive analysis is necessary: a single episode of state violence, captured on film, told numerous stories.

Jewish Israeli actors and institutions form the core of this study, with a par-ticular emphasis on Israeli soldiers and military units, and the right-wing Israeli publics that supported them, employing cameras to consolidate Israeli military rule and exonerate military perpetrators. In the process, this book continues the work that I began in *Digital Militarism* (co-authored with Adi Kuntsman): namely, to consider the ways that media technologies of the digital age have been conscripted into the everyday work of military occupation. In *Screen Shots*, employing a methodology of anthropological portraiture, I hew closely to the details of military voice and terminology (e.g., "victory image," or "Judea and Samaria" rather than "occupied territories"—the latter justifying occupation through a discourse of biblical inheritance). While such methodological choices might be thought to sit uneasily within a scholarly project that is framed as anti-colonial, I propose that attention to such modes of self-presentation is particularly crucial in a study of the military's representational ambitions, its drive to perfect the picture of Israel.

Cameras interest me as social forms because they often function as proxies, surrogates for the political dreams and anxieties of their users. In the process, they enable a reckoning with Palestine's colonial history. As postcolonial scholars have taught us, colonial history is closely tethered to technologies. Its textual archive is littered with scenes of wondrous "first contact" between colonized populations and technologies of various kinds, from phonographs to trains, with scenes of natives awestruck by their modernizing capacity.[64] Such encounters had a powerful pedagogical function, working to hail and retrain colonial subjects by rescuing them from the imagined time of pre-modernity.[65] So, too, in Palestine, where the ambitions of the Israeli settler–colonial project have long been reliant on technological discourses and developments, beginning in the early decades of Zionism, evident both in the nineteenth-century dream of an electrified Palestine and the twenty-first-century state dream of total surveillance. In Palestine, now and historically, the grandeur of technological innovation, or the promise thereof, has been employed to authorize the Israeli colonial project and obfuscate its constitutive violence. Cameras, I will argue, have been a crucial part of that project.

Thus, while *Screen Shots* chronicles the social life of photography in the context of the military occupation, it also studies photography's function as a political placeholder. In the pages that follow, camera dreams and breakdowns, at scales both large and small, are never only thus. I'm interested in the ways that military laments about belated images from the battlefield articulated a range of anxieties about Israel's global standing; how settler accusations about fraudulent Palestinian footage replayed a long history of colonial claims about indigenous fraudulence; how the verification practices of Israeli human rights workers, as they screened

Palestinian eyewitness footage, became a platform to negotiate what the Israeli political future should look like. The digital dream of the more perfect camera was a highly flexible surrogate: both the grounds for settler fantasies about Palestinian depopulation and activist hopes for a liberated Palestine. In turn, glitches and lapses in the realm of image operations, in the hands of all the Israeli and Palestinian constituencies and institutions studied here, were occasions to negotiate a range of concurrent political failures and anxieties. I am interested in what camera dreams and breakdowns make visible about the Israeli and Palestinian colonial present—and what they reveal about possible political futures.

Chapter 1

SNIPER PORTRAITURE

Personal Technologies in Military Theaters

BEFORE THE ARMY, NOAM WAS A SELF-DESCRIBED PHOTOGRAPHY enthusiast with a particular interest in urban landscapes.[1] During his army service, these interests would be channeled in new directions. "You know, every platoon has that guy that likes photography and goes everywhere with a camera. I always had it in my military vest—everywhere we went, whether a patrol in Hebron or training in the Golan." He was stationed in the West Bank from 2007–2009 on the heels of the second Palestinian uprising, serving in the Nahal Brigade. He spent considerable time in the occupied city of Hebron where, when the uprising was at its height, the military crackdown on the popular protest movement had been particularly fierce. He was not an official military photographer. Somebody else in his unit held that job. Nonetheless, his rudimentary digital camera—"a simple Fujifilm"—was always active, unregulated by his military superiors. He photographed voraciously, from snapshots of daily life in the security services to images of his unit commandeering a private Palestinian home as a temporary outpost. He only put down his camera during arrests or full-scale operations. On a few occasions, when the military's official cameramen were unavailable, Noam's superiors ordered him to use his personal camera for intelligence purposes, as they would describe it, instructing him to photograph Palestinian children during his unit's raid of a private home. Noam complied, putting his Fujifilm to work for the state.

Civilian cameras have a long history in military theaters, carried by soldiers onto battlefields and into military operations since the early decades of camera technologies in the nineteenth century.[2] But this phenomenon would change dramatically in scale and kind in the digital age, a shift famously chronicled by Susan Sontag in the wake of the Abu Ghraib revelations (2004) at a moment when photographic technologies, both newly affordable compacts and cellphone cameras, were beginning to flood military theaters.[3] Sontag wrote:

> A digital camera is a common possession among soldiers. Where once photographing war was the province of photojournalists, now the soldiers themselves are all photographers—recording their war, their fun, their observations of what they find picturesque, their atrocities—and swapping images among themselves and e-mailing them around the globe.[4]

Sontag noted a shift in the culture of soldiering that was, at the time of her writing in 2004, still coming into focus for onlookers outside the armed forces. As she observed, most of the infamous images of torture and abuse recorded by US soldiers at Abu Ghraib were taken with the compact digital cameras—so-called point and shoot cameras—that were becoming ubiquitous in the armed forces.

At a time well before the dawn of social media or smartphones, these infamous photographs and videos were first saved as JPEGs to hard drives or memory cards before they were uploaded and circulated by email.[5] Perhaps ironically, the very technological constraints of this moment enabled these digital images to bypass standard regulating bodies, "escap[ing] the control of both the Pentagon and the professional picture-making establishment."[6] Donald Rumsfeld, then the US defense secretary, would lament that soldiers were "running around with digital cameras and taking these unbelievable photographs and then passing them off, against the law, to the media, to our surprise."[7] It was only after Abu Ghraib's viral exposure that the Pentagon began to regulate the presence of personal photographic technologies, newly aware of their potential for public relations harm.[8] Rumsfeld's "surprise" is a crucial part of this story. For state officials across the globe at this moment in the early twenty-first century, the scale and significance of these proliferating consumer cameras in soldiers' hands caught them largely unaware.

A similar set of trends unfolded within the Israeli military context in this period, also catching the state unaware. At the turn of the twenty-first century, many of the Israeli soldiers patrolling the West Bank—including those charged with suppressing the second Palestinian uprising or intifada (2000–2005)—brought personal cameras with them.[9] They also carried them into Lebanon during the 2006 Israeli war, chiefly in the form of cellphone cameras, "tuck[ing them] into their cargo pockets . . . to call home or keep in touch with friends."[10] As in the US context, these trends were enabled by lax military regulations.

This chapter studies the migration of personal cameras and cellular technologies into Israel military theaters at the turn of the twenty-first century—and, in turn, the various forms of militarization to which these technologies were subject. I focus on the key Israeli military operations of this period in which these technologies were present in large numbers: the second Palestinian intifada and military crackdown on the West Bank; the 2006 war on Lebanon; the 2008–2009 assault on the Gaza Strip. The phenomenon of the amateur Israeli soldier-photographer was not new.[11] But in prior wars and military operations, they had been relatively peripheral actors. Now, with portable digital cameras becoming more affordable, they were becoming more prevalent, even commonplace figures in military theaters. At the core of this chapter are two former Israeli soldiers who served in the West Bank in the waning years of the second Palestinian uprising and brutal military crackdown. One photographed purely for personal ends, shooting images of daily life in the armed forces, while the other also served as his unit's official camera operator, tasked with using the wide range of military-issued optical technologies that were deemed necessary for surveillance and information gathering. Both would become founding members of the Israeli anti-occupation NGO Breaking the Silence, founded by former Israeli combatants who were radicalized by the brutality of military service.[12] The organization's inaugural project grew out of this camera history: an exhibition of soldier photography from the second uprising, intended to "expose the Israeli public to the reality of everyday life in the Occupied Territories."[13] The personal cameras of soldiers were highly flexible political technologies, at once instruments of repressive occupation and tools of radicalization.

Themes of photographic failure and photographic learning inflect this chapter throughout, including the considerable labor required by both soldiers and military officials to manage this changing media landscape and incorporate these private technologies into operational protocols. Military officials found themselves caught between civilian demands for policy leniency regarding the personal technologies of soldiers—stemming from the public desire to stay in touch with deployed relatives—and state demands for strict information security. After a spectacular Israeli loss during the Lebanon war (2006), blamed on insufficient military regulation of wartime media, Israeli analysts would chide the military for failing to understand the terms of the new digital media ecosystem. The contrast was stark during the 2008–2009 Israeli war on Gaza—at least, where military policy governing the personal technologies of Palestinians was concerned. In this policy arena, there was no trace of laxity.

The militarization of personal digital technologies at the turn of the twenty-first century occurred against the backdrop of the inverse: namely, the migration of violent technologies into consumer markets in new commodity forms, as advances in military technologies continued to feed the growing Israeli high-tech sector.[14] For the military, techno-fluidity was a distinct operational advantage. Soldiers on duty in the occupied Palestinian territories could, when need or whim demanded, employ an expansive toolkit, drawing on consumer cameras and habits. But such fluidity was also a state liability. The private cameras and cellphones of soldiers moved in and out of operational contexts in ways that military officials could not fully control. This chapter is a chronicle of these uneven processes.

MILITARY PHOTOGRAPHY: AN ABBREVIATED HISTORY

The interplay between cameras and militarism, and between photography and colonialism, has a considerable history in this geopolitical context. Its roots can be traced to late nineteenth-century Palestine, the early decades of both Zionist settlement and commercial photographic technologies, when cameras were employed as colonial instruments by Victorian travelers, documentarians, and ethnologists.[15] This interplay would take new forms in Palestine during the early twentieth century: in the tourist practices of Europeans visiting the Holy Land, armed with their Kodak snapshot cameras;[16] in the surveillance practices of the British imperial authorities (1920–1948);[17] in photography and cinema produced within Palestine's growing Jewish settler population, employed to cement the Zionist project.[18] In the ensuing photographic archives, Palestinians were typically expunged from the visual field or enframed by Orientalist tropes, providing the symbolic complement to the material labor of Palestinian dispossession.[19] Photography was also flourishing within Palestinian urban communities in the early twentieth century, and their intimate images of thriving community life generated a potent visual counterweight to Zionist visuality.[20]

Jewish military photography in Palestine emerged during the first decades of the twentieth century in the work of Zionist intelligence organizations, as Rona Sela has chronicled. This work began rather improvisationally in the 1920s, with the integration of ordinary commercial cameras into the intelligence operations of the Haganah, the forerunner of the Israeli Defense Forces.[21] By the 1940s, such work had been expanded to include a range of photographic techniques employed "to collect information about the Palestinian community," including "aerial photographs . . . and a photographer disguised as a Palestinian."[22] Subterfuge was essential. The Haganah's elite flight squadron undertook their aerial surveillance operations under the guise of a flying club to prevent Palestinian suspicion, while their scouting clubs were equipped with covert cameras and instructed to photograph Palestine's villages for intelligence purposes.[23] Scout manuals from this period offered tips on avoiding detection: "If you are unable to hide the act of photography, 'cover' it by taking pictures of your friends or the local people. In the former case, ensure that your friends do not appear [in focus] in the photo, not even from the back. . . . If, nevertheless, people do appear in the picture (as a result of carelessness), blur them on the negative."[24] Here, the tourist snapshot is explicitly redeployed as a military alibi (see Image 6).[25]

Zionist military photography would undergo a crucial period of institutionalization during the 1948 war for Palestine.[26] In August of 1948, two months following the establishment of the Jewish state, the nascent Israeli military formed its first official photography unit, sending photographers to accompany soldiers on the "battlefront"—joining photographers dispatched by the Israeli military journal *BaMahane* (In Base Camp).[27] The unit's mandate was broad, as one learns from their internal archives: at once "to prepare for military actions (such as training videos for patrolmen)" and to "document . . . special events characterizing life and missions within the IDF frame."[28] The head of military operations, Yigael Yadin, called upon all military personnel in the theater of operations to provide maximal assistance to military photographers: "Commanders of combat units, directors of different services, etc., are required to allow photographers and scriptwriters . . . every possible relief to facilitate their tasks, direct them to relevant military objects and order them to attend as many live military events as possible."[29] Battlefield victory, in other words, depended on successful wartime images, with a premium placed on live capture by embedded military photographers (a directive

IMAGE 6. Haganah Field Squad (*Cheylot Hasadeh*) on patrol in the Palestinian village of Kufur Salemeh. Approximate date: 1946–April 1948. Source: Haganah Historical Archives.

that anticipated the demands of the digital age). The timing of the unit's founding was telling, deemed so vital as to have been operationalized in the very midst of wartime efforts to secure Zionist territorial sovereignty.

The military's film unit remained active in the decades following the 1948 victory, entrusted with serving the Zionist national narrative.[30] During the 1982 invasion of Lebanon, this unit produced its most celebrated work, *Two Fingers from Sidon* (1985), a feature film that functioned, in Ella Shohat's words, as "a kind of promotional brochure for official Israeli policies and perspectives," advancing an exculpatory narrative about a military beset by moral quandaries.[31] The unit's work was deemed particularly urgent during the first Palestinian uprising (1988 to 1991–1993), particularly given the growing presence of foreign media in the occupied Palestinian territories. Their job was clear: to combat the "bad images" of Israel that were playing on TV sets across the globe, including scenes of heavily armed Israeli battalions facing Palestinian children. One military cameraman, Yariv Horowitz, faced punitive consequences when his probing interviews with military personnel yielded frank testimonials about their brutal attempts to quell Palestinian protests.[32] Horowitz would undergo an interrogation by military generals, his videotapes confiscated.[33]

IMAGE 7. Israeli soldier with Israeli tourists in the newly occupied Gaza Strip, posing with a captured Egyptian tank. 1 July 1967. Source: David Rubinger/Getty Images.

Throughout this history, official military cameras were accompanied by unofficial ones. Indeed, the figure of the amateur soldier-photographer pervades the popular writings on all of Israel's major wars and military operations. They appear in Israeli reporting on the 1967 war, with images of soldiers "wander[ing] around with a gun in one hand and a camera in the other," surveying newly occupied East Jerusalem, and in the 1967 victory albums shot by famed Israeli photojournalist David Rubinger, with images of soldiers celebrating the Israeli conquest in the manner of the tourist (see Image 7).[34]

Similar images litter the textual archive of Israel's 1973 war with Egypt and Syria. "When we ran to the tanks, I had a camera hanging around my neck," says a former soldier who photographed the 1973 war with a compact half-frame camera. This was something of a wartime anomaly "because not many people had cameras at all back then."[35] A decade later, during the Israeli 1982 invasion of Lebanon, the Israeli media grew fascinated by the Israeli soldiers navigating occupied Beirut with their personal cameras and tourist sensibilities.[36] Across these histories of warfare and occupation, the recoding of the Israeli soldier as a photographer was a convenient proxy-narrative that recast militarism as leisure. This figure was a vehicle of disavowal, and therein lay the roots of its recurrence.

By the turn of the twenty-first century, with the outbreak of the second Palestinian intifada (2000 to 2005–2008), the balance of military cameras would shift in accordance with changes in the global media ecosystem. Now, personal military cameras were more numerous than official ones. When the military deployed troops into the West Bank in massive numbers and force to stem the popular Palestinian protests (code named Operation Defensive Shield)—including invasions of Palestinian towns and refugee camps, shelling of civilian and government infrastructures, widespread imposition of curfew and closure—many soldiers had cameras in their vest pockets.[37] Once anomalous and even shocking, these civilian technologies had become an anticipated feature of military life. "You always had one or two people in the company who click every second," I was told by former combat soldier and Breaking the Silence founder Yehuda Shaul about his second intifada military service in the occupied West Bank. "They were just shooting their life." The state could regulate their official military photographers, but it had less control over their unofficial ones. And therein lay their threat.

SOLDIERS AT THE WINDOW

Noam grew up in West Jerusalem in a house on Bethlehem Road, the main historic route between Jerusalem and the Palestinian city of Bethlehem. In the 1990s, before the construction of the separation barrier, he could have driven into the West Bank in under twenty minutes, undeterred by legal or territorial constraints.[38] But these territorial proximities proved illusive, overwritten by ideological constraints. He would first travel into the occupied territories, and encounter Palestinians living under occupation, while serving as an infantry soldier in the waning years of the second Palestinian uprising (2006–2008). He carried his camera with him, as had other members of his family while in uniform. "My grandfather was a photographer, and my father is a journalist, so at my house we always had cameras, and we took a lot of photos." So, too, on duty.

Sitting together at a West Jerusalem café during our first meeting in 2013, we bent over the weathered laptop that housed his extensive personal archive from the second intifada period, the hundreds of photographs, and occasional video, that he shot during his military service. In the early months, he photographed his friends and their ordinary life. This part of his archive is filled with intimate portraits: soldiers during mealtime, humorous moments or expressions, bunkhouse antics. In these images, the military mission and its Palestinian targets are scarcely evident. But with the passage of time, his subject matter seemed to shift.

In the months that followed, he began a more somber study of military practices: combat soldiers applying camouflage paint; soldiers preparing for a stake-out; the interior of a military jeep on his way to an operation. These thematic shifts were unintentional, he said, something he had not really thought about: "At a certain point I started taking more . . . uh . . . political pictures I guess you would call them." He paused, remembering: "I used to walk around taking pictures during patrols, inside Palestinian houses. You know, everyday life under military control."

We linger on a collection of images shot in Hebron in the summer of 2008 in the waning days of the second Palestinian uprising. The Israeli military crackdown had been particularly harsh in Hebron during the uprising's early years. Palestinian residents of the city lived under relatively constant military curfews and closures that severely restricted their activities, while Jewish settlers enjoyed freedom of movement and state protection. Palestinians venturing out in violation of curfew faced the threat of lethal force. International human rights organizations decried the ensuing humanitarian disaster, with the city's families denied access to basic necessities.

In Hebron, as per military procedure, Noam's unit had commandeered a private Palestinian home as a temporary military outpost. It was a standard military operation, he explained, known in military terminology as a "straw widow" (*almanat kash*). In official military messaging, such operations were intended to "improve the IDF's control of territory by capturing and controlling positions and creating hidden lookout points."[39] In practice, they involved the forcible removal of Palestinian residents for the operation's duration: sometimes a day, sometimes weeks at a time. Noam was involved in many. When he wasn't actively participating in such operations, he was filming them: his unit's daily postures, rhythms, movements. He showed me a set of photographs of soldiers standing at the windows of the commandeered Palestinian home. They are pictured gazing toward the street, weapons at the ready, their position obscured by window netting.[40] Noam favored this vantage: images of fellow infantrymen from behind (see Image 8). In most of these photos, neither the city nor its residents are visible. We do not see what the soldiers observe, only that they are observing. "I couldn't take a picture of the soldiers from the Palestinians' point of view," he says, by way of explanation. "Only from my own."

We scrolled through numerous photographs Noam had shot from this stance, images that differed only minutely in details and angle. Some were artful shots, catching the light falling on the soldiers' bodies as they stand in wait, watching.

IMAGE 8. Israeli sniper takes position in a commandeered Palestinian home. Hebron. 2008.
Source: Breaking the Silence.

Some capture them in near-darkness, facial expressions only lightly sketched in
the shadows. Viewing these photographs again in 2013, Noam seemed surprised
by this tropological repetition. "So many window scenes," he mused aloud as we
viewed them together, as if struggling to recall his intentions. "Yes, we knew that
somebody lived there," he noted. After all, he said, the commandeered house
was fully furnished, with beds and mattresses and all the rest. "But we never
saw them." And then, as something of an afterthought, he added: "We liked that
house. It was comfortable."

    His photographic archive collaborated with these military logics and ways
of seeing. Echoing the operations themselves, he employed his camera to engage
in the micro-practice of dispossession by stripping Palestinians from the visual
field and replacing them with the military's gaze. Palestinians would become
more visible in his photographs during the subsequent months of his service, but
they were never his "preferred subjects," as he called them. Even in later images,
they were chiefly represented by what they have left behind: a pair of children's
shoes, laundry on a line. Traces.

When I spoke to Noam in 2013, he was an established activist with Breaking the Silence, a political stance he had only embraced in the years after he finished his military service. Nearly six years had transpired since he served in the West Bank. And although he frequently spoke to the Israeli and international public about his history as a soldier, and the violence of military rule, he found our interpretive exercise challenging. He had preserved hundreds of images from his military service in the Palestinian territories, each one labeled by date and location, all carefully saved on his computer hard drive. But he hadn't revisited them much since the time they were taken. Nor had he spent much time considering their implications. "You're asking many questions about things I've never thought about," he says.

He showed me a collection shot on his unit's last day in occupied Hebron in 2008. "I had some time off, so I went around with my camera and just took pictures of everything so I will have it for documentation." These images were different from those I'd seen before, as they moved well beyond the private spaces of military life. Everyday street scenes in urban Hebron, building exteriors, the details of private Palestinian homes. Many were out of focus, as if he was photographing in haste, trying to collect the images before his unit withdrew. I asked him about the rush to document that is so visually evident in this collection. "I think it a was a way to deal with my politics. In some of them, I was more aware, and in some less . . . I guess, during that time with your camera, you don't really understand what you're taking."

GEAR, ARCHIVES, TROPHIES

For the soldiers of the second intifada period, photography was a contingent practice. In the midst of full-scale military operations, when the demand for "operational alertness" was heightened, the success of every photographic attempt was uncertain. Many would describe the physical constraints of abundant military gear:

> First, I am wearing a uniform, a ceramic flak jacket, which is very heavy, on top of that a tight vest. And I have a radio, cartridges, and grenades on me . . . lots of equipment. Helmet, weapon, flashlight. . . . As I move around the alleys, the camera is in the pouch on my back, and if something catches my eye . . . then I tell them [the rest of the soldiers]: "Guys, stop! . . . go under right now," and they all lay down or squat. If I can reach the pouch, I will or

if not, I call one of my soldiers: "Moshe, please come get the camera out." He gives me the camera, I take a photo, and we continue.[41]

This soldier served in occupied Hebron at the height of the uprising, as we learn from his interview with anthropologist Regev Nathansohn, to whom he described the highly encumbered nature of the photographic act, his camera carried alongside heavy weaponry and telecommunications technologies. This interview provides an important counterpart to the portrait of Noam, who photographed during his West Bank "tour of duty" with the ease of a hobbyist, recalling the history of the Israeli soldier rendered as tourist. And Noam always photographed alone.

In this interview with Nathansohn, by contrast, soldier photography is portrayed as a necessarily collaborative practice. In the midst of full-scale military operations, assistance was required to get the shot right. It was an experience shared by other soldier-photographers from this period (again, in conversation with Nathansohn):

We often provided cover for the photographer, in an agreed upon fashion. He [the photographer] gets settled on the picture, which takes [a] few seconds, and meanwhile we stop to watch the roof. In urban fighting, you need to keep watch on doors and stairways, so each covers a different exit from which a terrorist . . . might appear . . . [that way the photographer] can put down his gun and take the photo at the right moment. . . . You don't shoot at all costs. It has to go through two filters: life and the mission. When it is appropriate, you take pictures. When you feel secure, you take pictures.[42]

Here, we learn that even a single photo could require the participation of many members of a military unit—"Moshe, please come get the camera out!"—particularly in a dense urban environment like Hebron. More than mere collaboration, these interviews point to careful orchestration, to photographic plans developed well in advance, in order to get "the photo at the right moment." They also suggest the perceived importance of photography, to these soldiers, as a military practice. No mere hobby or touristic endeavor, these soldiers stopped in the very midst of "urban fighting," coordinating lookouts on roofs and stairwells, in order to remove their cameras and get the desired picture.

As military photography spread within the Israeli armed forces in this period, informal archives of soldiering were coming into being. They had varied political

IMAGE 9. Israeli soldier takes a souvenir photograph in front of the partly demolished compound of Yasser Arafat. Ramallah. 22 September 2002. Source: Gil Cohen Magen/Reuters.

valences. Some were produced as souvenir or trophy albums and distributed to members of the unit as a commemorative DVD. Some repeated standard tourist idioms, with a focus on historic sites and picturesque landscapes (see Image 9). Others had a far more militarized stance. Casual snapshots of dead Palestinians were so frequent as to find "their way into private family albums" of military personnel.[43] Some of these archives were produced as vehicles of anti-occupation protest, although in a context of broad Israeli support for the brutal crackdown on the Palestinian uprising, they were in the decided minority. Among the reserve soldiers stationed in the West Bank were a set of budding documentarians, and some of their videographic work gave rise to a distinct genre of second intifada protest filmwork (e.g., *Jenin Diary* in 2003 and *Heavy Twenty* in 2004).[44] Although intended as critique, these films advanced an Israeli genre of "perpetrator trauma" that focused chiefly on the experience of the Israeli soldier.[45]

The most important protest archive of this period was curated by the founding members of Breaking the Silence. Yehuda Shaul was one of them. Like Noam, he was a committed photographer during his second intifada military service. Here is Shaul describing his tour of duty in Hebron in 2002 when the Israeli military crackdown was at its height:

> I saw what used to be a dentist's clinic. Soldiers had broken in and destroyed everything. There were broken syringes, shattered glass cases and mirrors. There was shit on the floor and it was smeared all over. This was the first time I encountered such brutality and I was shocked. I took out a camera I had in my gear and started taking pictures. When I went home on leave I had the photos developed and scanned them. A friend and I looked for Israeli journalists' email addresses; we opened an email account and sent the photos to journalists, saying, "look what's happening in Hebron."[46]

In 2004, with the help of veteran Israeli photojournalist Miki Kratsman, Shaul and other activists mounted a public exhibition of soldier photography from the occupied territories, shot on the personal cameras of soldiers and displayed alongside video testimonials from soldiers about their wanton brutality. The subject matter typified the range of this emerging military genre, from smiling snapshots of the platoon to souvenir images of dead Palestinian bodies. Images of bound and blindfolded Palestinian detainees were abundant, some with smiling soldiers at their sides, as were scenes of soldiers in commandeered Palestinian homes. Breaking the Silence had taken pains to anonymize the identities of both photographers and interviewees in an effort to prevent military retribution. Anonymization also generated a distribution of authorship, reminding Israeli audiences that these images could have been shot by any reserve soldier. These photographers were military Everymen.

The 2004 exhibit marked an important juncture in the Israeli visual record of military occupation.[47] Naively, echoing a history of Israeli public secrecy about its colonial project, many participating photographers spoke in the language of shock about the content of the images.[48] In fact, the perceived shock value was twofold: both the exhibit's content and its form. "[T]he first time he heard of soldiers taking pictures of themselves together with dead Palestinians, he was shocked," wrote an international journalist, describing his interview with a Breaking the Silence organizer. "But after a while he got used to it. He even heard of one soldier having his picture taken together with a severed head."[49] "Combat soldiers in action rarely use cameras to immortalize the moment," wrote another, laboring to make sense of the photographic exhibit. "Maybe because some ... prefer to forget. To repress."[50]

The "echoes of Abu Ghraib," exposed by soldier photography in the very same year, would be noted by many commentators.[51]

Military policy concerning soldier use of personal cameras had been vague in this period, as I explore in what follows. Nonetheless, a military interrogation of the exhibition's organizers would ensue, as would confiscation of the video testimonies and demands to provide the names of the anonymous interviewees. The military police claimed that they were "looking for evidence of crimes committed against Palestinian residents of Hebron."[52] For Breaking the Silence activists, the state message was clear: those soldiers using their cameras as a tool of protest would pay a price.

THE SNIPER'S CAMERAS

Before he joined the Israeli army, Eitan was a hobby photographer of sorts with a penchant for portraiture. During his military service in the West Bank from 2005–2008, he would carry his personal equipment with him, working with a set of midrange digital cameras favored by professional photographers. "I loved portraits of people, and I think I am quite good, actually. So when I got to the army, I took lots of photos during our training. You know, me and my teammates, our daily life": evenings in the bunk, routine training exercises, communal meals, humorous moments on base. All would become the subject of an ongoing photographic chronicle of soldiering that he shared with his unit.

He also used other cameras. In every unit, there was one member charged with implementing and overseeing the various photographic technologies and procedures required, and Eitan played that role. He served on the sniper team of a reconnaissance unit of the Nahal Brigade, stationed throughout the West Bank and Gaza Strip, and briefly in Lebanon, with the bulk of his service conducted in the Palestinian cities of Jenin and Nablus. The linkage between his personal and professional histories as a photographer was no accident. When it came to the selection of camera operators, the military preferred those with prior experience behind the lens as it lessened the learning curve.

Eitan's unit relied on a wide range of cameras depending on the needs of the moment, and he was responsible for all of them, including general knowledge of their workings and components and the ability to perform repairs or hacks in the field when required. The list of such cameras was considerable, including infrared helmet cameras employed to chart and learn a new terrain; closed caption cameras with remote screens; thermal cameras capable of photographic capture from miles away; and a surveillance device encased in rubber the size of a baseball that could be thrown into a room or through a window in order to shoot video, transmitted wirelessly.[53] They had only used the tossable device once, he said, in a hostage context. It was too much of a liability, as the device tended to get stuck under furniture and carpets. Sniping also depended on small CCTV cameras operated remotely with joysticks, installed on windows in positions that were deemed too dangerous to be manned. "That camera even saved my life once," taking fire that was intended for him. At the end of his service, Eitan would be asked to write a manual of sorts, documenting the best practices for optical technologies in the reconnaissance field—things like "how to use a thermal camera with an infra-red pointer, how to record, how many batteries you need." The manual hadn't existed when he began his service. He had been required to learn on the job.

As Eitan would describe it to me, each camera had its own operational function and photographic appeal:

> I had a lot of lenses. I had a tele 1000. It was an amazing camera. I'd use it for taking reconnaissance photos, taking photos of houses where we're going to do an arrest a couple of days later . . . you know, just to gather information. . . . [L]et's say, we arrested someone and he had guns and ammunition in his house. We'd take photos of that. Or when we were in Lebanon and did an operation and got really deep. I'd use it to take photos of Hezbollah repairing.

Having come into service with the fine-tuned eye of a photographer, Eitan was compelled by the images he was taking for the military. He found the reconnaissance images particularly appealing, those he shot with a high-resolution camera during operations. With the camera's long exposure, these images were particularly sharp. He would often take the camera's memory card home on the weekends and download everything to his personal computer, then return it to the military on Mondays for reformatting. He collected hundreds of them, he guessed, intended only for his own private viewing, unlike those photographs of daily life with his unit, shot on his personal cameras, that he regularly circulated and shared. Eitan was well aware that this was a violation of military protocol, as military guidelines clearly stipulated that reconnaissance images had to remain in the military context. Moreover, protocol dictated their deletion after the conclusion of any operation, except in the case of ongoing investigations, lest they prove a future risk to information security. But Eitan found a loophole: "I very quickly realized that nobody even cared what I'm doing with the camera and which photos I'm taking, as long as I give some photos to the intelligence officer at the end of every operation. You know, he just asked about photos of certain houses or streets."

He would be mildly disciplined by his regiment commander, but he was not deterred. The images were simply too appealing. "Some of those were really nice photos."

Eitan's unit conducted numerous "straw widow" operations, commandeering private Palestinian homes for temporary military usage. Because he was the unit's camera and technological expert, Eitan was charged with selecting the location of the house in question, based on a review of the available military imaging of the area. He relied on the military's computerized archive of aerial photographs of the Palestinian West Bank, an archive of tens of thousands of images, he estimated, stored on military databases and available remotely from military locations in the field. They were updated on a daily basis, sometimes hourly, by drone imaging to account for any changes in the built environment.[54] Every house in the West Bank had an associated number, he explained. "You have two kinds of aerial photos. You have the ones from above, and you have the one from an angle, so you knew the height of the house, and you could see the walls, the windows and the alleys around it. It shows you how to get inside. . . . I'd just choose a house that looked good for us."

He'd print the images and distribute them to the other teams, those who were also part of the operation, "so we'd have the same language." He looked for a house with big windows, facing the street they were asked to attack. Then, he would contact the Secret Service, identifying the house by its number.

During night raids for so-called wanted men, Eitan was tasked with thermal photography to identify the suspect. "My job was to look with the thermal camera and see if he's armed, or if he does something suspicious, and then I would give the okay to my snipers. . . . I would tell my snipers: 'Ok, you see that guy?' I give them the range, the angle, the wind. Then I tell them to set the aim." Yes, he'd need authorization from the platoon commander in order to proceed with the kill, but that wasn't difficult to obtain.

It was all filmed, producing an archive that the military had the capacity to review. His thermal-imaging camera was linked to a large screen, enabling his platoon commander, who sat behind him, to watch the targeting (and subsequent killing) in real time, "so he could tell us—'you have the ok to shoot.'" It was also linked to a recording device that filmed everything seen through the viewfinder, capturing the moment before and just after its activation.

In Eitan's early years as a sniper, before the technological advances that came later, these technologies were difficult to use. The videos could only be screened on the device itself, making them hard to review. The cameras were big and heavy, weighing up to 35 pounds including their tripod and batteries. And technological failures were frequent. Sometimes the screen would freeze, requiring the user to unplug it from the battery and then reboot, plugging it back in—a difficult and sometimes dangerous process in the midst of a nighttime sniper operation. In his later years in the field, cameras became lighter and smaller, using MP4 recorders that enabled users to download videos for screening. Review of the material became easier.

But often they were not reviewed at all, as Eitan would learn. Sometimes, in the wake of sniping operations, the platoon commander or intelligence officer would screen the incriminating footage. But not often. By and large, the images produced during these operations were rarely screened or reviewed, except during occasional training sessions with special forces, and only to give them a sense of the local terrain. "Nobody wants to see them."

FROM LAXITY TO LETHALITY

The growth of soldier photography in the first decade of the twenty-first century was made possible by numerous regulatory failures within the military where personal technologies were concerned. Israeli military analysts placed the blame on the military's very belated and flawed understanding of the new media environment within the armed forces, pointing the finger at military officials out of touch with everyday soldier practices. Others defended the military on this count, arguing that its implicit social contract with the civilian public, its commitment to enabling close connections between soldiers and families at home, made strict regulation impossible. Wartime losses in 2006 (Lebanon) would force the military to reconsider this policy leniency in the interests of information security.

Formal regulations regarding the personal technologies of soldiers were first codified in the 1980s, on the eve of the first Palestinian uprising. In 1986, the military chief of staff issued an order prohibiting soldiers from "taking photos or video filming" in or near military facilities and from filming "other soldiers performing their duty" without receiving permission from commanding officers.⁵⁵ The directive stipulated that "a soldier shall not possess a still or video camera or any other filming device while in a military facility or with a military unit unless he was given permission to do so."⁵⁶ Soldier violations constituted a criminal offense under Israel's code of military justice, and although this directive would remain in effect for two decades, amended in 2007 to include digital devices, it was rarely enforced.⁵⁷ During this period, there were several reported cases of hazing by means of cellphone cameras within combat units. While some of the soldiers involved were subject to disciplinary measures, none would be prosecuted.⁵⁸ In the shadow of such policy leniency, on-duty camera usage was allowed to flourish, virtually unregulated.

Cellphones were the most prevalent personal technology carried into military theaters by soldiers.⁵⁹ When Israel deployed troops into the West Bank during the second Palestinian uprising, "everyone brought his mobile phone along. . . . There was much variability among the phones. Some were old and heavy while others were thin, elegant, incorporated with a PDA. Some even had internet access enabling them to communicate with remote computer networks."⁶⁰ The Israeli commercial cellphone market actively responded to soldiers' needs. In May 2000, "[w]hen the Israeli army pulled out of southern Lebanon . . . some of the cellular operators reduced prices for calls originating from Israel's boundary with Lebanon, making it cheaper for soldiers arriving safely at the border to call home."⁶¹ This collaboration between the military and the private sector, a longstanding one in Israel, was deemed crucial to wartime morale.⁶² Within popular Israeli imaginations, the nation's ability to easily employ its mobile phones during wartime was represented as no less than a national right.⁶³

The absence of a comprehensive military ban on personal technologies was, then, not merely a policy failure but a willful calculation, a means of strengthening a perceived social contract.⁶⁴ Military commentators discussed this openly:

On the one hand, the [Israeli Military] Supreme Command several years ago issued a clear ban on the use of privately owned mobile phones while soldiers are engaged in military activities, including training and combat. This ban is owing to the fear of distraction by the device and the threat of revealing classified information, including the whereabouts of the soldiers, which the enemy might detect from signals emitted by the phone. During off-duty hours, however, the enforcement of the ban had been virtually im-

IMAGE 10. Israeli soldier with a personal cellphone, crossing from Lebanon to Israel follow-ing the cessation of the military operation. 15 August 2006. Source: Petr Josek/Reuters.

possible; hence the army's ombudsman, who was approached on the matter, has responded with a more liberal policy. Thus, soldiers can get in touch with their families and girl/boyfriends from wherever they happen to be, including outlying areas.[65]

Such loose enforcement was proudly embraced by soldiers as a crucial measure of the military's comprehension of their personal needs. "[T]he IDF understands our need to be available to our families at all times," wrote an Israeli reserv-ist-scholar in 2003, "so that even when on routine patrol duty we were allowed to answer our phones and hold short conversations, as long as we were careful to stop the patrol vehicle by the wayside."[66] Within military calculations of this period, the social cost of an outright ban was deemed too high, more than Israeli society could bear given its sacrosanct integration of military and civilian life.

Military policy in this arena would shift markedly in the wake of the 2006 Israeli war on Lebanon. This was the first active combat context in which Israeli soldiers carried their private phones onto the battlefield in large numbers and used them heavily for routine communication with family and friends (see Image 10).[67] Despite the availability of military-issued encrypted mobile phones, these personal technologies would also be retooled for occasional military usage when

need demanded.[68] Lebanon would be perceived as a decisive Israeli military failure, or so an internal state investigation would find in the war's aftermath, with
blame placed on the military's lack of media coordination and preparedness. Some
Israeli commentators argued that soldiers' lax cellphone usage had been decisive,
making them vulnerable to the enemy.[69] The military's post-war corrective was
substantial. Israel established a new government body, the National Information
Directorate, to centralize its media work and generate new regulations regarding
the personal technologies of soldiers.[70] The media lessons of the Lebanon defeat
were stark and lasting. Military commentators agreed that the cost of maintaining
national cohesion and social intimacy by means of personal soldier phones had
been impossibly high.

As social media usage grew in popularity, the perceived digital threat began
to shift.[71] Belatedly, the military targeted the dangers of mobile photography:
"Uploading video and photographed images has become a common phenomenon
among soldiers," wrote an Israeli journalist in 2008.[72] A new order targeting cellphone cameras would be issued that year, telegraphed succinctly in a headline:
Cellular Phone with a Camera? Not at Our Base.[73] The ban spurred a national
conversation about the dangers of mobile photography: "Many soldiers think
they are photographing their friends at the base, but are not aware of the great
dangers these photographs pose," wrote on Israeli journalist. "They can easily be
used by the enemy."[74] Some Israeli pundits pinned the problem on a lack of internal
military education, while others recommended dedicated "field security" units
to remove dangerous soldier images from the internet.[75] The belated nature of
the military's regulatory efforts did not escape their notice: "nice that someone
in the IDF has finally woken up."[76]

The media lessons of Lebanon would be tested during the 2008–2009 assault
on the Gaza Strip a few months later, representing the military's first systematic attempt, in a wartime context, to implement its new policies concerning the personal
technologies of soldiers. Military orders stipulated that no soldiers were permitted to
enter Gaza with their mobile phones or digital cameras, with violators promised stiff
penalties.[77] Information security was the military's primary objective, yet officers
also defended the ban in other terms, arguing its power to focus soldiers' minds.[78]
Again, enforcement proved both difficult and uneven. At the conclusion of the
military assault, confusion would ensue when the military endeavored to return all
the confiscated cellphones—suitcases upon suitcases full of them, it was reported
by the Israeli media—to their soldier-owners. Nor had the ban been systematic. In

fact, soldiers carrying their personal cellphones into the operation had produced
another informal photographic record of military atrocity during the course of the
operation, as Breaking the Silence would document.[79] The resonances from Breaking
the Silence's 2004 exhibit were striking to many. Once again, military policy laxity
had enabled the production of a damning perpetrator's archive.

The 2008–2009 Gaza war was also a telecommunications landmark in another
sense: it represented the first comprehensive targeting of Palestinian telecommunications infrastructures by the Israeli military. The forms of targeting were multiple, and the damage considerable, gravely impairing the Gazan telecommunications network. Among the related military tactics was a systematic incorporation
of private Palestinian phones into the military's battlefield strategy by means of
the "knock on the roof" policy, consisting of calls placed to Gaza residents on their
personal cellphones and landlines to warn them of an imminent bombing.[80] These
calls were lauded in military discourse as protective mechanisms with the ability
to dramatically decrease civilian deaths and trumpeted by analysts in Israel and
abroad as evidence of both "moral clarity" and "innovative" warfare.[81] Critics of the
military operation accused Israel of employing such calls to "legally [condition]
the battlefield" by converting civilian sites into legitimate military targets "whose
destruction would have been otherwise in contravention of the law."[82]

The Israeli military assigned a parallel legal function to the mobile phones
of Gaza's civilian residents. When held by a Palestinian at the wrong time and
place, these personal technologies provided the military with legal cover to bomb
a civilian residence by effectively redesignating their bearers as combatants.
Consider the following interview with an Israeli soldier regarding the military's
"rules of engagement" during the course of the Gaza incursion (questions posed
by members of Breaking the Silence):

Q: There are standard procedures for lookouts, or people with cell phones?

A: There's no such thing. *If I detect a lookout, someone holding binoculars or a
cell phone—he's an accomplice.* I must direct fire and take him down. Dress
is important, appearance, suspect signs. . . . *If he stands on a roof holding a
cellphone, that's suspect.*[83]

There were other corroborating testimonies. In what follows, an Israeli sniper
describes a military order given during the operation to "take down" any visible
"lookouts." The interviewer asks for clarification:

Q: What does that mean?

A: During the bombings, people either ran away or hid, so it was said that if anyone is out on a street where the IDF is currently present, *and he's holding a cell phone*—he must be a lookout. . . .

Q: But here, for example, it's someone holding a cell phone, not someone running towards you, armed.

A: That's right. But he is considered incriminated. We're not on routine security duty here, suspect arrest procedures. This is a type of war.[84]

When one reads these soldier testimonials together, a consistent military strategy becomes visible. The mere presence of cellular technologies rendered Gazans legitimate targets: their technologies "incriminated" them and they could be targeted for a kill. In Palestinian hands, personal technologies transformed the civilian into a combatant, able to be killed with impunity.

In the first decade of the twenty-first century, as this abbreviated history suggests, a wholesale shift in military policy was at work. Now, personal technologies were being designated as wartime actors in their own right, in new ways and degrees: variously as communications tools, regulatory objects, and targets. This history also illustrates the legacy of policy ambivalence and belatedness that attended the rise of mobile technologies in military theaters. It would take years before official bans and regulations caught up to the pace of personal technology usage within military ranks. In this gap between everyday technology usage and military policy, a generation of Israeli soldier-photographers flourished, in the stance of both willing perpetrators and anti-occupation activists. But policy laxity was highly selective. The leniency extended to Israeli soldier-photographers in Lebanon was not available to Palestinians living under occupation. Policy laxity was very unevenly distributed across the geography of occupation.

HOME INVASIONS

During their years of military service in the West Bank, both Noam and Eitan participated in numerous nighttime raids on private Palestinian homes. It was a standard feature of Israeli rule—and particularly prevalent during the military violence of the second intifada period—taking place in hundreds of Palestinian homes and neighborhoods, and sometimes numerous times a month for any given household. These raids often took the form of so-called mapping exercises (*mipuim*), thus designated in military terminology. "Mapping" involved not only forced entry and search of private Palestinian homes, typically in the early morning hours, but also full documentation of the residence: its dimensions and layout, the identities of their residents, the contents of the home, and so forth.[85] The military needed no specific pretense. These households were not suspected of committing an offense. The military simply required the documentation in the interest of Israeli security. Or thus was the official argument.

Cameras played a crucial role in such documentation practices. Typically, the military employed their official camera operators to do this job. But when these official cameras and operators were unavailable, other soldiers, using their personal cameras, were sometimes called upon. Noam described the operations this way:

> It's always at night. You enter the house, and you start writing down people's names, the description of the house, the drawing of the house. You're also taking pictures of the people. The idea is to put the names together with faces of people. And one of these times, I was asked to take these pictures, with my own private camera.... I did like twenty, twenty-five portraits of people.

Mapping procedures followed a standardized operational template, as one learns from the testimonies of former soldiers. They were mandated to collect personal data—"name, I.D. number and telephone numbers of all residents"— and to produce a visual record, to "photograph the people, the houses, so that there's intelligence information."[86]

As his unit's official camera operator, Eitan's role in such operations was crucial, both at the time of the home invasion and well before. The unit would first select a particular residence for the raid. Then, in days prior to the raid, he or a member of his unit would visit the nearest military headquarters to review the digital surveillance archive: aerial images of the targeted residence, shot from above and from a side angle, along with detailed military maps of the city or town. All this enabled them to plan their raid with precision.

Eitan became accustomed to mapping exercises. They were routine, as was his role as photographer:

> Eitan: If you have really nothing to do [no urgent operations] you would do mapping.... [E]ach team or platoon gets a street or a neighborhood [in the occupied West Bank] and you go and knock on every door, wake every family

up. And you're supposed to be nice. Be really nice. Don't knock the door down, just knock on the door. Take photos of every one of the family members and write down his name, his occupation, and a couple of details. And then you draw a map of the house with a pencil, and you move to the next house.

Rebecca: Now let's clarify the role of cameras here. You'd photograph everyone in the house?

Eitan: Yes. . . . You photograph the people that live inside the house and you draw the house on a piece of paper.

For a while, Eitan complied with military orders. It could be argued that his photographic work during mapping exercises drew on his longstanding interest in portraiture: these, too, were faces. But he began to have doubts about the necessity of this military practice:

Eitan: The first doubt I had about that operation is that you get like a piece of army paper that you need to fill—a form [on which you record] the details, everything. It didn't have a place to write the [identifying] number of the photo, so that when we got back to the base we'd know that . . . it's photo number 36 or something like that.

Rebecca: The form has no place for information about the photographs?

Eitan: Right. And I said, "hmmm, that's weird." I got back to the base and I went to the intelligence officer and I told him: "OK, let's download all the photos I took tonight so you can use them." And he said: "No, erase them. It's not really important." I gave them all the reports—you know, all the mapping, the drawing of the houses, everything. And he put it all in a shredder.

Such practices were recurrent, Eitan said. He'd already had a similar experience with his reconnaissance images, those shot during lethal sniper operations and ostensibly saved for military review. In practice, he said, nobody wanted to see them. In the case of the numerous mapping operations in which Eitan participated between 2005 and 2007, the military's failure to operationalize the images was more categorical. Noam told a similar story, as would numerous soldiers interviewed by Breaking the Silence.[87] None of the data collected during these home invasions, neither textual nor photographic, would be archived or processed. The military's disregard was systematic.

This is where Eitan pauses his narrative, where he locates its shock: not in the repressive terms of the military operation, but in the military failure to operationalize his images. He had accepted the routine violence of these operations, believing they were necessary measures, if regrettable ones, and had faith in the importance of cameras in such procedures. And he believed in the camera as a bureaucratic tool, a technology of data collection. But in the failure to operationalize, the military had broken a promise: both the promise that such operations were driven by security necessity and that cameras were indispensable tools in the process. In Eitan's telling, his radicalization came with the unraveling of this fiction. Yes, it was a crucial military technology in these operational contexts. But its success was not dependent on outcomes. Photographs would not be collected. Indeed, the camera didn't even need to function correctly. Point and shoot was enough. Breaking the Silence would summarize this issue succinctly in subsequent publications: despite military arguments to the contrary, mapping exercises were performative spectacles of military power, "demonstrations of presence" (*hafganat nochechut*).[88] The cameras were, in essence, designed to fail.[89] Their success lay in process, not outcome. These cameras were technologies of occupation in a more expansive sense.

I ask Noam to see his images, those he photographed on his personal camera during mapping operations. But he had erased them all, months after the operation, for reasons he could not really remember or piece together. Looking back as an anti-occupation activist, his regret is considerable: "One of the stupidest things I did. . . ." At the time, during his years as a soldier, he did not really understand their value, their political import. Had he preserved them, he could have mobilized them now as a kind of counter-archive. But that instinct, that understanding of the radical potential of militarized photography, would only come with time.

CONCLUSION: TECHNOLOGY TRANSFERS

For Israeli soldiers and military officials in the first decade of the twentieth century, the influx of personal technologies into military theaters, and the function of these technologies, was neither self-evident nor simple. Rather, their function had to be learned. The process was slow and error was frequent, as both soldiers and military officials labored to understand the political risks and potentials of this new media landscape.

Along the way, lags were frequent and challenges considerable. For soldiers serving in the occupied West Bank at the height of the second intifada, particularly those charged with a heavily mobilized crackdown on Palestinian protestors, the sheer logistics of amateur photography were considerable. Armed with flak jackets and weighed down with both weapons and telecommunications equipment—cartridges, grenades, radios—photography was a very encumbered art and often in tension with military directives. Under conditions of so-called counterinsurgency, even a simple snapshot often required the coordination of the entire unit. The challenging choreography involved, as whole units struggled to "get the right shot," suggests a military culture in which the drive to document was a growing compulsion, at once propelled and enabled by this shifting technological landscape.

Soldiers using their cameras as activist tools were also learning on the job, but differently. While Noam's photography was often compulsive and frenzied, it lacked a clear direction—or, at least, one he could articulate with any precision. Looking back at his photographs a few years later, through the lens of his radicalization, he was still at pains to reconcile his photographic gaze and his political orientation, struggling to make sense of his images: "uh . . . political pictures, I guess you would call them." Even his favored visual tropes, his obsessive attention to soldiers at the windows, were not clear to him. "You're asking many questions about things I've never thought about." Noam's interpretive confusion was shared by others, including some of the soldier-activists who participated in Breaking the Silence's 2004 photographic exhibit:

> Even when it was on the wall and you saw it all together, even then you didn't understand it all. And then you start to explain everything to the guys at the show, to tell stories . . . and every time around [the exhibit] you learn something else, another thing and then another. You rummage around in it more and you understand things better, get some perspective.[90]

Breaking the Silence activists came to the exhibition armed with an anti-occupation critique. But even so, they struggled to make sense of the images. Their interpretive confusion was born of mainstream Israeli ideology, reflecting the challenges of breaking through a public silence about the violence of Israeli military rule. But it was equally a struggle with the medium, indexing a moment before the normalization of photographic witnessing as a social practice. The same was true of Israeli audiences; they were shocked at the scenes of military violence but equally by the prevalence of consumer technologies that seemed out of place in military contexts. Both Israeli activists and audiences were laboring to reconceptualize amateur cameras as radical political tools.

The military was also learning the terms of this new media environment—and, as military commentators noted perpetually, they were often failing to get it right. In the years chronicled here, official policy regarding the personal technologies of soldiers fluctuated between the poles of willful leniency and grave miscalculations where information security was concerned, as demonstrated by the 2006 Lebanon war. The military's perceived social contract with the national public was deemed paramount in this arena, resulting in poor enforcement of existing bans and a slow pace of new regulations. Some military analysts read this policy legacy as a categorial failure, condemning poor enforcement and belated regulatory changes. Others supported the military's perceived social contract with the national public, of which, they argued, such laxity was necessarily born. Military policy always lagged well behind soldier usage. In this gap between policy and usage, a generation of Israeli soldier-photographers flourished, both in the stance of perpetrator and activist.

This chapter concludes with a scene of learning of a very different kind. Both Noam and Eitan would discover that the photographs they took during mapping exercises, in the midst of waking Palestinian families from sleep, would never be collected or reviewed. Radicalization would follow, as they belatedly understood the function of their personal cameras as blunt instruments of terror, technologies designed to fail.[91] In both this context, as within the context of the 2008–2009 Gaza war, the military was re-designating personal technologies as instruments of military occupation; personal cameras and cellphones were being conscripted into the military arsenal in new ways and degrees, variously as tools of military repression and, when held in Palestinian hands, as legal targets of Israeli warfare. This contrast is a reminder that military policy ambivalence regarding personal technologies was highly selective: only activated when it served perceived military or national interests. The permissiveness that Israeli soldier-photographers enjoyed on the battlefield in Lebanon, or in the West Bank with their personal cameras, used as tools of creative production, was not extended to Palestinian residents of the Gaza Strip. The difference was deadly.

A central Israeli mythology of the digital age lies at the heart of this chapter. In the years chronicled here, the Israeli state would proudly trumpet its technology transfers from the military into the civilian sector. These transfers were deemed a pillar of the Israeli high-tech advantage, as when drone technologies were given medical applications, or when surveillance infrastructures were retooled to protect the health of the Israeli population. In the process, lethality gave way to salubrious innovation, stripped of their deadly effects, or so the state narrative insisted.[92] Obscured by this narrative was the other axis of technology transfers, underway concurrently: namely, the movement of consumer technologies into Israeli military arsenals, policies, and battlefield plans. In the hands of the Israeli sniper, the "simple Fujifilm" camera was also a tool of occupation.

Chapter 2

CAMERAS UNDER CURFEW

Occupied Media Infrastructures

HUMAN RIGHTS WORKER MUSA ABU HASHHASH LIVED AND WORKED in Hebron during the second Palestinian uprising, documenting the Israeli military crackdown with his camera. Military restrictions on Palestinian movement in the city were severe and punishing in the service of protecting its Jewish settler population. Hebron residents lived under nearly constant closures and curfews, interrupted only occasionally by military sponsored breaks for procuring provisions, while settlers enjoyed Israeli state protection and unconstrained mobility.[1] Palestinians discovered breaking the curfew faced the threat of lethal military fire. International and Jewish Israeli photojournalists were scarce in these years, deterred by the perceived threat from "Palestinian militants." And as a result, Musa was often the only photographer working during military assaults on the city, electing to break curfew in order to create a photographic record. Military reprisals often followed in the form of detention or arrest, destruction or confiscation of his camera. Musa had several near-death experiences in these years, such as when a soldier took retributive aim at his camera with live fire, the bullet grazing his head. "I risked my life many times to film," he told me.

Even when he managed to capture the images or footage he sought, Musa encountered problems with delivery and circulation. He was working with the

Israeli human rights organization B'Tselem as their primary West Bank field-worker, documenting rights violations in the Hebron region. The nearly constant state of military closures and curfew meant that Musa was often unable to deliver his footage to the NGO's West Jerusalem offices, or even to transport his VHS cassettes out of Hebron, while the absence of reliable internet access in the West Bank usually foreclosed the possibility of a digital video transfer. Often, after the closure or curfew had finally been lifted and it was possible for him to travel, his footage was simply out of date, no longer of interest to the Israeli media outlets with which B'Tselem worked. In that window of delay, amid the fast-moving pace of the uprising, Israeli attention had turned elsewhere.

"I still have many cassette tapes from those days," Musa said, as we spoke about this years later in his West Bank home. "Many of the videos are still in my home today, because I couldn't send them in time." They remain in his residence, crammed into his small office. These tapes are both records and casualties of Israeli military rule.

This chapter chronicles the experiences of Palestinian videographers and camera-activists working in the occupied West Bank in the first decade of the twenty-first century (2000–2012), well before the proliferation of cameras or mobile digital technologies in Palestine. I focus on videographers who worked with the Israeli NGO B'Tselem (the Israeli Information Center for Human Rights in the Occupied Territories), Israel's most prominent human rights organization working within the military occupation context, which had been documenting Israeli violations of Palestinian rights since its founding in 1989 during the early years of the first Palestinian uprising.[2] In 2007, the organization launched a camera project that delivered hundreds of hand-held camcorders and rudimentary training to Palestinian families in particularly precarious areas of the occupied West Bank, where state violence was elevated, so they could document their frequent abuse at the hands of soldiers and settler populations.

For B'Tselem, the function and import of the camera project was varied. The NGO employed Palestinian eyewitness video as evidentiary materials in complaints and petitions filed with the military law enforcement system on behalf of Palestinians harmed by soldiers and used such footage as the basis for public advocacy and education in Israel and internationally regarding the military occupation. The NGO would abandon the legal component of this process in 2016, arguing that cooperation with the military's investigative process had effectively propped up the military regime: "Over the years, the military law enforcement system has developed the expectation that human rights organizations, including B'Tselem, serve as subcontractors for the military investigative system. . . . [W]e no longer want to serve as the occupation's fig leaf."[3]

B'Tselem's Palestinian partners had a rather different set of interests. They entered into the project on the basis of a wager about the relative political affordances of mediating their injuries through Israeli human rights channels, hoping that B'Tselem's intimate relationship to Israeli state and civil institutions, in both legal and media arenas, would help to advance their claims. They did so despite a military legal system that had, historically, enabled soldiers to harm Palestinians with legal impunity, and despite a growing awareness of the failed justice promises of the transnational human rights industry in Palestine, in ways Lori Allen has described.[4] It was a tactical and provisional wager born of limited political alternatives.

At the core of the B'Tselem camera project, a pillar of the relationship between the Israeli NGO and its West Bank team, was the demand for original copies of videographic materials shot by Palestinian camera operators: cassette tapes, data sticks, memory cards. In days when a suspicion about videographic provenance was beginning to grow and accelerate, originals were increasingly required in both legal and media arenas. As a result, any West Bank footage deemed usable, footage with strong images of Israeli perpetrators and Palestinian victims, had to be physically transported to B'Tselem's West Jerusalem office. Along this route, the footage moved through a network of Palestinian actors involved in this video ecosystem from point of capture to point of circulation: volunteer videographers, fieldworkers, cab drivers who delivered footage. It was a multi-sited circuit that began at the place of the human rights violation in the occupied territories and ended in various Israeli locations: on the NGO's social media feed; on the Israeli evening news; or, more occasionally, in the Israeli military court system, submitted as evidence against the Israeli authorities.

Or it might never circulate. Even after footage had been deemed strong and viable, Palestinian camera operators faced the challenges associated with its transport to West Jerusalem, regularly hindered by closures and curfews. Thanks to the restrictive terms of the Israeli permit regime in the occupied territories, most videographers could not travel into Israel and transport had to be outsourced to others (e.g., Israelis from the NGO's offices or Palestinians with Jerusalem IDs).[5] Infrastructural limitations of various kinds also stood in the way of timely delivery:

poor roads, missing electrical grids, internet outages.[6] All this slowed or, at times, wholly prevented the arrival of cassette tapes or memory cards.

Footage was also stymied or prevented at its point of capture. Palestinian camera operators in the West Bank were forced to navigate the perpetual gap between Israeli military law and military practice, where photography was concerned. By law, they were permitted to film routine military operations, save under "extraordinary circumstances" when the authorities declared a risk to military information security or soldier safety. But the daily experience of these Palestinian videographers was otherwise. Contra official Israeli state assurances, they faced the perpetual threat of retributive actions by police and soldiers in the form of violence to themselves or their equipment.[7] Between the poles of eruptive military violence in the form of soldier or settler beatings, and the slow violence of Israeli occupation in the form of infrastructural neglect, the ability of Palestinian footage to reach its target audiences was always in doubt.[8]

Such doubts are at this chapter's core. The chapter tracks the videographic ecosystem from point of capture in the West Bank to point of delivery in West Jerusalem, with a focus on the numerous forms of belatedness, constraint, and interruption that mired and complicated both production and circulation of the videographic record. The Palestinian camera-activists chronicled in these pages employed a varied toolbox of political tactics that enabled creative maneuvering. But Israeli military rule generated perpetual and flexible constraints. This chapter's counterpart, although largely invisible in the pages that follow, was the dream of liberation technologies. As my Introduction has noted, it was a dream that seized the imagination of anti-occupation publics across the globe in the early twenty-first century, catalyzed by the popular revolutions in the Arab Middle East and North Africa in 2011. Missing from this dream was an accounting for the difficult labor involved for Palestinians living under occupation as they endeavored to use their cameras as liberatory tools. Or rather: how the violence of occupation, in its myriad and flexible forms, made its mark on the project of Palestinian eyewitness videography at every point along the videographic circuit, often frustrating and impeding the footage's capacity to be distributed and publicly seen. This chapter is a chronicle of that often invisible violence.

PHOTOGRAPHERS AT RISK

In the occupied territories during the second intifada period, Palestinian journalists and camera operators labored under dangerous and difficult conditions.[9]

In addition to the frequent military closures and curfews, severely limiting Palestinian movement, the Israeli authorities were systematically stripping Palestinian journalists of basic press freedoms in an effort to block their access and control media narratives.[10] The Palestinian Center for Human Rights (PCHR) chronicled a pattern of wide-ranging and systematic attacks against Palestinian journalists during these years by members of the Israeli security services, including:

> beating journalists and subjecting them to other means of violence and humiliating and degrading treatment; arresting and holding journalists; denying journalist[s] access to certain areas and preventing them from covering certain incidents; confiscation of media equipment and devices; bombarding or raiding media centers and misusing their contents; preventing journalists from traveling abroad; and raiding journalists' houses.[11]

All this, the PCHR concluded, constituted a pattern of "willful and intentional [attacks] designed to prevent the objective coverage of incidents in the occupied Palestinian Territories."[12] Nine Palestinian journalists would be killed by the Israeli forces between 2000–2009, documented by the Committee to Protect Journalists (CPJ), while numerous others were shot and wounded.[13] The title of a CPJ report from this period telegraphed the issue: *At Risk: Covering the Intifada*.[14] Concurring with the findings of PCHR, they argued that "in at least some of these cases, IDF soldiers may have targeted journalists deliberately (the IDF denies this)."[15] The costs for Palestinian journalists and camera operators were high.

B'Tselem began their experimentation with cameras during this period. They started in the Hebron area—the West Bank's largest city and a hub of Jewish nationalist extremism, home to a settler population that had progressively grown in size and territorial holdings in the three decades prior, their presence safeguarded and cultivated by successive Israeli administrations. Musa, with whom this chapter began, was the organization's first fieldworker. In those days, he said, in keeping with global human rights protocols of the moment, the NGO did not understand photography's importance as an evidentiary or advocacy tool, viewing cameras as merely supporting technologies. Nonetheless, Musa carried several cameras with him as he worked, shooting both still images and footage, and B'Tselem would send the occasional clip to the Israeli media for review on the evening news. Musa experienced frequent military attacks in these years, particularly when his cameras were active. And as a fieldworker, he heard many similar stories from Palestinian members of the press. Here was one such testimonial from journalist 'Abd al-Hafiz al-Hashlamouni, who lived and worked in Hebron, as told to Musa:

> I saw six soldiers stop a Palestinian fellow and push him into a fence. His hands were raised. I began to take pictures of the incident and one of the soldiers saw me. The soldiers left the fellow and came over to me. They beat me and took the camera.... With another camera I had, I tried to photograph the soldiers and they noticed. A few of them came over to me, pushed me onto a car parked in the square and beat me. They kicked me a few times, punched me, and hit me with their rifle butts. The soldiers also took the second camera out of my hands.... Later, the soldiers left and threw the cameras on the hood of one of the cars.[16]

The experience was common. The very presence of a camera, in Palestinian hands, was a dangerous prospect, met with frequent soldier retribution. The military would deny the charge of systematic and willful targeting of Palestinian journalists and camera operators, often taking refuge in an argument about mistaken identity: cameras mistaken for guns. Such was their response to the 2008 killing of Reuters journalist Fadel Shana in the Gaza Strip:

> *The tank crew was unable to determine the nature of the object mounted on the tripod, and positively identify it as [either] an anti-tank missile, a mortar or a television camera....* In light of the reasonable conclusion reached by the tank crew and its superiors that the characters were hostile, and were carrying an object most likely to be a weapon, the decision to fire at the target... was sound.[17]

It was a lethal affirmation of a truism that Palestinian journalists knew well. In the estimation of the Israeli military, Palestinian cameras were dangerous political tools.

For Palestinians living in Hebron, daily attacks and harassment from Jewish settlers were also perpetual, particularly for families living in close proximity to settler homes.[18] In 2007, the NGO distributed cameras to some of these families, as both documentary and protective tools. In 2007, Rajaa Abu Aisha used one of these cameras to film the neighboring settlement of Tel Rumeida, infamous for what the Israeli media called a "reign of terror" against Hebron's Palestinians.[19]

Her footage was sharp and dramatic, shot from behind the metal screen her family had installed for their protection. Her camera followed settler Yifat Alkobi as she taunted Rajaa on the other side of the screen with the repetition of a single curse, delivered slowly and rhythmically in Arabic to consolidate the injury: *"sharmuta, sharmuuuuuta"* (whore). An Israeli soldier could be seen in the background of the frame, standing idly by.[20]

B'Tselem sent the footage to the Israeli news, and a viral media storm ensued.[21] At a time before widespread photographic technologies in the West Bank, Palestinian testimonial videography of this kind was still rare and arresting for Israeli audiences. The clip "set the country on edge," in the words of the Israeli media, with voluminous coverage and commentary in both the national and international press.[22] The militant nature of Hebron's settler population had a considerable and well-documented history, but Israeli commentators still spoke about the event in the language of shock. "TV viewers were exposed to an almost-physical experience," wrote a journalist for the Israeli daily *Haaretz*: "Pure human poison bubbling up from their television screen and directly entering their veins."[23] The footage traveled to the Israeli parliament where it generated a hearing before the Foreign Affairs and Defense Committee.[24] Comments from numerous state officials followed, including a public condemnation from the Israeli Defense Ministry and a call for a military investigation. The scale of the clip's virality even compelled a comment from the Israeli prime minister, Ehud Olmert, who endeavored to disavow state responsibility: "I saw it and I was ashamed. I felt very ill at ease because a soldier was standing by who had no authority to act. An incorrect impression was created . . . that the entire incident was under the regime's aegis."[25] Olmert also registered his surprise at the presence of the camera, deemed out of place in Palestinian hands: "Clearly, this is not the first time. Only this time, there was a camera . . . "[26]

B'Tselem launched a dedicated video project in the following year (2008), a response to the unexpected circulation of Rajaa's footage. The project was initially focused in the Hebron region, but grew massively in scale and spread in subsequent years, eventually involving communities from across the West Bank who worked in a volunteer capacity as videographers, overseen by a staff of paid Palestinian fieldworkers. The number of cameras distributed was relatively constant, a byproduct of an organizational decision to keep the project manageable, but the population of videographers was regularly in flux. Some grew tired of the work or simply became less active. In years when few residents had access to other photographic technologies, many families were eager to participate, and requests to participate far outpaced institutional capacity. While the NGO focused their relationship on a single volunteer within a household, cameras were designated as family property that was available for flexible usage and needs, both testimonial and personal. Thus, the same camera or cassette tape might contain footage of both settler attacks and baby namings, both military crackdowns and family road trips. This functional flexibility sometimes created tensions between the NGO and its volunteers, as when the NGO's demand for videographic originals, required for legal process, came into conflict with family desires to preserve private memories. This flexibility also made its mark on the institution's central video archives in West Jerusalem that functioned as a polyvalent repository of Palestinian life under occupation, with footage of violent assaults interspersed with those of daily Palestinian pleasures.

B'Tselem valued technological simplicity, arguing that cameras with basic functionality had the best chance for success in a crisis context. They began with rudimentary cassette-based camcorders that required manual digitization before files could be uploaded, eventually moving to digital cameras with memory cards. Cellphone cameras were categorically rejected as testimonial tools. Anyone could pick up a phone and photograph, the NGO argued, but they were investing in a cadre of trained and professionalized witnesses. They also hoped that more professional cameras had a security advantage, effectively identifying the operator as a human rights worker and thus moderating their treatment by the security services. These standard-issue camcorders with rudimentary zoom lens were particularly effective in urban locales or within interiors, when videographers filmed military violence from proximate vantages, like porches or windows, or within a family home.[27] But their usefulness diminished when a more powerful zoom was required for documenting violence at a distance, as in rural communities facing settler incursions or arson attacks in their agricultural lands. Given that their cameras lacked the capacity for long-distance precision, the footage shot by Palestinian camera operators in rural locales often lacked sharp images of assailants, chiefly seen as miniatures through their distant lens. In rural communities, perpetrator portraiture was a rarity.

The B'Tselem project was driven by an institutional investment in visible evidence of human rights abuses. But in those years, with few other camera technologies in most West Bank locales, the NGO argued that the security functionality was equally vital. As the project progressed, volunteers attested to the lighter

IMAGE 11. B'Tselem videographer films a demonstration against military restrictions. Hebron. 21 February 2014. Source: Oren Ziv/Activestills.

hand of Israeli security services when their cameras were active, driven by a fear of exposure. "The soldiers are now used to being filmed," a Palestinian fieldworker from the Hebron area noted in 2011. "They have accepted it." Most settlers, however, were not deterred. In the first few years of the video project, Palestinians armed with photographic technologies took Jewish settlers by surprise during their rampages on private Palestinian homes and lands—a surprise that was often registered on footage, as when settlers discovered mounted cameras perched in windows. A few years hence, settlers would be armed with their own photographic tools, activating them during raids on Palestinian homes and lands. They sought to respond to Palestinian videography in kind.

THE CAMERAS OF NABI SALEH

Although small in size, with a population of several hundred, Nabi Saleh became a focal point for West Bank protest after the second Palestinian uprising.[28] What started as a local nonviolent demonstration in 2009—a response to the seizure of village lands by the neighboring Jewish settlement of Halamish—grew into a broad-based political movement that drew residents from across Palestine, as well as a steady stream of Israeli and international solidarity activists and journalists.[29] The Israeli forces employed harsh measures to quell the weekly demonstrations, responding to protestors with tear gas, pepper spray, and beatings—and, less frequently, with rubber bullets and live fire. Arrests of demonstrators were common, with much more leniency granted to Israeli activists and photographers. Palestinians, subjects of Israel's military law, did not enjoy such leniency.[30] Military raids on village households suspected of political participation would also intensify as the popular protest swelled, as would detentions and arrests of suspected activists.

Bilal Tamimi, a resident of the Nabi Saleh with a longstanding interest in photography, was active in the popular struggle from its outset, employing his camcorder as a political tool. In the early years, he filmed the weekly demonstrations from the modest protection of his roof, or shielded by a porch or awning in an effort to avoid detection by the military.[31] Then, as the village's protest movement began to grow, he felt that political necessity dictated a retreat from the shadows. Soon, he adopted a strategy of filming in full view of the military, often from the very center of any confrontation with the security services. Although international journalists were present in growing numbers at the Friday demonstrations, Bilal believed that they had failed to capture the scale and import of their political struggle. Seeking greater exposure, he began an institutional affiliation with B'Tselem in 2010. They provided him with a digital video camera, a welcome change from cassettes and the associated work required to upload footage, and soon taught himself basic video-editing skills and launched a personal YouTube channel dedicated to the weekly protests and the village's encounters with the security services. He passed a large volume of footage to B'Tselem for review and processing in these years, for their legal or advocacy needs, but would also publish actively on his YouTube channel, including all the footage that the NGO was not using.[32] He kept his cameras next to his bed in accordance with his personal pledge to "document everything" pertaining to the village's struggle with the security services. "Wherever they went," he said, "I would follow them" (see Image 12).

When Bilal began his B'Tselem affiliation in 2010, he owned and operated one of the only cameras in the community. Two years later, many families had access to a photographic technology of some kind, and they proliferated at the Friday protests, although dwarfed by those of international journalists.[33] Most Nabi Saleh families now had internet access, with many sharing routers between households to enable cheaper connectivity, and many used social media to advance the

IMAGE 12. Israeli soldier blocks Palestinian video-activist and B'Tselem volunteer Bilal Tamimi as he documents a military crackdown on Nabi Saleh demonstrators. 25 August 2015. Source: Haim Schwarczenberg.

popular struggle. What was, as recently as two years prior, a political arena from which cameras and new digital technologies were virtually absent had quickly become a very crowded media theater with a robust social media presence.[34] The security forces had initially attempted to prevent Bilal from photographing with pepper spray, beatings, and arrests (see Image 13). But after a while, once he was a fixture at the ever-larger Friday protests and known to many military commanders, his presence was largely tolerated. He adopted a strategy of filming the forces at close range, always prominently displaying his laminated B'Tselem identification, proof of his affiliation with Israel's most prominent human rights organization. In the early years of the video ecosystem in Palestine, when much testimonial videography from the West Bank was identifiable by its shaking lens and blurry frames, measures both of fear and technological newness, Bilal's videographic work was an exception, always steady and assured.

Sitting together in front of his office computer in 2011, in the Palestinian Ministry of Education in Ramallah where he worked for a time, we screened some of his recent footage of the Friday demonstrations. A recent crackdown by the

IMAGE 13. Israeli border police detain Palestinian video-activist Bilal Tamimi following an anti-occupation demonstration. Nabi Saleh. 30 December 2011. Source: Anne Paq/Activestills.

Israeli authorities—on May 13, 2011—had been particularly aggressive and severe. Crowds of Palestinian and international activists had been beaten and showered with pepper spray, and tear gas had been fired directly into the crowd. Bilal's footage from this day was bold and aggressive, as it often was. He employed his signature strategy of following the Israeli authorities closely with his camera, capturing clear images of their faces and military insignia for means of better identification.[35] Some Israeli border police pushed him away—"move the camera!"—but Bilal persisted, relocating to a different vantage when necessary but always remaining in their midst in order to film the beatings and arrests from arm's length. Bilal's persistent proximity generated a remarkable collection of perpetrator portraits that most other B'Tselem volunteers were simply unable to replicate for reasons both tactical and technical. "I know I can't be far from the action," he said.

This 2011 clip was part of a growing videographic archive. Early on, at the inception of the weekly protest movement, Bilal had committed to filming every Friday demonstration. By 2019, he had amassed a record of 400 Fridays. The Israeli battalions serving in Nabi Saleh knew him well. In later years, he filmed wearing a bright yellow vest, imprinted with the insignia of the popular protest movement, for means of better self-identification. He had been injured on numerous occasions: shot by rubber bullets, live fire, tear gas canisters. Arrests were frequent, most while his camera was rolling, as were arrests of other members of his family.[36] Repeated military threats did not deter him. He credited his footage and mounting social media following with numerous political victories, including the release from prison of Palestinian youths falsely accused by the military. Perhaps more crucially, his camera had brought the popular movement much greater global exposure: "I know the value of this picture."

Among Bilal's most widely viewed videos from his early years as a B'Tselem volunteer was a January 2011 chronicle of a military raid on his family's residence, a videographic portrait of the home invasions in which the military regularly engaged in Palestinian communities across the West Bank. The military called them mapping exercises, conducted under the pretense of creating a security-driven record of the occupied population.[37] Bilal had known the soldiers were coming, as news of military actions traveled quickly in this small village, and he had been ready when they knocked on his door at 2:00 AM. His camera was already shooting as he approached the door to meet the waiting soldiers, and his lens remained trained on the scene as he woke his two young sons from sleep, one by one, under the soldiers' directives. We see their darkened bedroom and their sudden wake from sleep, before the camera pivots back to the security services. Only a very close observer of the footage could detect Bilal's terror. "Here," he points to the screen. "You see my hand is shaking because it was the first night raid on my house."

Bilal continued to film as the soldiers generated a textual and photographic catalogue of his family and their residence. One soldier asked the questions, lingering over correct spellings of names and ID numbers, while another recorded the findings in pencil: "How many children do you have? . . . Boys or girls? . . . What is their age?" Bilal's camera remained active as the soldiers photographed his sons, still half asleep and in their night clothes. His young son offered a partial smile, glancing between his father's camera and that of the soldiers', as if playfully refusing the military desire for repressive capture.

A four-minute clip from Bilal's footage from that evening's raid would be published by B'Tselem shortly after the event, and it circulated widely in both Israeli and international media.[38] Israeli viewers who watched the clip on the Israeli evening news praised the soldiers' restraint and measured temperament, welcoming this portrait of the occupation as mere bureaucratic necessity, while official military spokespersons responded that such raids were "necessary to maintain order and security."[39] The brevity of the clip belied the duration of the military presence in Nabi Saleh that night. The military raided six households that evening, and Bilal accompanied them with his camera throughout, after receiving begrudging permission from the battalion commander and a warning to behave ("No trouble!").[40] In the resultant footage, Bilal follows the soldiers into his neighbors' private homes—"I was still in my night clothes," he told me—their silent glances toward his camera suggesting that his presence was both expected and welcome, providing a modicum of security in these insecure times. Bilal's intimate footage of his family and his neighbors turned the military desire for a total catalogue against itself, generating a fine-grained portrait of the ordinary violence of occupation.

THE RIGHT TO PHOTOGRAPH

In the first decade of the camera project (2007–2016), B'Tselem was in regular contact with the Israeli authorities regarding the West Bank videographers with whom they worked. At issue was the perpetual gap between stated policy and practice where photographers were concerned. In their official documentation and memoranda, the authorities confirmed the Palestinian right to photograph the security services. But in practice, as this chapter has already suggested, Palestinian camera operators working in the West Bank faced the constant threat of reprisals and restrictions from soldiers and police on the grounds of alleged security necessity (see Image 14).[41] What resulted, for B'Tselem, was a highly regularized and bureaucratized struggle with the Israeli security services over the Palestinian right to photograph.[42]

The NGO's struggle over the right to photograph was a minor component of its larger institutional project: namely, documenting and combating Israeli violations of Palestinian human rights in the West Bank. In these years, this larger project involved regularized contact with the Israeli authorities, chiefly in the form of complaints filed on behalf of Palestinian claimants. B'Tselem described the process, and their mediating legal role, this way:

> [The] official position [of the military law enforcement system] is that any Palestinians who wishes to make a complaint against soldiers can do so easily.... Reality, however, is very different. A Palestinian who wants to lodge

IMAGE 14. Israeli army commander declares a closed military zone, from which journalists and activists were barred, during an anti-occupation demonstration in the West Bank. Kifl Haris. 1 August 2005. Source: Yotam Ronen/Activestills.

> a complaint against soldiers cannot do so independently and has no direct access to the military law enforcement system.... [T]he military law enforcement system forces complainants to contact it through mediators, be they human rights organizations or lawyers.[43]

For many in the organization, this mediating process was viewed as both a tactical necessity and a mechanism for accountability, a means of monitoring rights violations and shaping Israeli policy and public opinion regarding the Israeli occupation. But the limitations of this strategy were also abundantly clear.[44] Procedurally, there were the vanishing gains of working within the labyrinthian bureaucracy of occupation with its proliferating rules, regulations, and formalities bent on "controlling the lives of individuals and collectives through administrative violence," as Yael Berda has written.[45] But the political limitations were paramount, as many Israeli activists argued.[46] Not only were legal victories rare, with negligible rates of soldier prosecutions, but the legal process effectively normalized the Israeli occupation through a collaboration with its law enforcement system, thereby providing the Israeli regime with a human rights imprimatur.[47] This critique would be adopted as institutional policy in 2016 when B'Tselem ceased all formal work with the military law enforcement system.[48] In their own words, "[t]he organization does not wish to assist authorities in their attempts to create a false picture of justice being served."[49]

The bureaucratized struggle over the right to photograph was highly structured. The NGO would fax a complaint to the Israeli authorities, working with a range of divisions and units within the security services, regarding a breach involving a member of their Palestinian camera team.[50] The ensuing response would be saved within the institution's internal files. In each such response, the Israeli authorities affirmed the Palestinian right to photograph, save under extraordinary circumstances, and attested to their strict adherence to legal codes, rules, and regulations. So important were these state responses as to be distributed by the NGO, in hard-copy form, to its fieldworkers and photographers in the West Bank. They were encouraged to carry copies with them in the event of problems with the security services when they attempted to film.

In the following, I quote at length from a few of these responses to B'Tselem and the attorneys with whom they worked. Most involved incidents in the Hebron area where the camera project was active and soldier retribution frequent:

26 August 2008. " . . . In your inquiry, you described an event in which soldiers detained a photographer in Hebron because he photographed them and you inquired as to whether there is a guideline that prohibits photographing soldiers.... In general, *there is no legal prohibition against photography in the West Bank, including [filming] IDF soldiers,* even while they are engaged in operational activity, provided that the goal is not to collect sensitive or classified information, and [as long as] it does not disturb the security services' ongoing activity. . . . In the specific case that occurred on 11 August 2008, the photographer was detained due to the soldier's misunderstanding. It is important to note that this case does not indicate a general attitude or guideline. . . . I'll summarize by adding that as a consequence of this incident, guidelines were further clarified with the soldiers. We thank you for your inquiry."[51]

30 November 2009. " . . . In your inquiry, it was claimed that in the last few months, there were several occasions in which soldiers forbade Palestinians from photographing in areas of the West Bank . . . and *you argue that there's a gap between the official guidelines and the behavior of soldiers* on the ground. As an outcome of your inquiry . . . *it was clarified that photography is allowed in all areas of the West Bank, including photographing IDF*

soldiers, provided that it does not interfere with the activity of the [armed] forces nor gathers classified information. Central Command [Pikud Merkaz] places a high importance on maintaining freedom of movement and [enabling] photographers' activity in the West Bank and won't limit that activity unless there is a security or operational necessity to do so."[52]

8 January 2013. " . . . Regarding [your] general claims about the attitude of the soldiers serving in Hebron towards photographers and media: there is no change in the view of Central Command . . . Central Command views, with utmost importance, maintenance of freedom of movement and press across the West Bank. Therefore, *photography is allowed in the West Bank,* provided it does not disturb soldiers' work nor expose classified information. This policy has been clarified to commanders and soldiers serving in all areas of the West Bank, including Hebron."[53]

The official responses of this period are strikingly repetitive, a measure of the constrained terms of this bureaucratic genre, the stability of official regulations, and an iterative grammar of denial where rights abuses were concerned. Throughout, the Israeli authorities take pains to stress the lawfulness of photographic documentation by Palestinian civilians and their commitment to protecting this right.[54] In most of these state responses, the original violation addressed by B'Tselem escapes explicit mention, although sometimes appears on the margins of the text in an exculpatory register: "[T]he photographer was detained due to the soldier's misunderstanding."[55] In each official response, the legality of photographic work in the occupied territories would be reaffirmed, as would the authorities' commitment to protecting this right: "The basic premise is that there's no legal prohibition to photograph in the West Bank, including taking photos of IDF soldiers even if during operational activity. The area authorities, including IDF soldiers and border police, must act according to this understanding and in this spirit!"[56] This July 2008 memo from Central Command, the portion of the military responsible for its activities in the West Bank, asserted the right to photograph in a particularly emphatic register, graphically emphasized with boldface type and an exclamation mark, a rare moment of affective prose within an otherwise dispassionate bureaucratic genre.

These memos were also at pains to detail exceptions: namely, those events in which photography was not permitted and, by extension, those that merited detention or confiscation of the photographer or her gear. First and foremost were incidents involving "sensitive and classified information" or those that "disturb the forces' ongoing activity." In the July 2008 memo referenced above, the latter was illustrated by way of example: "incidents in which photographers enter a field and stand between soldiers and terrorists during exchange of fire," thereby "interrupt[ing] their routine activity and endangering them." Both were grounds for detention following a "warning."[57] When photographers disturbed routine operations, or came between soldiers and "terrorists," their equipment and materials could be legally seized. The same memo outlined the inverse: instances in which detention and confiscation was not permissible.

> (F) The force commander must ensure that the equipment is not damaged, including the camera, film, cassettes, etc. *Film or videocassettes should not be removed from the camera and definitely must not be destroyed.* The camera should be taken with the material inside it and be transferred, as is, to the care of the Israeli police. (G)[T]*he photographer is not required to present the photos or videos,* nor should [security services] operate the camera and browse through the images, unless in the presence and guidance of the Israeli police. . . . (H) If the on-site senior commander discovers that the photographer wasn't responsible for the violation attributed to him . . . and if it is clear that these photographs can't contribute to intelligence-gathering . . . *he must be released immediately and his equipment returned.*"[58]

This detailed discussion outlines the legal terms of confiscation or seizure of photographic equipment. But it is equally a set of rules pertaining to their preservation, working at the micro-scale of the photographic event to identify steps required, by the Israeli security services, to safeguard the photographer's work, materials, and associated gear. A legacy of malfeasance is evident on the document's margins within the mandate that the security services' refrain from "operat[ing] the camera and brows[ing] through the images." Here, in the dispassionate language of military guidelines, a set of routine abuses are inadvertently exposed.

Read against the daily experience of Palestinian videographers, these memos evidence the considerable distance between military law and practice, the perpetual "gap between the official guidelines and the behavior of soldiers" with which B'Tselem and their camera operators were forced to habitually contend. For the military, this bureaucratic cycle offered considerable gains: chiefly, a formalized mechanism for dispensing with the human rights complaint through an assertion of legal compliance. Each cycle of complaint and response, with its recitation of the terms of military compliance, functioned as a crucial performative platform for the Israeli authorities, an iterative occasion to reconsolidate a set of legal fictions pertaining to the Palestinian right to photograph. Indeed, state memos went well beyond the assertion of legal compliance by portraying the military as the benevolent protector of Palestinian photographers, committed to safeguarding their well-being and that of their photographic equipment ("make sure the equipment is not damaged . . . make sure that the photographer is not asked to present the photos . . ."). In the process, casting the photographer as a proxy for the Palestinian occupied population writ large, these memos also enacted a powerful fiction about military care.[59]

MASKED SETTLERS AND TECHNICAL CONSTRAINTS

The B'Tselem camera project was particularly active in the South Hebron hills during its early years. Victims of a history of Israeli state-sponsored de-development, most villages in this region lacked connections to water and power supplies, permanent housing, and rudimentary social services like schools and health clinics. The contrast to neighboring Hebron was stark. In 2011, a time when cellular technologies were proliferating within Hebron's middle-class neighborhoods, few families in the impoverished South Hebron hills had access to cellular or photographic technologies.[60] Here, the training of camera volunteers began with the basics.

Nassar, the NGO's fieldworker for this region, conducted these trainings. "In the beginning, it's the really simple things—you know, how to handle the camera, how to open it, how to use the zoom lens," Nassar told me in 2011. "Some people hold it upside down because they really don't know what it is." He worked with a diverse population of volunteers: young and old, men and women. In later years, as women increasingly filled the volunteer ranks, female-only workshops would be organized in an effort to boost their numbers. In these workshops, with the help of staff from the West Jerusalem office, fieldworkers would also train new recruits on basic compositional skills: the field of vision, the long shot and its advantages, how and when to move the lens, and so on. To practice filming under conditions of duress, they played a soccer game with new volunteers, urging them to track the ball with their cameras "in order to understand how to follow what happens in the field." The rapid movements of the game were meant as a proxy, the ball standing in for bodies in motion amidst a violent assault.

The exercise was a practical necessity. In this region, assaults by militant settler populations were frequent and fierce, bent on forcibly removing Palestinians from their lands. On 8 June 2008, Palestinian shepherds were tending their flocks in the South Hebron village of Susiya when Jewish settlers arrived from a neighboring settlement, demanding their departure. The herders refused and the settlers departed, returning minutes later in larger numbers, masked and wielding clubs. A shepherd's young niece, Muna al-Nawaj'ah, captured the ensuing violence on the family's camcorder, provided by the B'Tselem project.

The short video she produced, one of the first viral videos of the B'Tselem project, was vivid in its detail.[61] Muna's camera faced the oncoming settlers as they walked with a slow and confident gait toward their targets. Their faces were draped with colored fabric, with only their eyes visible. One was bare-chested and all carried clubs—the neighboring settlement, with its signature red roofs, visible behind them. Muna's elderly aunt and uncle appeared fleetingly in the foreground, clothed in traditional dress with arms at their sides, rocks in hands in anticipation of the impending assault. Her uncle turned suddenly from his attackers, standing his ground in defiance and averting his eyes—an image only partially captured by the camera's viewfinder. The settlers met him and words were exchanged (or so it seemed from the image, for the sound was inaudible, drowned out by a heavy wind). Then the beating began. Most of this attack would not be captured on film, as Muna dropped the camera in fear at the moment of the first strike.[62]

Muna's footage—with its shaking lens, subjects moving in and out of the frame, concluding suddenly with a camera dropped in fear—was part of a genre of amateur eyewitness videography that was just beginning to consolidate at this early moment in the Palestinian video ecosystem: namely, eyewitness footage visibly imprinted by the somatic terror of its producer. Often, the grammar of terror was registered in sonic form, audible in the sounds of quickened breath, in footsteps of flight, or the startled cries of the unexpected eyewitness. This testimonial footage would often be filmed in hiding, shot through windows and sometimes behind grates, or shielded by the enclosures of balconies, all of which would be visible in the resultant image. As in Muna's experience, the instance of heightened confrontation was often missing, foreclosed by a fallen camera, dropped in fright by the producer at the moment of attack, creating numerous challenges when the footage was used in the legal arena. The Israeli police, who arrived at the scene after the settlers retreated, confiscated the cassette tape, taking it into custody in the Hebron police station. It took a week before the

B'Tselem team, after filing an appeal with the police, was granted a copy. It was a rare case of successful retrieval.

As part of his routine work as a fieldworker, Nassar made regular visits to households participating in the camera project, assessing both their well-being and that of their cameras. Regular maintenance and repairs were required, batteries needed replacing, cameras needed upgrading. Refresher courses might be necessary, such as how to save a file or adjust a time stamp. New components would be provided, like memory cards or more powerful batteries, or rooftop surveillance cameras might be installed, particularly vital for families facing regular settler attacks from hilltop compounds. If technical needs could not be addressed on-site, support might be required from the West Jerusalem office, as when CDs were stuck in hard drives. Such technicalities were banal but crucial. If a battery was inadequate, capturing only an hour of continuous footage, the videographer might fail to record the entirety of a settler raid, as they often lasted over an hour. If a volunteer failed to set the date or time stamp correctly, problems could ensue in the legal arena when the NGO submitted footage for review with the Israeli authorities. Fieldworkers were aware that the political stakes in such technological matters were considerable.

Some technological problems were too difficult for fieldworkers, alone, to resolve. Challenges were acute in the aftermath of malicious retribution by soldiers or settlers, such as the attempted destruction or confiscation of cassette tapes or data-sticks. Sometimes the material could be retrieved with clever computer work, or tapes held in police custody might be recovered by the organization, after numerous appeals. But such resolutions were always uncertain. Such was the case for a 2012 camera volunteer from Hebron who was assaulted by Israeli forces while filming their clash with local Palestinians. He sustained serious injuries and was detained at the Hebron police station, his camera confiscated in the process. It would be returned after the fact, following a formal appeal to the Israeli authorities by B'Tselem, but only after the memory card had been wiped clean. The organization filed an official complaint with the military, calling for an investigation and reminding the authorities that "the Israeli military must permit video documentation in the occupied territories." The military responded to the B'Tselem complaint with their standard reassertion of the exceptionality of the event, confirming the right of Palestinians in the West Bank to use their cameras as documentary tools, unless they posed a risk for the security services. But despite support from the West Jerusalem office, the footage was never recovered.[63]

CONTINGENCIES OF TRANSPORT

At the core of the B'Tselem camera project—a pillar of its operations—was the movement of footage from the West Bank to West Jerusalem. The NGO required original footage—in the form of cassette tapes, disks or memory sticks, unedited and metadata intact—for its work with the Israeli military law enforcement system.[64] In an age of growing suspicion about provenance and authenticity, originals were also required by the Israeli media before footage could be aired. In the context of the highly militarized and regulated geography of military occupation, and given the restrictive time frame required by media bodies, the footage's capacity to reach Jerusalem on time was always in doubt.

The organizational procedure for managing and moving footage was distributed between numerous actors within the NGO. If the camera operator had strong footage, with clear images of perpetrators, she was required to phone the local fieldworker. Once the value of the footage had been established, the fieldworker would visit the volunteer's home to screen the material. Then, if they deemed the footage strong and viable, either as an advocacy or legal tool, they worked with the West Jerusalem team to organize its transport into Israel. In the case of a multi-sited attack within the West Bank, as sometimes coordinated by settlers, the labor was more complicated still. In these instances, multiple cameras would be involved, requiring the fieldworker to move from village to village to gather the materials. Timing was always crucial. If the fieldworker waited too long, the footage might be deleted by mistake, or perhaps the cassette tape would be reused for other purposes, a byproduct of the camera's flexible designation as a household tool. Sometimes the police arrived first, beating the fieldworker to the house and confiscating the footage. At that point, it was very difficult to retrieve. Social media made this process more complicated, as volunteers might elect to upload their footage directly to their online accounts or personal platforms, this despite an organizational protocol to the contrary. "We are always afraid of YouTube," I was told by a Hebron-based fieldworker. Once such footage was in the public domain, she said, having bypassed institutional verification protocols, the material had less potential function as legal evidence or was of little interest to the Israeli media. For all these reasons, she had to be ready to review the footage at any time. "Whatever the hour, I go immediately. My phone is never off."

In the early years of the B'Tselem video project, fieldworkers often relied on the transfer of computer files over the internet, usually by means of an FTP application, for initial assessment prior to its physical delivery. Given slow and irregular internet functionality in the West Bank, the process was enormously cumbersome, particularly so in regions suffering from basic infrastructural neglect. Even in Hebron, a city with a developed infrastructure and regular electricity, the internet was slow and file transfer unpredictable. At times, capture and upload took the entirety of the night, a process whose speed and success rate depended on the file size and type and was often unreliable. File degradation often resulted, including loss of metadata, such that it could not be assessed in the West Jerusalem office with the requisite precision.

Even if retrieval by the fieldworkers was successful, the question remained: How would it reach West Jerusalem? The regional fieldworkers, like the volunteer videographers they oversaw, were all Palestinian residents of the West Bank and did not possess permits for entry into Israel.[65] Sometimes, as a solution, they would deliver the materials to the nearest checkpoint where they would be met by B'Tselem employees with Israeli ID. If this was not possible, a range of other actors with the requisite permits or IDs were called upon to help. The organization relied upon a set of designated cab drivers for this job.

In May of 2013, I made this journey in reverse, traveling by cab from West Jerusalem to Hebron with one of B'Tselem's regular cab drivers, a man frequently tasked with manual footage transfer. As a Palestinian resident of Jerusalem, with an Israeli ID and license plate, he could move legally between West Jerusalem and the West Bank. The drives did not bother him, as he had learned from experience how to remain undetected. Although his Israeli ID shielded him from a certain level of scrutiny, he always hid the small cassette tapes he transported just to avoid unnecessary problems, fearing unwanted scrutiny by soldiers at checkpoints. "They would say: 'Why are you bringing it? Why are you working with them [B'Tselem]?' I know them and how they act. So I conceal the tapes and nobody sees." The trick, he says, is the empty cab. He made the drive to West Jerusalem unaccompanied, concerned about suspicions that a Palestinian rider might arouse. "The cab is empty, so I pass through the checkpoint without problems. Sometimes they ask me to open the trunk, and see that it's empty, and that's it. Nobody knows what I have in my pocket." The small cassettes of that period, like the memory sticks that eventually replaced them, could be easily concealed. He credited their size with his successes.

The media cycle, with its particular temporal demands and evaluations, also presented a contingency factor. With the passing of time, the Israeli or global media might lose interest in any particular clip, its perceived value superseded by footage of more recent settler incursion or military shooting. Within the constrained temporal demands of the media, footage from West Bank videographers might arrive to West Jerusalem too late: "If something happens in the afternoon in Susiya," I was told by the NGO's Israeli team, "and they [the fieldworker] get the material, do the capturing, send it to us and then we send to the media—it might be too late. The news is at 8:00 PM. You know how it works. If it's not from the same day, the television won't use it." Between the temporal constraints born of political violence and those imposed by the media, the ability to delivery materials on time was always uncertain.

CONCLUSION: MUSA'S OFFICE

The early years of the B'Tselem video ecosystem were not uniform. They varied greatly depending on the biography of the Palestinian videographer, the political history of her community, her relative proximity to settler populations, the availability of necessary infrastructure, and so on. Some of the footage filmed in this period reached large Israeli and international audiences, both through B'Tselem's work and later, as mobile networking technologies began to proliferate in the West Bank, via the social media platforms of individual videographers. Bilal Tamimi, the most seasoned and prolific of the Palestinian videographers chronicled here, whose work was closely tied to the popular struggle in Nabi Saleh, would garner a growing global audience. A savvy political activist, he had no illusions about the Israeli military justice system, well aware of the vanishingly low rates of indictment for soldiers accused of violence against Palestinians, including cases in which videographic evidence was abundant. As an experienced media actor, he also knew that even when his footage was strong, even when it arrived to West Jerusalem on time, and even when granted an airing on the Israeli evening news, as occurred numerous times in these years, it had little power to persuade most mainstream Jewish viewers who had, since at least the second intifada, grown tired of images of Palestinian victims. He brought the same political realism to his work with Israeli human rights actors and institutions, cognizant of both the limits and tactical capacities of the human rights paradigm. [66] While he employed his camera as a radical anti-occupation tool, he did so without illusions.

I have proposed that this chapter might be read as a counterpart to the global dreams about digital revolution that were in circulation in the early twenty-first century. In these years, footage from the scene of Israeli violence in the West Bank was becoming increasingly available to global audiences in something close to real time, filmed from the very midst of an Israeli incursion or bombardment. And in the process, a set of political dreams was activated: namely, that the media infrastructures of the digital age, seemingly annihilating space and time as never before, had a greater political capacity to move audiences and shift political landscapes. Or thus were the political investments of many.

This chapter, grounded in the ethnographic details of videographic production and circulation, provides a more sober assessment. In the West Bank, in the years chronicled here, Palestinian camera operators and video-activists labored amidst numerous constraints born of Israeli military rule. In the South Hebron hills, such constraints took the form of a legacy of Israel's state-sponsored de-development: broken roadways, missing electrical grids, and digital infrastructures. Settler violence produced different kinds of obstacles for Palestinian camera operators, manifest in the challenges of filming under conditions of eruptive violence. Cameras dropped in fear, in the face of such violence, generated additional problems when the footage entered a legal arena. Military restrictions on Palestinian movement often took shape as the theft of time, manifest in the stalled movement of camerapersons and videotapes.[67] All of these violences made their mark on the videographic ecosystem, stymying the movement of footage from point of origin in the West Bank to point of circulation in West Jerusalem.

Palestinian camera operators had creative ways to bypass these constraints, like concealing footage when crossing a checkpoint, or breaking military curfew to photograph, under threat of military force. But even then, they faced perpetual uncertainties, often violent ones. Would a soldier block her lens or seize her memory card? Would the new battalion be as lenient as the one prior? Would the movement of footage be stalled by a vengeful or lengthy search of her vehicle?[68] In the matrix of these multiple constraints, byproducts of military rule in its various forms, the capacity for Palestinian testimonial footage to reach its Israeli or international audiences was always in doubt. Contra the digital dreams of many, the testimonial camera offered no guarantees.

In conclusion, I return to Musa's home office. The space is crowded, filled with B'Tselem reports and cartons of videocassettes, footage filmed during the second intifada period in his early years as a B'Tselem employee. The videographic subjects were standard fare, he said: the routine military beatings of Palestinian protestors, the checkpoint violations, the detentions of journalists. Musa characterized some of the footage as "strong," with clear images of military violence in

Hebron, where he lived and worked. Others were less strong, particularly when he was filming under threat of arrest or gunfire. He had revisited some of these cassettes while writing reports for the NGO, but many had neither been reviewed nor seen by others. These were the videos that had not been delivered on time, constrained by closures and curfew, attacks and detentions. In this window of delay, Musa said, their perceived value had been superseded by the next Israeli rights violation. So they had remained here, in his home office, where they functioned as an informal archive of sorts, a chronicle of military occupation as registered through his camera's lens. But for now, at least, this archive had an audience of one.

Chapter 3

SETTLER SCRIPTS

Conspiracy Cameras and Fake News

ON 7 JULY 2008, A BOUND AND BLINDFOLDED PALESTINIAN DEMON-
strator, Ashraf Abu-Rahma, was shot at close range by an Israeli soldier in the
West Bank village of Ni'ilin.[1] Palestinian teenager Salaam Amira filmed the events
clandestinely from her family's back window.[2] A few days later, following the
assistance of an international activist who transported Salaam's cassette tapes to
B'Tselem, her footage would be aired on Israeli television. At the time, Palestinian
eyewitness video from the occupied territories was something of a rarity within
Israeli media spheres and still had the capacity to arrest Israeli audiences. They
took notice. Salaam's footage captivated Israeli audiences, spawning a national
conversation about military responsibility for the shooting. Was the soldier legally
responsible, pundits asked, or did responsibility fall to the commanding officer?

But a second storyline also followed the viral circuit: a story about fraudulence. The footage was fake, some Israeli pundits argued, digitally manipulated
by either the Palestinian videographer or the Israeli human rights organization
in order to defame the Israeli state: "[The] video was edited. . . . Shooting sounds
were added to the footage, it was shot on various dates, from several cameras. . . .
The video we see now is the result of this. . . . Whoever made this deserves an
Oscar."[3] Initially, this accusation of fraudulence emerged as a minor discourse in

the Israeli mainstream media. But the charge would grow in scale and volume over the three years that the Ni'ilin shooting remained in the Israeli public eye, picking up steam as the case moved into the military court, eventually supported by a minority decision from a judge. The stakes were considerable. Through the charge of fraudulence, accusers labored to revise the visual scene of Israeli state violence against Palestinians, removing the Israeli perpetrator and Palestinian victim from the frame. In the eyes of these accusers, the very future of the Jewish state was at stake.

This chapter studies the evolution of the fraudulence accusation as directed against video footage of Israeli state and settler violence in the first two decades of the twenty-first century.[4] I focus on the Israeli and pro-Israeli publics who leveraged the charge, including military spokespersons, Israeli settler media outlets, and Zionist conspiracy theorists in the United States. The accusation evolved into a social script of sorts, rooted in a repetitive set of narrative gestures, analytic operations, and logics of denial. Although repetitive, the script was also dynamic, flexible enough to change in accordance with shifts in the political or media landscape. The spread of the evolving script was enabled by an emerging cadre of self-styled experts from the military and private sector who, working both in legal and media arenas, provided the analytic and conceptual skills, including a body of forensic strategies, required to mount a persuasive repudiation charge.[5] The objects of their repudiation were scenes of state and settler violence, filmed by a variety of actors: Palestinian bystanders and human rights workers, Israeli and international activists and journalists, stationary CCTV cameras, and so forth. For the accusers, this emerging archive would be grouped under the singular rubric of enemy footage. By the end of this period chronicled here, their repudiation script, taking aim at so-called enemy footage, had migrated from the conspiratorial blogosphere into the halls of the Israeli parliament. Once a marginal internet fantasy, it would be adopted as the language of state.

At the core of this chapter are some of the most widely publicized repudiation campaigns of this period. All involved shootings of Palestinians by the Israeli security forces and all were caught on camera: the 2000 killing of Muhammad Al-Durrah; the 2008 injury of Ashraf Abu-Rahma; the 2014 killing of two Palestinian youth in Beitunia. I am interested in the social history of these campaigns as they made their way through Israeli media and legal spheres, moving fluidly between radio talk shows and military courtrooms, in the hands of conspiracy theorists and state spokespersons alike. In both media and legal arenas, the script proved to be relatively immune to countervailing evidence, regardless of the volume of corroborating video, its precision, or its clarity.[6] As such, the charge of Palestinian fraudulence functioned as a kind of performative speech-act: installing the effects it named.

This script has a considerable history. As we know from postcolonial studies, the repudiation of indigenous claims of various kinds (to history, land, humanity, etc.) was a foundational logic of all colonial projects: namely, the charge that the indigenous claim was inauthentic or fabricated in some respect.[7] Such forms of repudiation were crucial in enabling the violence of colonialism in its various forms. This dynamic was also at work in the early history of Zionist settler nationalism and would have a lasting hold on dominant Israeli ideology in decades hence.[8] The accusation also winds its way through the history of photography, traceable to the very onset of photographic technologies in the nineteenth century, magnifying in scale and precision in the digital age.[9] Such accusations would proliferate in the digital age, fueled by the rise of photo-editing software. In the social media era, the charge would become so widespread as to underwrite the visual field at every point along its networked circuit, shadowing the digital image as a kind of co-constituent.[10]

This chapter is interested in the interplay between these histories—namely, the history of colonialism on the one hand and digital visuality on the other. The growth and spread of the fraudulence charge in the first two decades of the twenty-first century can be understood as an attempt to recalibrate the terms of the longstanding colonial project of denial to meet the considerable threats posed by the digital media moment. In the first two decades of the twenty-first century, greater numbers of Palestinians were filming the scene of state violence with their personal cameras, and their footage was circulating virally. The perceived threat to Israel's public image was considerable—or so Israeli right-wing publics, and their international supporters, believed. This chapter, then, tracks the ways that the Israeli charge of Palestinian fakery, with its long colonial history, was being recalibrated in the smartphone age.

Like other chapters in this book, this is a study of media emergence: more pointedly, the emergence, growth, and popularization within Israel of a politicized discourse of videographic fakery. These were years well before the perceived threat of so-called deep fakes. Within human rights communities and legal arenas in both Israel and Palestine, as on the global stage, protocols for authenticating videographic evidence were still emerging.[11] And all this occurred well before the onset of what would become, in the Trump era, the prevalent charge of fake news, a narrative that the Israeli repudiation script anticipated and preceded by almost a decade.[12] Today, at the time of this writing, the very ordinariness of the fake news charge, now widely deployed as a tool of right-wing populism, threatens to mask the history of its evolution as a political tool. In the case studied here, the repudiation script had to be cultivated and learned before it acquired its broad intelligibility. This chapter is a chronicle of such cultivation.

PALESTINIAN THEATRICS

The Israeli repudiation script, taking aim at the videographic field, had its roots in the early days of the second Palestinian intifada. The event in question was the infamous shooting of 12-year-old Muhammad Al-Durrah on 30 September 2000, trapped with his father in a crossfire between Israeli troops and Palestinian gunman in the Gaza Strip.[13] This 45-minute incident was filmed for French television by Palestinian correspondent Talal Abu Rahma, and images from his footage would rapidly go viral, beginning with the scene of Muhammad crouching in terror with his father, shooting underway around them, and culminating with the child's crumpled body in his father's lap. The scale of the footage's reach was virtually unprecedented in the history of the military occupation, "broadcast from Malaysia to Morocco, from Frankfurt to Tokyo," appearing on "the front pages of the world's newspapers and . . . plastered on walls throughout the Palestinian territories."[14] "Palestine's emblematic child," wrote *Le Monde*.[15] For Muslim audiences in the Middle East, for whom the footage was perpetually repeatedly replayed on television news, Al-Durrah was mourned as a martyr, an icon of Palestinian victimization.[16] Within Israeli state and mainstream imaginations, the event would be read through a hasbara optic, with an emphasis on the deleterious implications for Israel's public image.[17] In this storyline, the viral frames would be credited with severe media damage, "fix[ing] Israel's image as a brutal and bloodthirsty country" and "inciting violence against both Israel and Jews."[18] Within Israel, the event would be widely perceived as a public relations disaster, one of the most damaging media incident's in Israel's history.[19]

The campaign to repudiate the Al-Durrah footage would unfold gradually in the years that followed, waged chiefly from France and the United States (see Image 15). Repudiators pointed to a myriad of supposedly suspicious elements: blurry frames at the moment of the shooting, cuts made to the footage by the French production crew, the question of why filming ceased when it did. All these issues,

IMAGE 15. Part of international conspiracy campaign against the veracity of the Al-Durrah footage. No date. Source: Breitbart News.

they said, begged the question of veracity. In 2000, at the time of the incident, the Israeli military had taken responsibility for the shooting, stating that "this was a grave incident, an incident we are all sorry about."[20] Their stance would change in 2005 when they "publicly retracted the original admittance of IDF responsibility in the alleged incident."[21] In 2008, the director of the Israeli government press office, Danny Seaman, would cement the military retraction, as telegraphed by the title of his op-ed in the mainstream Israeli media: "Palestinian Industry of Lies: Media Manipulation Has Become Strategic Arab Weapon Against Israel."[22] Israeli media pundits advanced the accusation, reminding their audiences that "an image, even a video, may be the perfect lie."[23]

At the helm of the Al-Durrah campaign was a small cadre of self-styled experts in Palestinian media manipulation, as they put it. American academic Richard Landes was among them, working closely with physicist Nahum Shahaf.[24] Here is Landes describing his 2003 screening of the original footage, accompanied by an Israeli cameraman who had worked with the original French TV crew:

Much of the footage had a familiar quality: it resembled the footage I had seen in Shahaf's studio, either boring or staged. At one point a Palestinian adult grabbed his leg as if he'd been shot and limped badly. Here, for the "scene" to work, a half-dozen others should have picked him up and run him past cameras to an ambulance. But only kids gathered around him who were too small to pick him up. The man shooed them away, looked around, realized no one's coming, and walked away without a limp. [The] Israeli cameraman laughed. When I asked why, he said, "It seems staged." I replied, "Everything seems staged." And then the other shoe dropped. . . . *At that moment I realized the full-double-extent of the problem: Palestinians stage all the time,* and Western journalists have no trouble with that.[25]

Faked injuries, comical limps, staging practices. Landes would coin a neologism to describe such processes of tactical theatrics: "Pallywood," his term for "the Palestinian national film industry in which 'militant' journalists and street actors produce staged news as propaganda."[26]

The international campaign against the Al-Durrah footage, centered on a theory about tactical theatrics, would both set the stage for all subsequent repudiation campaigns and provide a roadmap that suspicious publics could follow. It would take over a decade for this storyline to gain popular traction in Israel. In those years, the narrative would eventually consolidate into a script that could be easily employed by Israelis at home, and their supporters abroad, as a means of managing their country's international image in the age of viral video.

THE SCRIPT TAKES SHAPE

Return to the footage with which this chapter began: the shooting of Ashraf Abu-Rahma by an Israeli soldier in the West Bank village of Ni'ilin, filmed by Salaam Amira in July 2008.[27] The incident emerged out of a history of Israeli military aggression and Palestinian struggle. Two months prior, Israel had renewed construction of the separation barrier in the Ni'ilin area, threatening mass expropriations of village lands. The community responded with a wave of nonviolent protests that drew hundreds of local, Israeli and international activists into Ni'ilin's fields. The military crackdown was swift and harsh: tear gas and rubber bullets, beatings and arrests, closure and curfew.[28] In the course of the months that followed, two Palestinian youth would be killed by the Israeli security forces. A spokesperson for the Israeli border police, responding to B'Tselem calls for an official inquiry, defended the military's actions, arguing that "anyone who enters a danger zone is putting themselves at risk."[29]

Salaam Amira's footage begins with a Ni'ilin protest against the Israeli authorities. Abu-Rahma is visible at the demonstration's center, waving a Palestinian flag as journalists look on. There is a break in the footage, resuming with the image of Abu-Rahma detained at a checkpoint, sitting bound and blindfolded in the hot sun, military personnel standing by. Another break in the footage and Abu-Rahma has been moved upright, an officer's hand firmly on his arm. An adjacent soldier lifts his gun at close range, facing the detainee. The sound of a shot fired. The ensuing frames are blurry because Salaam dropped her camera in shock, her gesture registering as a series of blurred and black frames. When her footage resumes, Abu-Rahma is shown lying on the ground, soldiers bent over his injured body. He sustained a foot injury and was released.[30]

Ni'ilin was under curfew at the time of the shooting, preventing the movement of residents and the transfer of Salaam's footage. As a result, her original cassette tapes remained in her family's home for two weeks before they could be transported to B'Tselem's Jerusalem office with the assistance of an international activist. Once received, B'Tselem lodged a formal complaint with the Israeli military police, demanding a full investigation, and then sent the footage to the Israeli media for a possible screening. Salaam's family suffered numerous reprisals as a result of the ensuing publicity, including arrests and denial of work permits. B'Tselem "accused the Israeli army of seeking revenge for the girl's role in exposing the actions of its armed forces in the West Bank."[31]

The Ni'ilin protest movement had garnered little national attention in the Israeli media, but Salaam's footage received broad coverage. While most Israeli audiences focused on the role of the military in the incident, concerns about fakery and digital manipulation were also persistent, although in a more minor key. Mainstream media pundits led the charge, with television anchors and radio hosts addressing "the element of video editing" and inviting B'Tselem spokespersons to address the accusation.[32] Many took aim at the footage's belated arrival to the B'Tselem offices, raising questions about the two-week delay in investigation and publication.[33] Other Israeli commentators queried the "suspicious" black spots on the footage following the sound of gunfire, asking "what happened in the second after the camera blacked out?"[34] B'Tselem responded with detailed information about their standard verification process, including a media dossier outlining their protocols for forensic analysis and subsequent findings of videographic authenticity.[35] As they noted to the media, the Israeli police's criminal forensic unit, with the assistance of their "number one expert on digital photography," had found the tape "authentic and undoctored."[36] But their critics were not mollified, insisting that something malevolent had happened behind the scenes to produce these "horrendous images."[37]

The charge of fraudulence entered the military courtroom during the trial and sentencing phase of the soldier and commanding officer involved in the shooting.[38] The defense drew heavily on the expertise of Nahum Shahaf, a veteran of the Al-Durrah repudiation campaign, who "accuse[d] B'Tselem of forgery."[39] Pulling from the Al-Durrah playbook, Shahaf argued that the nature of the forgery was twofold, comprised of both digital manipulation and Palestinian theatrics. Drawing on acoustical analysis of the audio track, he contended that "[t]he sounds of gunshots were produced in post-editing" and argued that his forensic analysis of "the geometry of the path of the bullet" had proven that Abu-Rahma's alleged injury was a physical impossibility.[40] Shahaf's arguments also cast doubt on the very body of Abu-Rahma:

> I examined the video frame by frame ... [and] he did not fall immediately to the ground as you might expect from a man with an injured foot. He turned away. You can see him standing on two legs and resting precisely on the left injured leg. Then, the film was cut with apparently deliberate editing and you see him lying down on the sidewalk. *I want to stress that there is no photographic evidence of the alleged left-toe injury.*[41]

In the hands of the defense, the charge of videographic inauthenticity worked by banishing all traces of military violence from the original incident. Abu-Rahma's injured body, Salaam's camera dropped in fear, the video's belated circuit, as a result of military closure—all were read as signs of malfeasance, evidence of Palestinian or human rights trickery, rather than as byproducts of military violence in its various forms. Shahaf's findings would receive considerable Israeli mainstream media coverage—"Physicist: Ni'ilin Shooting Tape Doctored," in the words of one headline.[42] This analysis, "proving that the film had been doctored," would be covered in minute detail, while B'Tselem's investigative dossier, backed by the findings of the Israeli police's criminal forensic unit, were largely excised from the national conversation.[43]

B'Tselem would decry the outcome of the legal trial, with the lenient sentence issued to the soldier and commanding officer involved, arguing that the policy of impunity within the military justice system fostered such incidents of violence against Palestinians.[44] The court rejected the charge of videographic inauthenticity. Two of three judges in the case sided with the prosecution, ruling that the defense had presented insufficient evidence to support the doctoring charges.[45] But the third judge dissented, leaning heavily on Shahaf's dossier: "I suspect that the publicly presented film includes, in fact, a combination of some films taken in different places and at different time periods. I further suspect that the film blurs and omits parts that were filmed immediately after the shooting."[46] This judge also ruled Salaam's testimony not credible, arguing that "[t]he Palestinian woman's argument, that she did not film after the shooting because she accidentally dropped the camera, is contradicted by other evidence."[47] This minority opinion would set the stage for legal ratification of the repudiation script in years to come.

During the course of the Ni'ilin incident, from the time of the video's initial circulation through the three-year military trial, the repudiation script would develop and mature. The charge of fraudulence had been a persistent storyline in the national media in the aftermath of the video's release, but only in a minor key. By the time of the trial's conclusion, this accusation had received the legal imprimatur of the Israeli military court, albeit in the form of a minority opinion.[48] The script was beginning to capture Israeli imaginations, starting to function as an important political tool in the national fight against, in the estimation of some, Palestinian lies and incitement.

"THE BOY WHO WASN'T REALLY KILLED"

In May 2011, I visited the Jerusalem offices of the Israeli military's social media team, then housed within the division of the military spokesperson unit. Their work with social media as a hasbara platform was only three years old, having begun spontaneously during the 2008–2009 Israeli war on the Gaza Strip.[49] I had come to their offices to interview the head of their social media team, but, having arrived early, I was invited to join their team's consultation session with Richard Landes. He was well known in those offices for his Pallywood work, the focus of two English-language blogs that he maintained.[50] They sought Landes's advice on matters of anti-Israeli media bias and Palestinian media manipulation.

The timing of Landes's visit was crucial. The Israeli military was still stinging from the aftermath of the highly publicized voyage of the *Mavi Marmara* in May 2010, a naval convoy of activists who had attempted to break the Israeli blockade of the Gaza Strip.[51] Israeli commandos had raided the convoy, killing nine activists. The images of Israel's lethal assault, filmed by activists with their personal cameras and shared on social media, had been a viral scandal for the military. Their own visual record of the incident reached global publics a day later, mired by infrastructural challenges and internal state debates. In that lag time, activists had gained the media upper hand. A familiar lament was replayed: Israeli was losing the media war. Now, at the time of Landes's visit, a military media win was desperately needed.

I was led to a small conference room where Landes's informal lecture was already underway. The room was crowded, with a dozen uniformed soldiers, men and women, seated on chairs and tabletops. Most of those present were recent Israeli immigrants from France, England, and Germany who were selected for work in this unit because of their ability to communicate with international publics in their vernacular. Landes's lecture began with Al-Durrah, the case that defined his multi-year crusade against Palestinian fraudulence. He walked his audience through his findings with the aid of a small television and VCR, showing clips from the short film he produced on the subject. The boy wasn't really killed by the Israeli military as Palestinians and the international media claimed, he contended. "You see this blood? It should be darker." The whole thing was a set-up, he argued, an elaborate staging for the international camera. Here, as in his writings, Landes described a case of media manipulation that, in his rendering, was the rule rather than the exception where Palestinian claims of death and injury at Israeli military hands were concerned. He explained to those present that he had been making inroads with the Israeli government on such issues, working through military spokespeople.

Lances had a rapt audience, eager for his advice on media matters. He urged them not to lose sight of history: namely, those prior media events when false Palestinian accusations gained international traction. He provided a list of some notable instances: the Jenin massacre of 2002, the *Mavi Marmara* in 2010. These and others, he said, required careful scrutiny by their unit. "Documenting the past is very important. Go back and ask, did the media get it right?"

Those in the room had many comments and questions. The head of the social media team noted the numerous "false accusations" that had been leveraged during the 2008–2009 Israeli military operation in the Gaza Strip. Landes concurred, reminding them of Palestinians claims that Israel had targeted a United Nations' school during the course of the bombardment. In fact, he said, the Israeli

mortar strike had landed outside the school, and thanks to the work of "scrupu-
lous Israeli bloggers," the UN was forced to issue a retraction.[52] A soldier in the
room added another false accusation to Landes's list, citing a 2006 claim about
a Palestinian girl killed by the Israeli military. Later, the soldier noted, the girl's
death would be attributed to injuries sustained from falling off a swing.[53] Yes,
that was also a victory, Landes said, and the military's media team needed more
victories like these, more successful retractions and renunciations. "Pallywood is
everywhere," he added. "There is a serious price to pay for telling the truth about
Palestinians, but no price to pay for lying about Israel."

The response within this military crowd was charged. They listened closely,
raising questions and sharing ideas about media strategy, implementation, and
narrative focus. One soldier proposed an "ongoing series called Media Watch"
while another suggested that they prepare materials in advance, ready to be deployed when the need arises. Landes recommended working with bloggers to
spread the military's narratives:

> Landes: They will be a magnifier for your story. Use them to amplify your
> media reach.
>
> Soldier: But should our focus be empirical refutation of these events, or
> spinning new stories?
>
> Landes: Depends. What do you have in mind?
>
> Soldier: Like, the goods going to Gaza through Israeli checkpoints. We could
> play up that stuff.

It was a storyline about state humanitarianism in which the Israeli government
had already invested considerable energy, an attempt to defray the "bad press"
that had resulted from Israel's blockade of the Gaza Strip.

Landes liked the idea. "When you emphasize the good stuff, we [bloggers] can
help you. You provide the stats, we can do the work." He spoke about the overblown
nature of international media coverage of the Israeli occupation, citing their persistent failure to report on Israeli military restraint. This, too, should be the subject
of their work. "Show just how disciplined the Israeli army is. Document it. And
if there are some articles you need written, we would be happy to write them."

A suggestion from the crowd: "What about going out in the territories and
filming photographers, watching what they are doing?"

Landes agreed, this was crucial element of the overall media strategy. "Pay attention to the NGOs. They are also cognitive warriors," he said, employing a phrase he employed frequently during this lecture.[54] "You should go to the weekly demonstrations at Bi'ilin and see what the photojournalists are doing." He rehearsed his trademark argument about Palestinian theatrics for the camera, a staple of his blog, about the ways "they stage scenes of people being shot in cold blood." As a corrective, he proposed employing a "team of forensic experts" to examine all video evidence published by Palestinians and the Israeli NGOs that support them.

"Journalism is a theater of war," he said, wrapping up. "And western journalists are being manipulated to tell the story that Palestinians want to hear. They are being intimidated to tell this story, but they can't admit it." The military team must be ready to counter these stories—to discredit Palestinian staging and outright lies. And unlike some recent military failures in the domain of public diplomacy, in which they had been outflanked by their enemies due to media delays, their work had to be immediate.[55] Timeliness was of the essence.

"Think of it like a chess game," he concluded. "You have to imagine what their next move will be."

Throughout the course of the two decades studied here, the Al-Durrah incident remained at the heart of the repudiation paradigm, the touchstone for all further campaigns. By extension, the state's perceived missteps in their initial response to the incident—namely, their apology for lethal violence—worked as a crucial cautionary tale for state actors. In all these respects, the case would set the terms of the repudiation script as it consolidated and gained a national foothold.

In 2012, a government review committee would be convened by Prime Minister Netanyahu "to examine the Al-Durrah affair in light of the continued damage it has caused to Israel"—a committee whose supposed expertise, "comprised of numerous specialists," would be praised by the Israeli media.[56] Neither the testimony of Jamal Al-Durrah, father of the slain boy, nor any other Palestinian witnesses present at the scene would be solicited, nor would the committee heed the family's calls to exhume the dead boy's body. In the report produced the following year (2013), the committee's ostensible experts would cast doubt on Palestinian claims, concluding that the Israeli military was not responsible for the child's death. In the words of the government's press release: "The review revealed that there is no evidence that Jamal [the father] or the boy were wounded in the manner claimed . . . and that the footage does not depict Jamal as having been badly injured. In contrast, there are numerous indications that the two were not struck by bullets at all."[57] The report paid close attention to the Palestinian bodies involved, arguing that despite their best efforts to play dead, their bodies gave them away: "The raw footage shows clearly that in the final scenes, the boy is not dead. In the final seconds of the footage, the boy raises his arm and turns his head in the direction of Al-Durrah [the father] in what are clearly intentional and controlled movements."[58]

The state commission exonerated the Israeli security services in Al-Durrah's death. But, they also went further to insist that he wasn't actually dead. Right-wing Israeli newspapers put it succinctly in their headlines: "Muhammad Al-Dura: The Boy Who Wasn't Really Killed." Netanyahu praised the outcome: "There is only one way to fight lies, and that is with the truth."[59] In 2013, with the findings of the state commission on Al-Durrah, the repudiation script had gained a state imprimatur. The stakes were considerable, as Netanyahu made clear following the findings of the state commission. The Al-Durrah incident, he argued, was a theater of war against Israel:

> [It] has come to symbolize the ongoing propaganda against the State of Is-
> rael. While this war does not involve bullets and missiles, it is, nonetheless,
> as vicious and as destructive. This war, being fought in the sphere of public
> diplomacy, propagates lies and libels in an effort to cast Israel as an interna-
> tional pariah and strip her of all legitimacy and credibility . . . [60]

The war on Palestinian fakery was nothing less than a struggle for Israel's political survival.

THROUGH THE SETTLERS' LENS

Jewish settlers in the occupied Palestinian territories, and the media organizations that represented them, were relatively late to employ cameras as political tools in any organized fashion. In May 2013, I paid a visit to an Israeli media center based in West Jerusalem (Tazpit) that was working to correct this problem, laboring to present the settler's perspective.[61] They began in 2010 in an explicit attempt to counter the cameras of B'Tselem—which, as they saw it, had a camera monopoly in the region. "In those early days," Tazpit staff told me, "everything that you saw was from [B'Tselem's] perspective. But there are two sides of the story. There's B'Tselem with their agenda. They believe that Jews don't have the right to be in Judea and Samaria. We believe that Jews should be in Judea and Samaria." They referred to the West Bank by their biblical names, as was standard settler practice, a means of grounding contemporary Israeli sovereignty in biblical history. The name of their organization articulated their goals succinctly. "Tazpit," meaning "observation post," marked their interest in an alternative political vantage point. It also denoted their rootedness within a settler ideology in which Jewish Israeli control of territorial heights was a strategic priority.[62]

In Tazpit's early years, it focused on changing the Israeli and international media narrative by means of alternative photographs shot from the settlers' perspective. They began slowly with a handful of untrained volunteer photographers working with basic digital cameras "that weren't that great and didn't work well." At the time of my 2013 visit, the organization boasted a team of thirteen Israeli reporters and photographers, most living in West Bank settlements, all with press credentials. In the three years since their founding, they had fashioned themselves into a hub for camera distribution within the settler population. In addition to their certified reporters, they worked with over a hundred volunteer photographers, situated throughout the West Bank ("where are we located precisely? I can't tell you"). Together, these paid employees and volunteers were generating a counter-archive of settler images, a counterweight to those produced by Palestinians and their Israeli partners in the West Bank. Their photographers filmed chiefly "in their own communities." But their cameras were everywhere, they said, "throughout Judea and Samaria."

Existing media portrayals of settlers and settlement life were riddled with falsehoods, they argued, erroneously painting them as violent extremists. As a corrective, the organization aimed to present a fuller picture, including portraits of everyday settler lives, cultural exploits, and humanitarian ventures. On the day of our conversation, Tazpit employees were scrambling to file stories about the fatal stabbing of a Jewish settler by a Palestinian man in the northern West Bank. "In international reports," I am told by a member of the organization, "he [the settler] was referred to as a hard-liner, some kind of extremist. In reality, he was also an actor who was part of a theater troupe. There's a lot more to this person than just the tag 'settler.'" Her article about his theatrical exploits would be published two days later.[63]

Tazpit leadership told a story of rampant visual manipulation by "the other side." It wasn't just the Arabs who did it, said Amotz Eyal, the organization's founder (he avoided the term "Palestinian"). Rather, their Israeli and international supporters were equally to blame. Manipulation took numerous forms: sometimes as image repurposing or fraudulent captioning, as when Arabs used photographs from Afghanistan to frame the Israeli military for crimes they didn't commit.[64] Other times, it took the form of malicious misattribution of violent events. For example, he argued, Arabs frequently cut down their own trees and blamed settlers, employing fraudulent images as evidence. The same was true of car-torching incidents that were attributed to Jewish extremists. "Feuding Arab clans," he insisted, were chiefly to blame.

The story of Palestinian theatricality for the camera was prominent within the organization. Amotz provided the example of a prominent Israeli film producer who worked as an activist in the Hebron area. "It's all a set-up," he said, referring to his footage of settler attacks on Palestinian civilians. "He's a professional and directs the whole thing." Tazpit camera operators refused to engage in such theatrical tactics and, as a result, found themselves at a media disadvantage. Without the elaborate choreography employed by Palestinians, "our images tend to suffer."

Sitting with Amotz in front of his office computer, we screened a collection of Tazpit footage from the Friday protests in the Palestinian village of Nabi Saleh—an epicenter, he argued, of Arab fakery. He pointed to a figure on the screen, identifying a Nabi Saleh photographer who regularly filmed the weekly demonstrations: "Here's the B'Tselem cameraman, standing here." He let the video play for several minutes, eager to stress the thematic contrast between Tazpit's video archive, and that of his enemies. "Now, you see the stones and the slingshot in their hands?" He pointed to a small group Palestinian youths in the image, many of whom he could identify by name. "The B'Tselem camera appeals to the pity of people: '*What a poor child.*' But sometimes they have slingshots or Molotov cocktails." These are the kinds of images, he said, that B'Tselem would never show. This accusation suffused Tazpit's work: namely, the claim that the Israeli human rights community was systematically distorting the visual field.[65] Tazpit's most senior photographer, a settler from Ofra, made the argument this way:

> They [B'Tselem] show only the Palestinian side, only what they want to see. At the moment, we are the only organization that is showing the Israeli side [in the territories], the Jewish side, the silenced side. . . . So, if I stand next to a B'Tselem's photographer, we would take pictures of the same object. He

would definitely show something other than what I show. In their footage, the soldiers never look good. Never.

At the core of the Tazpit repudiation paradigm was the concept of "what came before." The phrase was repeatedly invoked by those in the organization as we sat around their office computers discussing B'Tselem footage. Had the videographer turned on the camera earlier, or if B'Tselem hadn't edited the initial frame, the argument went, we would have seen the originating Arab violence—that which preceded, and justified, the soldier shooting or settler beating. "What came before" denoted all that had been excluded from the videographic frame through a manipulative foreshortening of the event, either by the Palestinian camera operators themselves or the Israeli human rights image brokers. This pre-event was invariably a provocation or act of "incitement" from Arabs or their Israeli supporters, consistently clearing the ostensible Israeli perpetrator of wrongdoing. In this imagined zone of pre-footage, the political record was always set straight.

At my behest, I joined Amotz and several Tazpit employees to screen footage shot by B'Tselem's Palestinian camera operators in the West Bank. We started with a 2008 beating of Palestinian shepherds by masked settler youth in Susiya, filmed by Muna al-Nawaj'ah.[66] We had just concluded a conversation about Pallywood—the accusation of Palestinian tactical theatrics for the camera—and I asked Amotz if this accusation would apply here. He paused before answering: "Okay, not in this case. It's not a set-up," he conceded. "But it *is* incitement. I can promise you that the Arabs started it by shouting and cursing. It's just that no one showed them on film." Another Tazpit employee chimed in:

Tazpit employee: It's all about timing, the timing of the documentation. Usually when you see B'Tselem videos, they are showing you the response to Arabs throwing rocks or something, so you just see the soldiers reacting, but *you don't see what led up to it.*

Rebecca: So for the sake of argument, what if you saw the entire thing? These are pretty horrific images. For a US audience, it brings up all sorts of associations. If you saw the whole thing, would that possibly exonerate the masked men?

Tazpit employee: I think it would give a more complete picture of what's going on. When you just see certain excerpts, you're getting a completely misconstrued idea of what's happening. There's more to this than what you're seeing—that's what we're saying.

Amotz: Look, there's only one minute here—one minute from, let's say, a thirty-minute episode.

Tazpit employee: [quoting the title of another B'Tselem video] "Palestinian Boy Injured by Israeli Army." Okay, *but what did he do before?*

"What came before" was a repudiation tool of last resort, called upon when other accounts of visual manipulation failed. It was a highly flexible accusation, easily marshaled, almost regardless of the nature of the incident in question. The temporality of this accusation was crucial to its success. "What came before" referenced the past, but in very vague terms—maybe a minute, maybe an hour, before the clip in question—and did not require temporal specificity. Nor was it predicated on visible evidence. And herein lay the argumentative tautology. The invisible evidence of "what came before" could be surmised by the accuser even though it could not be seen, surmised less on the basis of visual clues than ontological ones. "It's just the way they are," the argument seemed to go. The claim merely required a reassertion of that old colonial truism: the lying nature of the Arab.

At the time of our 2013 interview, Amotz was hopeful about Tazpit's larger political project of correcting the visual record. By producing their own images, he argued, they had successfully changed the photographic balance of power: "Once, the cameras were only on one side, and it was very easy to produce a forgery. Today it's more difficult." Even the mere threat of Tazpit's presence in the field, he argued, helped to dissuade dissimulators. "If we are there, it's harder"—harder, he meant, for the other side to generate their visual forgery, deterred by the knowledge that settlers were now armed with cameras and ready to document. Yes, he conceded, there were "still nine Arab news agencies working in the territories," far outnumbering settler media outlets. But he believed that they were making a difference, providing a truer story of life in "Judea and Samaria." "We are saying to our people: the camera is a weapon. And if we don't learn to use it, it will be used against us."

COUNTERING REPUDIATION

For the B'Tselem staff, the allegation of fraudulence was a constant presence. "It's always on our minds," said Sarit Michaeli, the NGO's spokesperson, in 2011, "always impacting the work we do." During the years chronicled here, it was the rare B'Tselem video that had not been met by public suspicion, by charges of video tampering and fraud: the accusation, and anticipation thereof, perpetually cast its shadow on the institutional work of verifying Palestinian testimonials, filing official complaints with the Israeli authorities, conducting human rights advocacy in the mainstream Israeli media. With every video they published, as Sarit noted, their detractors were organized and ready: "There is a whole industry around obscuring harm done to Palestinians and the damage of the occupation project," she said, referencing the work of NGO Monitor, a right-wing Israeli organization that targeted human rights projects in the occupied territories as a means of defending against (in their own words) the "demonization and delegitimization of Israel."[67] The military also frequently employed this script after B'Tselem footage aired: "It appears that the clip was edited tendentiously and does not fully reflect the unraveling of events," said a military spokesperson in 2012, after the organization released footage of an officer head-butting a Palestinian youth.[68] The suspicion was frequent, predictable, and repetitive in its logic and narrative form. Sarit rehearsed its central refrains: "How can you be sure that your photographers aren't lying to you? Or, the footage is only from the Palestinian angle. The image is taken out of context. Or, the Palestinians are provoking the security services and then filming them. And 'what happened before'? That's a frequent one."

In the estimation of some within the organization, particularly those working on the camera project, the formal qualities of Palestinian eyewitness videography sometimes abetted the work of their detractors. In addition to frequent starts and stops in the footage, a byproduct of much amateur videography, this footage often registered the bodily terror of its producer in the form of jerking lenses or dropped cameras. It was not uncommon for the moment of heightened confrontation to be missing from the resultant video, foreclosed by a camera's fall. These interruptions to the filmic narrative, sometimes evident as a black screen on the footage, were particularly prone to repudiation. In this political climate, the degree of verification conducted by the organization had to be "obsessively high," as Sarit noted. "We're so obsessed with credibility and making sure we don't issue anything that is even remotely edited. We always err on the side of caution."

The maturation of the repudiation script did not alter B'Tselem's work. Their verification and complaint process continued as before. But the growth of repudiation did produce some minor adjustments in institutional protocols. In the early years of their social media work, B'Tselem tended to publish short excerpts from videos shot by their West Bank team, focusing only on the moments when the human rights violation was visible. In 2012, they began uploading full clips to their YouTube channel: "everything that was filmed," sometimes many minutes before the soldier beating or settler injury began. Some members of the organization hoped that this shift might dissuade their detractors, disarming the "what came before" storyline. They would be mistaken, as Sarit noted: "That didn't stop all of the people out there from trying to discredit us, from saying: okay, but what happened ten minutes earlier?" The "what came before" storyline was flexible enough to adjust to such changes.

In 2011, Sarit was a realist, but also hopeful: "Even a strong video doesn't help with these kinds of suspicions. Unless the solider himself confesses." But she believed that the right evidence might have the power to alter the course of proceedings with the military justice system. "There would need to be very good material evidence—not just video footage, but ballistic or forensic evidence." In the years that followed, even that hope would be largely abandoned.

THE SCRIPT IS NORMALIZED

In 2014, in the West Bank town of Beitunia, two Palestinian youths—Nadeem Nuwara and Mohammad Abu Daher—were fatally shot by the Israeli security services during an annual demonstration commemorating the Palestinian Nakba, and their deaths were captured on camera.[69] By 2014, amidst the growing spread of cameras throughout the West Bank, footage of military killings of Palestinians was no longer a rarity. But this case was different due to the sheer number of camera operators and photographic technologies trained on the scene. Two photojournalists and four stationary security cameras, installed on a Palestinian-owned business in the immediate vicinity, had captured the day's events. What resulted were not only multiple angles on the killing but a massive volume of footage: 3 hours of video and 21 gigabytes in total.[70] One Israeli journalist called the incident "the most documented and forensically corroborated murder in [the] IDF's history."[71] Israeli and international human rights organizations condemned the Israeli security services for its unprovoked killing of unarmed Palestinians, and the UN called for an "independent and transparent" investigation of the events.[72] Human Rights Watch concluded that "[v]ideo footage, photographs, witness statements, and medical records indicate that two 17-year-old boys . . . posed no imminent threat to the forces at the time."[73]

IMAGE 16. Image from the B'Tselem dossier documenting the lethal shootings of Nadeem Nuwara and Mohammad Abu Daher by the Israeli security forces. Circles identify two CCTV cameras. 15 May 2014. Source: B'Tselem.

The Israeli authorities denied responsibility for the deaths, insisting that its forces had used only nonviolent crowd control measures in compliance with official rules of engagement, rather than live ammunition.[74] Drawing on the large body of associated evidence, B'Tselem refuted these claims, accusing the Israeli security services of responsibility in the killings and raising concerns that "the killing was willful."[75] In addition, they argued, CCTV footage disproved military claims about a threatening provocation preceding the shooting: "Security camera footage of the incident proves that at no stage were security services endangered by any of the four victims, or by anyone close to them at the time of the shooting" (see Image 16).[76] The autopsy report was issued several months later, confirming the killing of Nuwara by live fire.[77] Many in the organization had considerable faith in the ensuing legal process due to the voluminous nature of the corroborating evidence: forensic, material, ballistic, videographic. In the words of their media spokesperson, "I thought it was an open and shut case," she says, gesturing to B'Tselem's dossier on the killing. "You know, it's all documented."

The Israeli public disagreed. Indeed, the volume of corroborating evidence did not still the Israeli public debate about the day's events. Rather, it seemed to fuel it. State actors were among the first to join the chorus.[78] Following the first publication of video—it would be released in stages—Israeli Defense Minister Moshe Ya'alon assured the Israeli public that the footage was fraudulent. Indeed, he argued, such fraudulence was foretold in advance: "I've seen lots of films that were edited [to distort what had happened]. This film I've not yet seen, but I know the system."[79] Israeli Foreign Minister Avigdor Lieberman cast doubt on matters of timing: Why had there been a delay in the video's release? Did this not, he asked, raise considerable suspicions about videographic authenticity?[80] He argued that there was no need to even investigate the incident. Official military spokesmen concurred: "[T]he film was edited and does not reflect the reality of the day in question."[81] Military correspondents spoke to Israeli audiences about the probability of "forgery," the likelihood that "the film may have been staged and faked."[82] In the studio of the Israeli evening news, an Israeli ballistics expert reviewed the footage frame by frame, arguing that the signs of videographic manipulation were clear (see Image 17).[83]

Throughout the course of the Israeli and pro-Israeli conversation about the Beitunia killings, state actors and media pundits found themselves returning to the Al-Durrah example. Many drew the linkage explicitly: "[T]he Nakba [Beitunia] killings are a new version of the al-Dura blood libel," in the words of one Zionist magazine.[84] The right-wing media solicited the opinion of so-called experts with experience in the Al-Durrah case, who attested to the numerous parallels between the incidents.[85] Headlines in the Israeli press articulated the linkage clearly: "An Expert from the Muhamad al-Dura Incident: 'The Beitunia Videos Are Fake.'"[86]

Other echoes from the Al-Durrah case were more implicit, including the recurrent focus of accusers on the bodies of the Palestinian youths. Many argued that their gestures and movements, particularly at the moment of death or injury, rendered their fraudulence clear (see Image 18). Here is one military correspondent speaking to Israeli audiences as he screened the footage on the evening news: "Notice how he [the Palestinian victim] reaches his hand forward to counteract the fall—something that looks like it just might—maybe—be a fake."[87] No real injured or dying body falls that way, was the implicature. International commentators in the Zionist blogosphere added to the chorus: "[P]erhaps he [the Palestinian victim] *was instructed to fake a fall* as soon as he heard a shot . . . his fall seems inconsistent with being shot in the chest with a live bullet."[88]

Tonight, we asked Yosef Yekutiel,
a weapons expert,

IMAGE 17. Israeli ballistics expert assessing the Beitunia footage on Israeli television news and declaring it fraudulent. Channel 2. 22 May 2014. Source: Channel 2 (Israeli television).

Others cast doubts on the volume of blood evident in the video, former Israeli Ambassador Michael Oren among them:

> But again, looking at those pictures and . . . the way the bodies fall, the fact that there's no blood, someone who was hit in the back by a bullet has an exit wound, there is a tremendous amount of bleeding. There's no bleeding in the picture. There are many, many inconsistencies.[89]

Oren would go further than some repudiators by casting doubts on the boys' death—that is, even after footage of their funerals had been aired and autopsy reports had been analyzed. Military correspondents agreed with his assessment: "There are still some question marks here . . . The two we see here fall here: are the two dead? No one has a sharp and clear answer to this question."[90] The echoes from the Al-Durrah case were strong and recurrent. Al-Durrah's body had given itself away as fake with insufficient blood quantity and color and suspicious movements. So, too, here.[91]

IMAGE 18. Annotated image from CCTV footage of the Beitunia killing, an element of the international conspiracy campaign against its veracity. The dead body of Nadeem Nuwara is seen on the left. No date. Source: Israellycool.com.

For Israeli left activists and journalists, the accusation was familiar. But the scale of such assertions was something new. Throughout the course of the Beitunia case, as it wound through both the media and the Israeli military legal system, they would endeavor to counter repudiators by drawing on the case's abundant evidence: forensic, ballistic, videographic. Some anti-occupation journalists took a different tact, imploring Israeli onlookers to look beyond the voluminous public debates over videographic authenticity:

> The question of the number of cameras, the volume of video . . . where the cameras are located, to whom they belonged, whether the material is edited or not, and by whom . . . comparisons to Muhammad a-Dora, endless debates about . . . why there are not more cameras on our side. And *not a single question about the countless events that just aren't filmed.* They die and no one records.[92]

B'Tselem's spokesperson agreed, as she noted to me. In her words: "The battle over the [video] content . . . is a supreme effort to avoid discussing the real issue, which is ending its control over the territories."

The Israeli officer responsible for the shooting would be indicted for manslaughter in the killing of one of the two Palestinian youth, Nadeem Nuwara.[93]

Three years hence, the officer would accept a plea bargain, the manslaughter charge dropped.[94] As a result of the plea, the court was unable to rule on much of the videographic and forensic evidence against him. He would be sentenced to nine months in prison: "You could get a harsher punishment for texting while driving," tweeted Ahmad Tibi, Palestinian member of the Israeli parliament.[95] Those in the B'Tselem organization who had initially been hopeful about the fate of the legal trial, believing in the justice capacity of the unprecedented volume of corroborating evidence, were forced to revise their conclusions. But in disappointment, there were also political lessons learned, as their spokesperson noted to me:

> Today, a lot of people [Israelis] are willing to believe that someone staged twelve hours, or got dressed up like soldiers in jeeps and had Palestinians run around throwing stones in order to simply like invent this. More people are willing to believe that, than believe a soldier fired at Palestinians. I think that's a good indication of where we are as a society.

In part, what distinguished the Beitunia repudiation campaign from those of the past was the early involvement of state actors. In this case, they stood at the campaign's helm, from its very early days. In the process, they helped reconfigure the repudiation script as the language of state—a process that had begun with the State Commission of Inquiry on Al-Durrah, but which Beitunia would concretize. This development was evidenced during the Israeli aerial bombardment on the Gaza Strip a few months later (summer 2014), when Prime Minister Netanyahu would infamously accuse Palestinians of staging their own deaths for the camera: "They [Hamas] want to pile up as many civilian dead as they can, because somebody said they use—it's gruesome—they use telegenically dead Palestinians for their cause. They want the more dead the better."[96] By 2014, the script could be easily employed by state actors when need emerged. The accusation of Palestinian fraudulence was now readily available whenever Israeli state violence on camera went viral.

CONCLUSION: COLONIAL LOGICS OF THE DIGITAL AGE

This chapter has traced the consolidation and normalization of the repudiation script during the first two decades of the twenty-first century. The process was gradual. In the first few years following the Al-Durrah killing, the accusation of Palestinian fraudulence remained a relatively minor discourse, chiefly deployed on the margins of the blogosphere, propelled by a small cadre of conspiracy theorists in both Israel and abroad. The script would develop and spread over the next decade, as evident during the course of the Ni'ilin shooting and subsequent military trial. By the time of the Beitunia killings (2014), a year after the state commission on Al-Durrah issued its final report (2013), the accusation had received the imprimatur of the state. Over the course of these decades, as the storyline gradually captured mainstream Israeli and Zionist imaginations, an inversion was at work. What was once a fringe conspiracy theory had become normalized. Moreover, the allegation was now anticipated whenever Israeli violence against Palestinians was captured on camera, as Israeli investigative blogger Eishton noted in 2017: "Any new video which surfaces, depicting wrongdoing by Israel, is presumed to be Pallywood, until proven otherwise beyond unreasonable doubt."[97] The script had become a social default. Now, images of dead or injured Palestinians were treated as mere weapons in the war against Israel (see Image 19).

Normalization took considerable work. In the years charted here, Israeli and Zionist publics would gradually learn the fine art of repudiation, schooled by the small cadre of self-styled experts in Palestinian media manipulation that were appearing with increasing frequency in Israeli media outlets and legal arenas. Each repudiation campaign functioned as a pedagogic project, a public lesson in best practices for hoax detection. Recall, again, the range of analysts that testified after the Beitunia killings, substantiating their fraudulence claims through close readings of the videographic frame. In the process, they were retraining the Israeli mainstream public to see the visual field with a new degree of precision, providing them with the analytic strategies required to detect Palestinian manipulation with ease. Another pedagogical domain was more forensic in nature, focusing on how to analyze the crime scene, with a particular emphasis on how to sort fake deaths from real ones on the basis of bodily gestures and blood volume. In the process, video forensics became a layman's art that could be practiced at home, with the confidence of an expert, in front of the computer.[98] Israelis were being taught to read the visual field of state violence as a locus of probable, rather than merely possible, fraudulence.

Throughout the history charted here, repudiation was relatively immune to countervailing evidence in its various forms.[99] That is, such accusations tended to function as immutable, installing the effects they named ("hoax!"). In military courtrooms, where amateur footage of the crime scene was being introduced in

Posters4Israel
@Posters4Israel

#Pallywood: When that award winning photograph of "#Palestinian Resistance" is not what it appears.

Is this a "resistance"?

Or the red carpet at the Oscars?

And who is he about to throw that rock at?

10:40 AM · Jan 5, 2014 · Twitter Web Client

IMAGE 19. Meme accusing Palestinians of "Pallywood": namely, staging their victimization, injury, or death for the media. 5 January 2014. Source: https://twitter.com/posters4israel.

new ways and degrees, the longstanding pattern of judicial and state disregard for the violations committed by Israeli soldiers against Palestinians persisted, with negligible rates of conviction for the accused, as Eitan Diamond has noted:

> [T]he Israeli political and security establishment, backed by the state judiciary, have denied or diminished allegations of unlawful killing *even when they were supported by forensic analysis of video documentation from three different angles, or by the overwhelming convergence of multiple audio-visuals, still photographs and autopsy findings, as well as a host of other cases in which video documentation was produced to support allegations* that Israeli troops had used unlawful force against Palestinians.[100]

For many human rights workers, these judicial outcomes were a sobering corrective to the hope attached to the proliferating eyewitness cameras of the digital
age. To their dismay, they would find that the growth in camera penetration in
the West Bank was directly proportional to the popularization of the repudiation script. As Diamond noted, "denial persist[ed]" in legal arenas "by morphing
to adapt to heightened levels of transparency."[101] The script was a flexible political tool that could adapt to this new legal environment.

The script was as repetitive as it was flexible, reliant on a set of recurrent
accusations that differed little in their details. In part, such regularities can be
traced to the small body of conspiracy theorists who figured centrally in these
campaigns. In each incident, they cast doubts on both the veracity of the footage and the body of the alleged victim, alleging that both were manipulated to
frame the Jewish state. Such repetition was crucial to the success and longevity
of these campaigns: they required perpetual iteration in order to be nurtured and
sustained. But underlying such repetition was something of a tension pertaining
to the locus of the Palestinian hoax, as evidenced by the findings of the Israeli
state commission on Al-Durrah:

> . . . . TV cameras at the site recorded several instances in which *Palestinians
> acted out scenes of being injured* by Israeli fire and evacuated. The behavior
> and movements of those supposedly injured immediately prior to and after
> being "wounded," *the lack of blood or any other evidence of injuries,* the man-
> ner and speed of their evacuation, and the behavior of those around them,
> make it clear that *these were mostly attempts to stage scenes* for the benefit
> of the journalists on site.[102]

Here, two stories competed for prominence. The first focused on malicious dra-
maturgy: "Palestinians [who] acted out scenes of being injured by Israeli fire." In
this rendering, that staple of the Pallywood playbook, the Palestinian hoax was
located in practices of tactical deception. Indeed, the term "staging" appears no
less than nine times in the state report. But the second storyline was more ontological in nature, situating the hoax in the Palestinian body: "lack of blood or . . .
other evidence of injuries." Repudiators were particularly interested in these
moments of bodily noncompliance, when bodies didn't behave as they were instructed. Recall the Al-Durrah report: "In the final seconds of the footage, the
boy raises his arm and turns his head in the direction of Al-Durrah [the father]
in what are clearly intentional and controlled movements."[103] Or in the Beitunia

case, when the Palestinian youth didn't fall like a dying body should. Their bodies gave them away, was the recurrent claim, despite their best efforts to play dead. Their bodies can't help but lie. That's just the way they are.

A larger argument was at work, here. What was being diagnosed as fraudulent was the Palestinian condition itself. In the process, repudiators of this period were activating a longstanding colonial ideology about native fraudulence: fraudulent claims to land, peoplehood, history. The script, in other words, was merely a new variant of a very old colonial storyline that had been updated to address the perceived threats of the early twenty-first century. Colonial denial had been given a new digital dressing.

Chapter 4

THE EYES OF HUMAN RIGHTS

Curating Military Occupation

IN MAY 2011, A COLLECTION OF PALESTINIAN EYEWITNESS FOOTAGE
reached the Jerusalem office of B'Tselem, the Israeli human rights organization,
documenting the weekly anti-occupation demonstration in the West Bank village of Nabi Saleh. The police and military crackdown had been severe on that
particular Friday—beatings, stun grenades and pepper spray, tear gas—and two
demonstrators had been seriously injured by the impact of a tear gas canister, fired
by the Israeli security forces at close range.[1] With the footage in hand, a group of
B'Tselem staff huddled around an office computer for a preliminary screening,
those with Arabic skills assisting those without. They were particularly interested
in the tear gas shooting, deemed the day's most substantive rights violation.[2] If
the video was strong, with clear images of both perpetrator and victim, it would
become part of the evidential basis for a complaint filed with Israeli authorities.
Illegal tear gas usage by the Israeli security forces was becoming more frequent
across the West Bank, and sometimes with lethal consequences.[3] The military
perpetually denied the charge, insisting that policy regulations were always up-
held: "There is no disparity between the declared policy . . . pursuant to which
tear gas is not to be aimed directly at demonstrators, and the manner in which
the forces behave in the field."[4]

The footage was powerful, including graphic scenes of the Israeli border police beating protestors and attempting to prevent them from filming ("Move the camera!").[5] But the tear gas shooting, the chief object of their scrutiny, hadn't been clearly captured on film. Eli, one of the B'Tselem team involved that day, described the collective screening and ensuing disappointment:

> We were trying to figure out if we could see it. Frame by frame. Pause-play, pause-play, like watching stop-motion animation. We realized that the camera had been tilted at the moment of the shooting [of the tear gas], so we couldn't exactly see the shooter. We could only see the smoke and the general angle of the guns. And we were like: "Damn! I can't believe it—" Everyone was so bummed.

Eli was tasked with reviewing the footage after the collective screening concluded, identifying any usable segments. Aware of the numerous cameras on the scene, he had mined social media for corroborating material and found video shot that day by two veteran Nabi Saleh video-activists. There, he found the images he needed.

"So here, I can see the injury," he pointed to the original footage, "but I can't see the soldier shooting. When I found the online version, I could see the same incident from another angle." Manually sequencing the videos, he was finally able to place both perpetrator and victim in the same visual field. The materials would be a crucial element of their complaint with the Israeli authorities. One year later, the authorities would close the file "due to insufficient evidence."[6]

This chapter is an ethnographic study of videographic assessment in human rights contexts.[7] It focuses on the daily labor involved as human rights workers in B'Tselem's West Jerusalem offices—chiefly, Israeli Jews—watched, verified, and brokered Palestinian footage of state and settler violence. After footage arrived in Jerusalem from their West Bank team—a journey that, as previous chapters have chronicled, was often stymied and delayed by the violence of occupation in its various forms—the assessment process began. Chronologies would be produced, geographic coordinates verified, actors identified. This work was painstaking and slow. Eyes on the screen, staff studied the footage for images of human rights violations that were clear enough, strong enough, to form the basis of their legal or advocacy work. Some clips would form the basis for official complaints filed by the organization with the Israeli authorities, and a portion of these would yield criminal investigations of the officers involved.[8] Others would be sent to the Israeli media for review and potential screening. Their institutional mandate was clear. Working in accordance with international human rights standards, they sought visual evidence of harm committed by the Israeli security services against Palestinians, or visual evidence of what they termed "state-backed settler violence."[9] In these years, their advocacy work focused on Jewish Israeli publics. As they reviewed footage for possible screening on the evening news, it was these publics whose attention they sought.

It was a perpetually uncertain process. The team of West Bank volunteer videographers with whom they worked, whose footage was the subject of their review, filmed under conditions of fast-moving violence: large-scale settler incursions or arson attacks, crackdowns by soldiers or police. As a result, the ensuing images were often partial: the result of cameras dropped in fear, soldiers blocking the lens, or videographers skirting an impending attack. That is, there was often something missing from the videographic frame, or only partially rendered, that redoubled the labor involved in assessment and increased the uncertainty of outcomes in both legal and media arenas.

During the years studied here (2011–2014), the integration of digital videographic technologies and human rights institutional practices was still in its nascency, both in Jerusalem and globally. Protocols were still being developed, including standards for videographic authentication, models for protecting visual privacy, and ethical standards pertaining to mediated witnessing. The New York-based NGO WITNESS, "help[ing] people use video and technology to protect and defend human rights," was leading the global effort. As it noted in a 2011 report, the integration of "human rights, video and technology" was

> challenging long-held assumptions about how human rights documentation and advocacy functions. . . . Those seeking to create lasting impact will need to develop new skills and systems for creating and handling human rights video, online and off. . . . Ethical frameworks and guidelines for online content are still in their infancy and do not yet explicitly reflect or incorporate human rights standards.[10]

Human rights standards, norms, and labor practices were being recalibrated alongside shifts in the global media ecology.

The nascency of this integration—human rights work with videography—was evident in the B'Tselem offices. The labor of footage processing was still a slow and rudimentary affair, chiefly conducted manually, as technological resources were limited. In these years, the NGO's spokesperson still regarded Israeli television news as the media gold standard, their most prized outlet. But the changing media ecosystem of the West Bank was beginning to make its mark on assessment practices. Personal camera technologies were starting to proliferate within Palestinian communities, although slowly and unevenly, as were surveillance cameras, both state technologies intended to regulate Palestinian residents and those mounted on private Palestinian businesses by their owners. In the process, the volume of footage emerging from the West Bank was growing. Once, scenes of Israeli state violence, captured on camera, had been something of a rarity. Now, they were becoming an anticipated part of the political landscape. After any given incident, B'Tselem staff would increasingly expect footage from multiple angles and scales. For those sitting behind screens, this new visual landscape had to be learned. Practices of assessment and curation had to be updated to accommodate this changing media field.

But B'Tselem's central challenges were more political in nature, particularly so given the organization's advocacy emphasis on Jewish Israeli audiences. They were working in a political context in which human rights work in the occupied Palestinian territories was not merely unpopular but increasingly vilified by right-wing Israeli politicians and activists. In this political landscape, the labor required to bring Palestinian testimonials into mainstream media spaces was considerable. Within dominant Israeli imaginations, in keeping with a colonial epistemology at the heart of the Zionist project, the credibility of any Palestinian witness was always in doubt. Committed to Israel's destruction, Palestinian or Arab testimonials simply could not be trusted, or so the mainstream argument went. Palestinians were deemed impossible witnesses: incapable of bearing witness to their own victimhood, to scenes of their own subjection at the hands of the Israeli authorities or Jewish settlers.[11]

This colonial logic was effectively built into the legal structure of the military occupation, as B'Tselem documented: "A Palestinian who wants to lodge a complaint against soldiers cannot do so independently and has no direct access to the military law enforcement system. . . . [which] forces complainants to contact it through mediators, be they human rights organizations or lawyers."[12] During the years studied here, B'Tselem was among the many bodies playing that mediating

role vis-à-vis the Israeli authorities. It was a role they had played since their founding in the late 1980s, but its terms were changing in the digital age. Now, B'Tselem
was also acting as what Zeynep Gürsel calls an "image broker," functioning as
an "intermediary for images" produced by Palestinian camera-operators in the
occupied territories.[13] The organization critiqued the political logic that made
such mediation necessary but was also party to its workings.

The practice of watching is at this chapter's core: namely, the labor of sitting
before computer screens, alone or in groups, as B'Tselem staffers parsed and brokered the videographic field produced by their West Bank team. The Israeli political
climate of the moment enframed and inflected this work throughout. Even as they
assessed footage with an eye to compliance with human rights standards or its
evidential potential in a military courtroom, staffers were also asking, what is the
best strategy for representing the occupation to Israeli publics? Namely, within a
political landscape in which mainstream publics widely agreed on the disposability
of Palestinian life, how could the organization draw national eyes to the scene of
state violence against these same "disposable" subjects? This chapter began with an
Israeli abuse of power, captured on camera, that couldn't be clearly seen in the ensuing frame. This study focuses on precisely this: the multiple forms of uncertainty,
contingency, and failure that attended the NGO's work as videographic curator and
broker. Their foremost failure was political. This chapter is chiefly a chronicle of this:
the ways that the Israeli logic of Palestinian disposability enframed and constrained
the daily work of videographic processing for those sitting behind their screens.

THROUGH ISRAELI EYES

Since its founding in 1989 during the first Palestinian uprising, the Israeli NGO
B'Tselem built its legal and advocacy work on oral testimonials from Palestinians living under occupation. In the organization's early years, such testimonials
were collected and preserved in written documentary form, as was the protocol within human rights institutions of this period. By the second decade of the
twenty-first century, amidst the changing media landscape of the digital age,
the NGO was increasingly reliant on videographic materials for evidencing an
Israeli human rights abuse, both in legal and advocacy arenas. "Ten years ago, if
B'Tselem published something, it was based on oral testimonies," I was told by
the NGO's spokesperson in 2012. "Today, I won't even try to document a story if
there isn't a substantiating image." Proliferating cameras and videography were
changing the nature of the human rights field.

In B'Tselem's West Jerusalem office, video processing began when the original footage arrived from the West Bank in the form of data-sticks, memory cards, and videotapes. The ensuing labor was considerable: metadata analysis, authentication and verification, written summaries, oral testimonies employed as corroborating materials. The work was done collectively, drawing on staff in many branches of the West Jerusalem office. In the years studied here, most were Israeli Jews, aided by a much smaller population of Palestinians with Israeli citizenship. Middle-class Ashkenazim and Jewish immigrants from the United States numbered heavily among NGO staffers, in keeping with the broader demographics of the Israeli left. Most were Tel Aviv residents, having little tolerance for Jerusalem's religiosity and social conservatism.[14] Some had refused to serve in the Israeli military on political grounds, while others came to the job as military veterans, putting these skills to work in new ways: "In the army, I was working in aerial reconnaissance and visual intelligence, observing Palestinians through the viewfinder. Ten years later, I find myself looking at Palestinians again through the viewfinder."

Some of these Jewish Israeli staffers were activists who regularly traveled into the West Bank for anti-occupation demonstrations, sometimes shooting footage that would be part of the NGO's legal and media work.[15] Others had little personal experience of the occupied territories, save what they encountered on the job, and knew their West Bank team through their videography alone. Such was the experience of Natela, curator of B'Tselem's video archive: "She tends to stand and argue with soldiers at the checkpoints while her camera is running," Natela says, speaking of a veteran Palestinian videographer from Hebron. She described another videographer with a quieter style who "preferred the long shot," and another who filmed chiefly from her balcony. Through repeated screenings of the footage, Natela had also become familiar with the contours of particular Palestinian villages and cities, the route and routine of Friday anti-occupation demonstrations, the layout of private living rooms, made visible by videographers during military night raids of their family homes. She viewed her archival work as an education into the daily experience of Palestinian life under military rule, studied from the vantage of her computer screen.

In years before cameras were widespread in the West Bank, and well before eye-witness footage shot by Palestinians living under occupation was widely available on social media, footage shot by the NGO's Palestinian teams achieved a kind of brand effect within the Israeli media ecosystem. "Whenever they see shaky footage from the West Bank on television, they [Israeli Jews] perceive it to be a B'Tselem video,"

I was told in 2011 by a member of the video project, "even if it's not." This framing of videographic provenance ("a B'Tselem video") was telling. The ability of such videos to reach mainstream Israeli audiences was enabled by this reattribution of author-ship, by which the imprint of individual Palestinian videographers was replaced by the imprint of the Israeli NGO. At times, this logic was echoed by the organization, however inadvertently, when clips were uploaded to their website without the name of the Palestinian videographer.[16] The oversight echoed a mainstream Israeli logic with a long colonial history: the Palestinian as an impossible witness.

THE WORK OF WATCHING

Doron worked in B'Tselem's department of data coordination, tasked with gath-ering corroborating materials about human rights violations in the occupied territories. At the time of our interview, he was assigned to the "killing desk," as he wryly termed it, assigned to investigate fatal shootings of Palestinians by the Israeli security forces. He collected the associated evidence—including eye-witness testimonials, forensic evidence, photographs, statements from the mil-itary, and so forth—established the chronology, identified the actors involved, engaged in the necessary verification and cross-checking, often working closely with fieldworkers in the West Bank. If merited, Doron would also draft a letter of complaint to the authorities or pass documentation to the appropriate state offices. In his early years with B'Tselem, some of this work did not involve video. As years progressed, alongside shifts in human rights protocols, the absence of footage became increasingly uncommon.

When video of a violation was available, it would eventually reach Doron's desk. Then, his slow labor of watching began. Sitting over his computer in the West Jerusalem office, he described the challenges involved:

> Often, you have a video, but it's not totally clear what you see. Because even if I do see someone get injured, it might not be useful. Sometimes, the cam-era angle does not show the shooter. In the case of CCTV [surveillance foot-age], the picture might not be that great, and effort is required to decrypt it. I try to connect all the dots, add additional information that you can't see in the video or that you can only see when you're checking it carefully, which the normal viewer would not. Then you have the fuller picture . . .

The work required to "connect the dots" was considerable. In these years, Doron was still relying on video time stamps to produce the chronology of an event, albeit with an awareness of the frequent human errors this introduced. The video's soundscape often proved useful in producing a chronology, like the sound of shots being fired or cries at the time of an injury. Protocols for evidence assessment were changing, as they were in human rights organizations across the globe. B'Tselem was increasingly turning to social media for corroborating visuals, particularly the YouTube accounts of Palestinian and Israeli activists who were active with their cameras at the weekly demonstrations. The organization was also drawing more heavily on surveillance footage from the growing number of cameras mounted on homes and businesses by Palestinian residents, often in an attempt to monitor petty crime. Work with Google satellite maps was also in its early phases, occasionally consulted as a means of making sense of the West Bank territory and terrain. In the years that followed, all of these digital tools and platforms would become a regularized part of video assessment in the Jerusalem office.

Screening through a human rights lens wasn't intuitive, Doron said. Over his years with the organization, he had developed the screening literacies that the institutional, legal, and political conditions demanded, honing his capacity to understand and parse this kind of violent footage. In the beginning, he lacked requisite knowledge of military rules and regulations, like the flexible breadth of military authority in the occupied territories and the range of rights violations that occurred in the field. Gradually, he would understand what to look for in footage of a demonstration or settler incursion, how to read the behavior of the security services, how to identify the moment of a bullet's impact. Surveillance footage required its own kinds of literacies, chiefly because it lacked crucial sound cues, like the noise of a weapon discharging or the victim's cry. In all these domains, he had been required to train his eye, learning to identify human rights violations with accuracy and precision. Over time, he had acquired the skills necessary to watch Palestinian eyewitness footage through the particular optic of the human rights paradigm.

Despite these literacies, and the range of digital tools at his disposal, the footage was often difficult to understand. Doron had become accustomed to this: the blurry frames from videographers on the run, the cameras dropped in fear, the visual fields produced under conditions of threat and fear. As a result, as he noted, "it's not totally clear what you see"—this despite the fact that footage arrived at their office after a full narrative of the violence in question had been provided by the West Bank fieldworkers. Yet it was often hard to match the images with the oral testimony. Another data coordinator provided this example:

> The fieldworkers said—hey, I brought you this tape of a soldier hitting a kid. We said, "No, we already watched it and there's nothing in it." They insisted, so we watched it again. This often happens. Like when the data-coordinator says, "I know what is happening in this tiny spot on the video: a soldier is hitting a boy. I'm sure of it." But in fact, nobody can really see it. We don't have the kind of technologies that the police have, like in CSI—to enlarge an image and all that. We have to use the material as it is.

This particular video would prove unusable—sent neither to the media nor pursued in legal channels. The image of the violation was deemed too difficult to see.

Sometimes there were other kinds of visual challenges, particularly during episodes of heightened military crackdown when the volume of footage was high. "Nobody in the office watches it all," confided another data coordinator, describing the accumulation of unwatched video following a week of settler attacks. "They won't tell you this, but they don't." Doron also described the challenges associated with habituation, including the weekly footage he received from Palestinian videographers in West Bank towns where anti-occupation protests were regularized: "They walk to the wall, they demonstrate, the army opens fire." Such predictability, he said, dulled his viewing process. Herein lay an irony that data coordinators frequently faced: the very routinization of military rule, that which the organization was working so hard to chronicle, made it harder to see.

In the spring of 2014, B'Tselem turned its attention to the fatal shooting of two Palestinian youths by the Israeli border police in the West Bank town of Beitunia.[17] Doron was tasked with processing the videographic material. At first glance, the event resembled many other military killings that had been captured on film. But what distinguished this incident, he said, was the sheer number of cameras and volume of resultant footage, generating what one Israeli journalist called "the most documented and forensically corroborated murder in [the] IDF's history."[18] I watched this footage with Doron in the NGO's Jerusalem office, and he described the labor involved:

> What did I look for in this video? Things like, what the victim did prior to his injury, and his exact or proximate surroundings. I tried to identify the shooter, the context, [whether it was] a demonstration or confrontation, whether there was use of force, whether or not medical help was provided for the injured [and so on]. . . . I want to know everything I can know about

it, so I watched it over and over again, frame by frame. And, when possible, I tried to see the same thing from different angles.

Doron employed meticulous cross-checking in order to establish the reliability of the video, working with footage from all of the cameras. He had manually synched the video on two monitors, focusing on the twenty minutes prior to the shooting. His handwritten notes evidence his close scrutiny: "11:19—burning of a tire. 11:21—first gas grenade. 11:43—youth gathering . . . 13:02—young man injured. 13:40—the youth run away." Not all the footage was clear, and disputes arose with others in the organization over the events in the frame, as his notes in the margins indicated: "11:20—I doubt that this is Muhammad 'Azzah [one of the young men shot and wounded during the events]." Numerous questions had to be answered: How many youths were present? Was the population of protestors stable or did it change? Was there something in the hand of the future victim and might it be a weapon? That is, were the youths involved in a provocation with the security forces as the state claimed? This work was tedious and emotionally draining, as he would note in our conversations ("Do you know how many hours I have watched this?"). Sitting in front of the computer, screening the footage tens of times with an eye to the minor details, Doron watched the youth die over and over again.

Sometimes, he conceded, the work was maddening. With every bystander armed with a camera—at least, in the more recent years of their work—they sometimes faced "a staggering volume" of footage and struggled to keep up. "You are literally going crazy," another data coordinator confided during a period of elevated settler violence, "watching all those settler attacks. For a while, when it was piling up, I found that I couldn't do it, this weekly chore of watching. Okay—I made myself watch, but it was difficult, another video and another." Given the volume of the material involved, and the labor required, their review would sometimes culminate after national interest in the incident had peaked, consigning their footage to relative invisibility. In this political climate, it was just part of the job.

The everyday practice of assessing, curating, and brokering footage functioned within a protracted temporality: the temporality of waiting. For Doron, from the division of data coordination, videos only reached his desk after a violation had been determined, and he knew the relevant details of the case before he sat down to screen. As a result, he usually engaged in a kind of anticipatory viewing, watching the screen and waiting for the violence to come: "The first watch is kind of superficial. I just sit and wait—is it going to happen now?" But within the political context in which he worked, this anticipatory process was twofold: both waiting for the shot to be fired and waiting for responses from Jewish Israeli audiences. Such responses tended to follow a predictable storyline: the charge of videographic fraudulence, the defense of the Israeli perpetrators ("they had no choice"), the accusation of treason against the Jewish human rights workers.[19] As he sat in front of his computer screen, both were the objects of his meticulous gaze: the details of the shot and the highly constrained terms of the national political landscape. Eyes on the screen, Doron was always anticipating the footage's inability to persuade the national audience of state wrongdoing. In this political environment, such inevitable failures were just part of the job.

CINEMA AS SOLUTION

The NGO's advocacy work followed a standard pattern. Clips deemed strong, with clear visual evidence of state or state-enabled setter violence, would be sent to the Israeli media for review. Several clips a month would get a nation-wide screening on Israeli television news, sometimes to viral effect. The video division studied these viral cases, eager to learn from prior successes. Footage rejected for media consideration, but nonetheless deemed important, would be uploaded to the organization's website and shared on social media, but only tele-vision ensured a broad national audience. Curatorial decisions rested in a stan-dard media calculus, with a premium placed on video with the requisite hook to draw an audience. The political challenges were paramount, as the NGO's spokesperson noted in 2013: "Most of this footage doesn't cause any real stir ex-cept among the people who still care about these things. Most Israelis are past caring and past pretending to care."

Time and again, the solution seemed to lay in cinema. Many in the NGO argued that only the visual grammar of cinema, with violence rendered in spectacular terms, would draw mainstream Israeli viewers, effectively bypassing their political disregard for Palestinians under occupation. As evidence, they pointed to some of the organization's unexpected viral successes from the early years of the video project. Footage shot by Muna al-Nawaj'ah in 2008 of a violent settler incursion onto her family's land was one such example. Muna's frames were sharp and vivid, capturing images of the bare-chested and masked settlers, carrying clubs and walking slowly from their settlement to mount their calculated attack on their Palestinian neighbors. They approached, words were exchanged, and then the beating began. Within the legal arena, the incident ended as many others had: with arrests of the two suspects, but without a prosecution. No charges would be filed.[20]

Within the Israeli media, the incident had a more substantive imprint, with the footage replayed on Israeli television news and featured on the front page of a prominent national newspaper. "It was the first time that Israelis saw masked Jews," those in the video department noted. For national viewers, it was a surprising inversion of the visual iconography of the first Palestinian uprising with its recurrent images of masked Palestinian youths, denoting thuggery in the mainstream Israeli visual lexicon. "Average Israelis were shocked . . . they'd heard about the violence, but never seen it in such a graphic way. These were settlers?" In years hence, settler masking would become a common tactic, rapidly assimilated into the visual iconography of Israeli militarism.

Within the NGO, the footage's success was unexpected, even startling. The video team, eager to make broader inroads with the Israeli public, considered its lessons. It would be read as a case study in viral capacity. In 2011, I screened Muna's footage with the head of the video division, Yoav Gross. He was a filmmaker in his own right, and he drew my attention to the video's opening sequence: a long shot of the masked settlers approaching Muna's family from the neighboring hillside, their figures coming very gradually into focus as they near the Palestinian family, clubs in hand. "It's very cinematic," Yoav suggested, pointing to the screen. "Just like something from *The Good, the Bad and the Ugly*. Like a scene from the Wild West (see Image 20)." Of course, he said, it was a visual accident driven by expediency and the lack of a proper zoom lens, a byproduct of the rudimentary cameras that B'Tselem was distributing in those days. But the resulting visual field was classic, he said, both the timing and physical gestures of the villains, and herein lay its mainstream appeal, enabling its broad circulation within the Israeli media. The form effectively bypassed the content.

This argument was also adopted by the media division. "I'm up against an Israeli media that would prefer not to show things," I was told by B'Tselem's spokeswoman in 2013. "Actually, it's not the media, but their awareness that their audiences don't want to see it. So I'm trying to get dramatic footage."

"The dramatic," in her estimation, tended to cohere chiefly in scenes of eruptive violence: marauding settlers, violent military assaults, police confrontations with a Palestinian civilian. Provided they were rendered in spectacular terms, they had viral potential:

IMAGE 20. Still from eyewitness video of masked Jewish settlers beating the al-Nawaj'ah family. Filmed by Muna al-Nawaj'ah. Susiya. 8 June 2008. Source: B'Tselem.

Someone shot and injured is dramatic. Someone being killed is dramatic. Beating is very dramatic, so evocative of many historical moments. Settlers and Palestinians clashing is dramatic. Cynically, I would say more intense violence is what the media want. You know, they want to get closer to the violence. . . . and we're also trying to give our videographers better training to capture those images in a way that would be better, technically or cinematographically.

The optic of comedy also had cinematic potential but was harder to come by. She pointed to the inaugural footage of the B'Tselem video project: a short clip documenting one Palestinian family's brazen verbal abuse at the hands of a neighboring Jewish settler, filmed by teenager Rajaa Abu Aisha.[21] This, too, was a crucial lesson in media impact. At the time of the footage's viral success, B'Tselem's standard work on settler violence was making few inroads with the Israeli public. In sharp contrast, Rajaa's footage was widely consumed by Israeli audiences—but chiefly through the lens of dark comedy, a reading focused on its central images of the vulgar, profanity-spewing settler. The video quickly entered Israeli popular

IMAGE 21. Still from eyewitness video of settler harassment of Palestinians. Filmed by Rajaa Abu Aisha. Hebron. 16 January 2007. Source: B'Tselem.

culture, spoofed on late-night satirical shows.[22] B'Tselem viewed this clip as one of its greatest media successes, albeit accidentally so. "Now, it's a classic," Yoav told me. "Everybody knows it" (see Image 21).

Occasionally, there were other inadvertent comedic opportunities, culled from the violent landscape of military rule. Such was the case with footage of settler vandalism at a Hebron checkpoint, shot by B'Tselem volunteer Susan Jabber from her second-story window. It was an act of settler revenge against rock throwing by Palestinian youth—dubbed a "price tag" attack (*tag makhir*) in the settler lexicon, a proud act of vengeance against Palestinians under occupation. Such attacks were recurrent, and perpetrators were rarely prosecuted.[23] Jabber's clip began with a settler vehicle speeding into view. It stopped suddenly and two settlers exited, running in the direction of the fleeing youth. The camera followed them as they exacted their revenge on Palestinian property: smashing car windshields and tossing a case of eggs, removed from the back of the private vehicle of a Palestinian grocer. The police arrived while the vandalism was underway, but they ignored the perpetrators, as they often did, only questioning the Palestinians present. Jabber, a seasoned videographer, took pains to capture a clear shot of the settler license plate, aware of its legal value should an investigation ensue.[24]

I screened the footage with B'Tselem's spokesperson the day after it reached their offices from the West Bank. The national appetite for their footage was particularly constrained at the time of our meeting in 2014. A few months prior, the Israeli military had launched yet another attack on the Gaza Strip, widely supported by the Jewish Israeli mainstream public. With national eyes turned toward the "existential threat to the Jewish state," as the government would frame it, the Israeli tolerance for images of Palestinian victims was particularly low. She hoped that this footage, with settlers cast as comic actors, might enhance its media appeal. She paused on a single frame: eggs raining down on the Palestinian vehicle. "This is a great shot, well filmed and clear. It looks like slapstick, like the keystone cops. It's all a little ridiculous. And this is the reason that I think it will work."[25]

In the B'Tselem offices, the limits of this tactic were abundantly clear. Staff knew that the visual grammar of cinema was risky, threatening to collude with the Israeli state by subsuming the Palestinian experience of military occupation beneath the veneer of spectacle. They understood the ironic resonance with their right-wing detractors who employed the charge of Palestinian "theatrics"—arguing that Palestinians "staged" their injuries for the camera—to undercut the veracity of Palestinian eyewitness footage.[26] But the potential political gains, they thought, were worth the risks. They hoped that the accidental grammar of cinema might be a means of bypassing the standard national relationship to the visual field of Palestinian suffering and Israeli perpetration. It was yet another tactic for maximizing Palestinian visibility in these highly constrained political times. The spokesperson described it this way: "We try to find every crack in the wall. If they don't let us in through the door, we are going through the window—in order to show these snippets of reality to the Israeli public, regardless of who wants to see and who doesn't, regardless of the conclusions they draw."

CURATORIAL CONTINGENCIES

The labor of video assessment was rarely a solitary project. Rather, it was often done collectively, bringing many B'Tselem actors, forms of expertise, and ways of seeing around a shared computer screen. Often, Palestinian fieldworkers in the West Bank were part of the conversation by phone or email. Decisions had to be made about the footage's value, its evidentiary potential in the military courts, or its media capacity, including which clip to send to Israeli television for possible screening on the evening news program. Disagreements were frequent, regarding both the content of the image ("Is that a settler?" "No, that's a Palestinian"), and its advocacy potential. These collective viewings were curatorial endeavors that were crucial in determining the institutional value of any given piece of footage.

On the morning of 30 April 2013, a Jewish settler from the extremist settlement of Yizhar, well known for its violent ideology, was stabbed to death by a Palestinian at a bus stop. It was the first deadly attack on an Israeli citizen in the occupied territories in several years, and the mainstream Israeli media framed it as a watershed, shattering a period of political "calm."[27] Settler reprisals quickly followed in the form of so-called price tag (*tag mehir*) attacks, a settler practice of "exact[ing] a price from local Palestinians for violence against settlers" or their physical infrastructures.[28] Across the West Bank, in the hours after the killing, dozens of settlers rampaged through Palestinian cities and villages, raiding residences and damaging property, stoning cars and school buses. Palestinian communities in the vicinity of Yizhar were their primary targets.

Two days later, a collection of footage from these settler attacks, shot by Palestinian videographers from across the West Bank, reached B'Tselem's central offices, its arrival delayed by a military closure.[29] Those in the B'Tselem office had known it was coming and had a good sense of its content from conversations with Palestinian fieldworkers. But the quantity and quality were a surprise, shot by numerous volunteers in the varied Palestinian communities across the West Bank that had come under simultaneous attack. With the footage in house, several members of the video team gathered around a set of computers to begin the viewing, and I joined them.

Much of the footage was clear, with images of male settlers gathered in large numbers to conduct their assaults on the villages in the vicinity of Yizhar settlement: 'Urif, 'Asira al-Qibliya, Burin. Most of the settlers were masked, some shirtless to enhance the masculinist threat, carrying stones and petrol canisters, fuel for the fires they planned to start in the arid hills. Soldiers were visible in the background, making little attempt to intervene while settlers mounted their assault. Footage from the village of 'Urif was particularly sharp, with scenes of a coordinated attack on a primary school, already evacuated. The camera lens jostled as the videographer ran up the school stairs, panting as he moved. He pointed his camera through the school's barred windows, capturing scenes of masked settlers throwing stones in his direction from an adjacent hillside. The audio track was vivid, with sounds of rocks hitting the bars and protective wire mesh, sometimes breaking the glass. Through the mesh, only partially obscured in the frame, were images of the soldiers standing by. Later, the videographer would ascend to the roof of this school, his camera panning the adjacent area, now surrounded by the attackers. He would be injured in the midst of this rampage, struck in the head by a rock, but continued to film.

This was the first screening of this footage, and the mood was electric. The magnitude of this coordinated settler attack, and the strength of the images, was only now becoming clear to staff ("wow ... that's strong"). This group of B'Tselem staff included both Israelis and Palestinians, with varying degrees of familiarity with the settler communities in question. For the Arabic speakers among us, the images were augmented by a vibrant soundscape, including shouts and conversations as the terror unfolded. But there was no time to translate, let alone think about providing subtitles for future audiences, something that was not regularly practiced within the video team in those years, chiefly due to limited labor. On that day, there was just too much material to review.

As they watched, they endeavored, with some difficulty, to generate a clear sense of the timeline, the location of each assault, the settlers involved. Six Palestinian videographers working with the B'Tselem project had been filming that day, stationed across the northern West Bank, generating a total of some sixty clips and hours of footage. Numerous questions arose:

"Where is this?"
"They are in 'Urif now [West Bank village]. . . . "
"Who is that? Palestinians?"
"No, those are settlers. . . . And there's the soldier."

On our second viewing of the 'Urif footage, the contours and scale of this coordinated assault are coming more clearly into focus. Now, some of the B'Tselem team thought they could identify particular settler attackers. But they were chiefly interested in the soldiers, deemed the most crucial players in this scene of state-sanctioned violence. To the dismay of those present, the videographer had not focused his attention there. In his footage, the soldiers moved in and out of the frame, his lens focused on the settler attackers:

"Let's look again at those clips of the soldiers and the settlers together."
"Okay . . . "

"What makes this newsworthy is the soldiers standing there . . . "

"Here—here it is."

As they screened the materials, the B'Tselem team tried to fill in the pieces: tracking the soldiers' movements, noting refusals to protect Palestinian civilians from settlers' assaults and destruction of property. These details would prove crucial in the complaint they would file with the Israeli authorities, demanding a military investigation into the military's failure to "adhere to the obligation to effectively defend the Palestinian population from revenge attacks."[30]

Hours of screening had now passed, and the team was concerned. To overcome the general national disinterest in the material at hand, B'Tselem couldn't afford delay where their work with the media was concerned. Receipt of the footage had already been impeded by a military closure, and the sheer volume of videographic materials had further slowed the screening process. Such delays came at a considerable cost. Most television news programs would not air footage that was not filmed on the day of the broadcast. It just would not be seen as relevant. For the organization, it was a recurrent and nearly impossible tension. Amidst the belabored temporality of occupation—a landscape of closures, checkpoints, movement of Palestinian persons and footage perpetually constrained—such delays in video processing were frequent, inevitable.[31] This temporal struggle was part of the fabric of their videographic work: the battle between the media demand for timeliness and the belated time of life under military rule.

The spokesperson entered the room, updated by those present. We watched the scene from the primary school again, in her presence. Again, we watched the panting cameraman ascend the stairs of the school, surrounded by settlers. Again, we saw settlers throwing stones, the videographer's view partially obstructed by the mesh window. This was the footage on which they decided to focus, sending a clip to the Israeli television for review. Selections from the remaining footage would be uploaded to the B'Tselem website, accompanied by textual documentation—the arson attacks, the stoning of school buses, the settler rampage of village homes and businesses. But consigned to the website, most would not be seen by their target audience. Culling was a necessary part of the job. Not everything could be seen.

THE EVERYDAY OCCUPATION

"Do you give the media what they want?" It was the subject of some disagreement within the organization. When eyewitness footage took an accidentally cinematic form, it had the potential to arrest Israeli audiences. But such clips were often at odds with organizational priorities, as a staff member noted in 2013:

> Last week, for example, we received footage of settlers running rampant, burning fields, throwing stones. Now, this is the image that the public wants, and it gets on the evening news because it's sensational. But from a human rights perspective, it's not relevant. What's relevant is the fact that right next to them, standing and doing nothing, is a soldier. But that's not going to go viral. Everybody wants the first image, but the second is the actual human rights violation. The second is the crux of the matter.

Amidst a steady stream of violent extremism from the Jewish settlements in the occupied territories, the organization had no shortage of such footage: scenes of masked settlers vandalizing Palestinian homes and businesses, torching agricultural lands, raiding villages—filmed by their West Bank camera operators on a weekly and sometimes daily basis. But their institutional priorities as a human rights organization were otherwise: namely, state and state-backed violence in its varied forms.[32] Organizational priorities were often at odds with media appetites:

> Eruptions of violence can get a lot of views. But the occupation is not necessarily about people getting killed or injured, about the big or dramatic eruptions. It's not always spectacular. The real occupation is about the daily reality—the reality of having soldiers coming into your house, or having to wait hours in the checkpoint on the way to school or on the way to work, or having to drive 20 extra miles because the two exits to your villages are closed, or the crazy bureaucracy. It's daily harassment. Daily limitations. This is the real occupation. And how do you portray this? How do you portray the routine nature of occupation?

This question had very practical implications. In weeks when footage from the territories was plentiful, the organization was forced to make difficult decisions. Which clip of Israeli state or state-backed violence, of the many available, should be sent to Israeli television for a potential screening on the evening news? Such was their dilemma in February 2012, when B'Tselem received information about a settler attack on the West Bank village of Luban al-Sharqiya in the early hours of the night. Footage from two mounted security cameras corroborated the account, showing a settler vandalizing a Palestinian business, stabbing through building materials with a knife. A follow-up investigation by the Israeli police found graffiti on the walls of the shop—"Muhammad is a pig"—also attributed to the assailants.

This particular settler attack "caused a lot of inside turmoil inside the organization," I was told later by a data coordinator:

> I thought it was ridiculous. They just vandalized—and stupid vandalizing, not something major. I mean, compared to regular settler violence and the everyday violence of the occupation, it was nothing. Just petty. This is not occupation.

Others disagreed, arguing that petty violence was a crucial element of the political story. It was a clear example, they argued, of lax Israeli law enforcement where settlers were concerned.[33] The latter argument prevailed, and the footage would be published.[34]

This was a perpetual challenge within the organization: namely, how to make visible "the everyday violence of the occupation." There were numerous Israeli violences in the West Bank that simply did not "photograph well," as they put it: the structural violence of de-development, exploitation of natural resources, normalization of the settlement infrastructure, and the list went on.[35] Nor was the Israeli public interested: "Infrastructural violence is something that people don't want to see . . . it's the boring stuff."

Sometimes, there were viral surprises that defied these logics. Such was the case of a video shot in Hebron in 2012 by the al-Haddad family, documenting a military night raid on their family home. Like other night raid footage shot in the West Bank, it was an intimate portrait of family life under military occupation: the children woken from sleep by masked soldiers, the private corners of the home overturned for late-night inspection. It was equally a portrait of military violence rendered absurd. The camera, moving between the hands of various family members, recorded the soldiers' seemingly aimless search through the mundane objects of family living in a search for evidence of their alleged misdeeds. Some soldiers rifled through cups of coins and knickknacks, others overturned blankets and pillows, asking the family to move their sofas and unlock their closets. In the midst of the raid, the al-Haddad family attempted to restore a sense of proportion. The eldest son presented the contents of a mug—a string of beads, a keychain—in compliance with military demands: "Please, have a look. You—the commander. Please, look!" As the camera rolled, the family made a subtle mockery of the military mandate.

In 2012, when the video department first received the footage, its visual power was clear. But they were challenged by its unconventional form. A long take of twenty minutes could not be screened in its entirety on the evening news. Nor did it contain eruptive violence that might draw an audience. B'Tselem sent a short segment to the media and posted it online, but the footage acquired few views and little journalistic interest. Its power and impact would only emerge belatedly, requiring a wholesale reconceptualization of its form, framework, and target audiences. Rather than working with the national media cycle, the video team produced the footage as a short film in collaboration with the al-Haddad family—*Smile, and the World Will Smile Back*. Hewing closely to the original long take, the film was screened broadly on the international documentary circuit and met with considerable acclaim.[36] For B'Tselem, the film's success was a lesson in both the visual potential of everyday occupation and the formal constraints of the testimonial genre. Over the years, the consolidation of human rights videographic genres, fed by a media calculus, had effectively produced a set of governing conventions that made certain images and storylines visible, particularly violence in eruptive form, while consigning others to the media shadows. The framing of documentary film was less encumbered by these constraints.

Media demands had other secondary effects. The visual idiom of violent eruption worked within a fleeting temporality, predicated on a logic of sudden violence that had to be quickly witnessed or captured by the camera before it disappeared. As such, this media-favored storyline bolstered the state-sponsored myth of the military occupation as a merely temporary political form, a narrative long embraced as a means of complying with international law and masking Israeli political ambitions. The pacing of the al-Haddad footage—capturing the ordinariness of this manifestly arbitrary invasion—illustrated military rule as slow, habituated, still emergent. Media predilections, by contrast, colluded with state fictions.

CONCLUSION: ARCHIVAL ALTERNATIVES

In B'Tselem's West Jerusalem office, the work of videographic assessment was never about verification alone—or rather, not in any strict sense. Sitting in front of the screen, as staffers struggled to make sense of the footage before them ("Who fired the shot?"), they were also asking larger questions about the visual field of Israeli military rule. As a human rights organization, bound by international protocols, these were chiefly normative questions. Namely: what is the

THE EYES OF HUMAN RIGHTS   121

nature of the rights violation at issue, and which clip most clearly illustrates its terms? Which sorts of violence should appear in our institutional frame and, by extension, what kinds of images exceed our human rights mandate? But as an anti-occupation organization, these questions also took a more prescriptive form: What *should* our institutional rendering of the occupation look like? While normative questions hewed closely to the content of the image, prescriptive questions aligned with the capacity of their intended audience. Namely: what kind of footage has the capacity to bypass national ideologies and ways of seeing? What are the visual conditions under which the violence of the Israeli authorities could be seen *as such* by Jewish Israeli publics? These larger political questions about Israeli political capacity always lay just beneath the surface of the assessment project—sometimes articulated explicitly, sometimes muted by the exigencies of the day's work. The NGO's daily labor of watching, curating and brokering Palestinian eyewitness videography was, then, always a performative practice. As they sat before their screens, staffers were actively shaping the visual contours of Israeli military rule.

In this work, B'Tselem was frequently caught in a videographic bind. In the digital age, footage was increasingly required to substantiate claims about Israeli human rights abuses in the occupied territories, in both legal and media arenas. But such footage often failed to persuade their target Jewish Israeli audiences of state wrongdoing. The reasons for failure were varied: a busy news cycle, a large-scale military operation that directed national attention elsewhere. But as years progressed, as the Israeli population moved ever-rightward, failure increasingly took a far more basic form, rooted in the colonial ideology of Palestinian disposability. What failed, in this framework, was neither the persuasiveness of any given footage, nor the work of its Israeli broker. Rather, it was Palestinian humanity that had failed, and ontologically so. Herein lay the organization's most insurmountable bind. Not even the most powerful clip of state or settler violence, even when rendered in highly cinematic terms, or bolstered by abundant forensic evidence, had the political power to overcome this colonial commitment.

Nonetheless, many B'Tselem staffers remained hopeful. Like the Palestinian videographers in the West Bank with whom they worked, many harbored a set of recalcitrant hopes—arguably, a tactical set of hopes—about the project of rendering state violence visible. Even as the Jewish Israeli population moved ever rightward, many continued to invest in the radical potential of Palestinian eyewitness footage in Israeli media and judicial spaces. The legal limits of their work were an ever-present reality: namely, a military court system in which soldiers and Jewish settlers who attacked Palestinians, or damaged their property, rarely faced prosecution.[37] The advocacy limits were also clear, particularly so in the years studied here, as human rights institutions and advocates grew increasingly vilified in the eyes of the mainstream Israeli public. Despite these vanishing odds, many in the NGO celebrated their "human rights achievements," determined to "learn from what works" about best practices for advocacy and legal work.[38] Many working in the video division continued to place great stock in the dream of more perfect evidentiary video—namely, footage with both perpetrator and victim in the same frame—arguing its power to persuade even the most politically recalcitrant of Israeli audiences. Hope of this kind persevered in the face of vanishing political odds.

As the NGO curated the visual field of Israeli military rule, it was also determining its limits. For every clip selected for media review, there were hundreds passed over. The reasons were varied and multiple. Sometimes, the footage was not deemed relevant to a human rights framework. Or it was considered insufficiently arresting for Israeli television audiences, lacking "a good hook." Perhaps the assailant was beyond the camera's range, or the scene was just too poorly lit. Once identified as unusable, provided it was no longer the subject of a legal investigation or being used to produce an internal report, all videographic materials moved to the institution's archives, housed in the West Jerusalem office, where footage would be catalogued and tagged. On rare occasions, data coordinators would revisit this collection for internal research purposes. But more often, it was used by documentarians, researchers, and the occasional artist who sought images or footage of the military occupation.[39] At the time of this research, B'Tselem's archive housed thousands of hours of footage: all the materials shot by their Palestinian team in the West Bank. Deemed unusable within media or legal spheres, the archive gave this videographic material a potential second life.

The archive worked according to a very different set of logics. This footage was not subject to the organization's curatorial or brokerage interventions—neither enframed by the demands of the Israeli media nor by human rights protocols. It could not fail as a body of testimonial material, as it was not intended for an Israeli audience. Rather, as a collection of all the supplemental materials that neither courts nor Israeli media could use, it was chiefly organized by the Palestinian videographers themselves: their movements and choices during an anti-occupation protest, their camera tactics during a military night raid on their private home, their experience during settler incursions. Often, their footage of Israeli state violence shared space, on a single videographic record, on a single cassette tape or memory stick, with scenes filmed for personal reasons, particularly in years when other cameras were not available: family weddings, baby namings, road trips, and village celebrations. The archive as videographic compendium offered a rich portrait of Palestinian living at the intersection of state violence and everyday Palestinian pleasures. Indeed, as one of the video project's Israeli curators proposed, this archival portrait of the everyday occupation, ill-suited for national airtime, may have been the project's most powerful contribution.

Chapter 5

THE MILITARY'S LAMENT

Combat Cameras and State Fantasies

BARAK RAZ, A LEADING SPOKESPERSON FOR THE ISRAELI MILITARY, had a keen interest in cameras. He oversaw the military's West Bank division and was often in theater with his iPhone, ready to capture images that could be uploaded directly to the military's social media accounts. Raz believed in the power of official military messaging when translated into a popular idiom. He was a heavy social media user and frequently posted content under his military designation during years before such practices were constrained by official policy. His playfulness and informality on Facebook were something of a personal signature within the offices of the military spokesperson. "The beauty of social media," he noted to me during a 2013 interview in his Jerusalem office, "is that it's not just Captain Barak Raz with the beret and the uniform. It's also the Barak Raz that goes out in Tel Aviv and uploads an Instagram photo of the beach. Not just the riots and the protests and everything else." The result, he believed, was the military's capacity to connect online with individuals and communities "on a personal level. You know, to understand where I'm coming from." His playful tactics proved prescient. In years to come, personalization would be adopted by the military as a concerted social media strategy, a means of translating official doctrine into a vernacular register. On the military's social media feeds, the traditional idiom of state speech would be increasingly replaced by selfies.[1]

But while the smartphone era afforded the Israeli military certain advantages, Raz believed that it also posed a considerable threat. Within the Palestinian West Bank, the volume of personal technologies was growing markedly. Anti-occupation demonstrations—"we call them riots," he corrected me—were now dense with networked-enabled cameras: those of Palestinian activists, Israeli human rights workers, international journalists. The result, Raz thought, could be damning for Israel. Soldiers in the field agreed. The growing volume of Palestinian cameras in operational contexts was constraining the military: "A commander or an officer sees a camera and becomes a diplomat, calculating every rubber bullet, every step," a soldier would note to the Israeli press in 2012. "It's intolerable, we're left utterly exposed. *The cameras are our kryptonite.*"[2]

In Raz's estimation, the solution was clear. The military needed enhanced media production from operational arenas in order to respond to their enemies in kind: "All you have to do is film, and it'll be broadcast back to our servers, and then we'll pull what we need." While the formula was simple, the process of operationalization was less so. Raz conceded that the military's recent efforts had been plagued by errors, miscalculations, and "unfortunate technological issues." Nonetheless, he placed great stock in a possible correction: more military camera operators, better media infrastructures, and faster circulation of ensuing images. The military simply required the right technological fix and political solutions would follow.

This chapter studies the Israeli military's evolving media strategies during the first two decades of the twenty-first century. I am interested in the steep learning curve involved as the military attempted to narrow "the gap between the documentation abilities of the enemy and those of the IDF," a gap evident since the first Palestinian uprising (1987 to 1991–93) but widening in the digital age.[3] As network-enabled cameras proliferated among Palestinian populations living under occupation, the military grew ever more concerned. In 2011, writing in the military's professional magazine (*Maarachot*), a former spokesperson warned about the gravity of the enemy's media capacities:

> [C]*ameras are everywhere now and everybody . . . is constantly document*[*ing*] *our forces' activities.* This documentation is instantly distributed on social

media, blogs, news websites, news agencies, and traditional media. Sometimes it's even broadcasted live. . . . Developing operational documentation
[*tiyud mivtza'i*] is vital for victory. *Today, documentation is a weapon which
is no less important than tanks and planes.*[4]

This concern would be repeatedly recited by military officials in the first two
decades of the twenty-first century. Their enemies seemed to be perpetually "winning the media war" through sheer technological volume and speed,
employed to deliver "false information from the battlefield" in an "attempt
to undermine [Israel's] legitimacy and restrict the IDF."[5] In the estimation of
these analysts, what was required was a whole paradigm shift in military media production and distribution. The military needed more robust "operational documentation" (e.g., documentation of military activities) in wartime and
battlefield contexts.[6]

Over the course of the first two decades of the twenty-first century, the military would attempt to make the necessary changes in their media policy. Michael
Shavit described the ensuing process this way:

From 2000–2014, [the Israeli military] underwent *a process of intensive mediatization* that transformed the media into an interpretive grid for many
of its military activities, and media and media logics became increasingly
entwined with its identity formation, organization, structure and the social
construction of warfare in Israel. . . . [T]he IDF became extensively engaged
in the social construction of warfare in the new media ecology of the twenty-first century.[7]

The daily work of mediatization was centralized in the office of the Israeli military spokesperson (Dover Tzahal), their professional media arm.[8] This unit
was charged with "disseminating military related information to the public, instructing IDF [Israel Defense Forces] personnel in matters pertaining to PR, and
developing relationships with media outlets and accompanying them to military
events."[9] Their advocacy mandate was proudly broadcast to the public: namely,
to "report on the accomplishments and activities of the IDF to the Israeli and international public" and "nurture public confidence" in the Israeli military.[10] "[T]
he IDF defends the country," a spokesperson noted in a public forum, while "we
defend the IDF."[11] It was widely acknowledged within Israel that this unit wielded
a "total monopoly on information concerning the military."[12]

But mediatization was not a simple task. There was a need for new policies and protocols befitting the digital age, greater numbers of camera operators in military theaters, more robust training, and better technologies. Along the way, missteps and policy miscalculations were recurrent at scales both large and small. The media victory that the military sought proved elusive. As Israeli military analysts and scholars lamented, the Israeli security services continued to be outwitted in media matters by their digitally savvy enemies.[13]

This chapter focuses on this repetitive lament about media failure as attached to some of the key Israeli military operations of the early twenty-first century: the invasion of the Jenin refugee camp (2002), the naval interception of the *Mavi Marmara* (2010), the Shalom Eisner affair (2012), and the 2014 war on the Gaza Strip.[14] In each case, the lament followed an episode of intensified military aggression that was caught on enemy or media cameras. The images or footage would go viral, and international condemnation would follow. The military would declare a public relations crisis, bemoaning the damning images and registering their negative impact on Israel's global image. Then, military officials and analysts would take stock and envision a solution. The blueprints for such solutions were relatively stable over the years, shifting chiefly in scale or degree: more plentiful military cameramen and cameras, better digital infrastructures, faster delivery of military images to global audiences, and so on. The message was: better technology will save us from the incendiary cameras of our enemies, preventing their threat to the Jewish state. Out of the ashes of military melancholy over the belated state of its media operations came utopian dreams about media futures. This pattern was recurrent over the course of the two decades studied here: media failure, media lament, media solution.

At the core of this military storyline was a logic of proxy, whereby military violence was replaced by a story about the PR damage: that is, the ostensible violence of the image. Each lament drew national eyes away from the scene of militarism, refocusing them on the scene of its mediation. The proxy logic inverted the structure of victimization: replacing those that the Israeli military had targeted within the military operations in question—variously, Palestinians under occupation and international anti-occupation activists—with the victimized Jewish state, injured by malicious visuals. The proposed military solutions were consistent with the proxy logic, offering technological rather than political solutions: more cameras and camera operators, enhanced digital infrastructures, faster circulation and image delivery. Within military imaginations, the resolution to the crisis in

Israeli legitimacy, posed by enemy cameras, was perpetually deferred: always just one innovation away.

Much of this chapter grows out of interviews I conducted with current and former Israeli military spokespersons and ethnography within their Jerusalem and Tel Aviv offices on those relatively rare occasions when I was granted research clearance. My relationship to the spokesperson's office, like that of other researchers and journalists, was highly contingent. As I was told by a senior Israeli military correspondent, although off the record, "those who are liked will be allowed in and those who are critical will have a hard time doing their job." My work was also bound by these constraints, even as it was enabled by an ethnonational logic that allowed a Jewish American researcher to gain access to the military and its archives in ways that most Palestinian scholars never could. It need hardly be remarked that, within their shabby offices, Israeli military rule of Palestinian people and places was never discussed as such. The term "occupied territories" was missing, replaced by biblical nomenclature for the occupied territories embraced by settler populations and their supporters (Judea and Samaria), while military brutality and repressive rule was refigured in the language of deterrence and terrorism, or actively displaced through the tropes of innovation and humanitarian engagement. In these offices, the daily violence of Israeli military rule functioned as a carefully guarded public secret—known by all, acknowledged by few.[15] As the military investment in cameras increased during the years chronicled here, they would become increasingly important players within the technology of public secrecy, employed to support and sustain state fictions.

HASBARA FAILURE

The second Palestinian uprising would prove a crucial juncture in Israeli military media policy. In an effort to suppress the popular Palestinian protest movement, Israel launched a heavily militarized invasion of the West Bank, codenamed Operation Defensive Shield (2002). Israeli public opinion provided the authority to act with near impunity against Palestinian civilians. During the course of the operation, Israel massively deployed tanks and shelled civilian buildings in its largest military operation since the Lebanon invasion of 1982.[16] By the end of Operation Defensive Shield, the military had killed dozens of Palestinians, detained thousands, and left many hundreds of civilians "imprisoned in their homes without food and water."[17] The disproportionate nature of the Israeli assault was widely condemned by international human rights organizations.[18]

For the military, the foremost public relations challenge of this operation was Jenin—more particularly, the global condemnation that followed the military's lethal invasion of the Jenin refugee camp (April 2002), a central node in Operation Defensive Shield.[19] In the course of the Israeli invasion, fifty-two Palestinians would be killed by Israeli forces, chiefly civilians, and the camp's infrastructure would be devastated by military bulldozers.[20] Palestinian eyewitnesses accused the Israeli military of a calculated massacre. The global outcry was swift and sharp. Human rights organizations accused Israel of war crimes, decrying their use of "indiscriminate and disproportionate force."[21] The global media would be consumed by Jenin for weeks and months after the Israeli invasion concluded. Images of Palestinian survivors in the rubble of their homes, leveled by military bulldozers, aired on televisions across the world, while journalists in the international media debated the massacre charge.

The Israeli public was also consumed with Jenin. But with a difference. Eager to turn eyes away from the scene of Israeli brutality, scholars and journalists read Jenin through a public relations optic, focusing on its damning implications for the Jewish state in the theater of public opinion.[22] Israeli politicians accused Palestinians of fabricating the massacre accusation and denounced "the malicious lies spread about the event," in the words of the Israeli foreign minister.[23] "Bad images" of Israeli soldiers were dominating international screens, many Israeli pundits warned, and the effects were dangerous: "When the world will see the pictures of what we have done there [Jenin], it will cause us enormous damage."[24] Much Israeli denunciation focused on Mohammed Bakri's 2002 film, *Jenin, Jenin*, based on Palestinian testimonials from the refugee camp. Initially, the film would be banned by the Israeli censor—a decision that was later overturned by the Israeli Supreme Court.[25] On the floor of the Israeli parliament, lawmakers debated best practices for protecting the Israeli military from Palestinian defamation, culminating in the passage of libel legislation intended to protect soldiers.[26] Such legislative efforts would persist for years to come.[27]

Within Israel, a consensus emerged: Jenin had been a seismic "public diplomacy problem," a "resounding hasbara failure."[28] The volume of commentary was voluminous, both within the military and among the Israeli public. Policy papers would abound (e.g. "The Case of Jenin: How Poor PR Planning Led to False Charges of 'Massacre'").[29] Some Israeli commentators focused their blame on the military's "lack of strategy for media policy," including its failure to understand the "part played by the Internet and cell phones . . . during the Jenin operation."[30] The military's policy of restricting journalists from "battle zones" also came under considerable criticism, blamed for ceding the media advantage to the Palestinians: had journalists "been permitted to enter Jenin in the early stages of the battle, Palestinian accusations of massacre would have had a different reception."[31] The argument was echoed by many: "though Jenin was sealed to the press, pictures of the battlefield, shot with local amateur video cameras, were broadcasted, mainly on Arab TV."[32]

In this media vacuum, most Israeli commentators agreed, enemy images were allowed to gain the upper hand. "There is a war being waged against the state of Israel," concluded a former military spokesperson, reflecting on the lessons from Jenin. "The world looks at us through the lens of the camera . . . and these lenses are mostly Palestinian."[33] And the damage was lasting: "The dramatic pictures of the operation's outcome haunted Israel's public diplomacy efforts long after the operation itself had ended."[34]

Among the proposed solutions was a fuller integration of embedded military photographers in operational theaters to provide countervailing state-sponsored visuals, combating the cameras of the enemy.[35] Israeli analysts returned to this point frequently in the postmortem that followed Operation Defensive Shield.[36] "A camera is a cannon . . . part of the arsenal," wrote celebrated Israeli military analyst Ehud Ya'ari, reflecting on the lessons of Jenin (in one of the numerous academic conferences—many co-sponsored by the Israeli military—that would be dedicated to the subject).[37] "The question is, in which direction does it point and who is behind it. The ultimate question is how we can ensure that most of these cannons are to our advantage."[38]

A BATTALION OF CAMERAMEN

For the military, the hasbara failures suffered during the second uprising would yield a rethinking of its approach to media production: its strategies, operational protocols, associated technologies. Current and former military spokespersons would call for a wholly new approach to operational documentation. A month after the Al-Durrah killing (2000), a former military spokesperson, writing in the military's professional magazine, urged the military to make a bold shift in media policy:

> Let us imagine that the IDF had a battalion of television cameramen
> equipped with 500 cameras, and that each camera had a team of two peo-
> ple: a cameraman and an audio recorder. At the outbreak of the riots, they

would disperse to all clashes and friction points, and their job would be to collect videographic testimonials about the clashes. The filmed material that the battalion commanders collect . . . [could] expose the truth about what is going on in the confrontation with the Palestinians. The raw material could then be transferred to foreign broadcast stations with a short explanation of where they were filmed. The raw material could also be edited for hasbara films.[39]

Writing in the immediate aftermath of the viral damage caused by the Al-Durrah footage, this former military spokesperson imagined a future battlefield that was dense with military cameras in "all clashes and friction points." In his vision, the proposed "battalion of cameramen" would "uncover the truth" that foreign journalists and Palestinian amateur photographers had obscured and distorted. The author made a budgetary argument as well, noting that "cameras are much cheaper than a Merkava tank or an assault helicopter," but conceded the considerable work required to develop the relevant photographic skills and strategies. The military's longstanding fears also had to be overcome: "We don't need to be afraid of the cameras. We just need to learn how to use them and deploy them in all the relevant arenas."

The military's first training course for "photographer-warriors" was launched the next year (2001). The soldiers involved were "trained in photographing under battle conditions and instructed how to get photos that were attractive to newspaper editors and news broadcasts."[40] They would be installed in military theaters the following year (see Image 22). But the project suffered from numerous shortcomings, as military analysts were quick to point out, including a lack of adequate equipment and training, and failure to move images quickly from operational contexts. And because these military photographers lacked requisite combat training, they could not accompany troops onto the battlefield, a guideline that had also prevented military photographers from chronicling the 2002 Jenin operation.[41] In 2003, one of these so-called photographer-warriors would be killed in Gaza, drawing national attention to the program's serious limitations.[42] In the eyes of military commentators, the project required a wholesale reconceptualization.

One such blueprint would emerge in the immediate wake of the Jenin operation. In a policy paper entitled "Implementation of Conclusions," distributed to the Spokesperson's Commanders Forum, a former military spokesperson made the case for an ambitious approach to operational documentation:

IMAGE 22. Israeli soldiers with shock grenades, accompanied by a combat photographer, during a demonstration against the separation barrier. Marda. 26 May 2005. Source: Yotam Ronen/Activestills.

> Every IDF operation should be documented for dissemination in video and stills [where] emphasis should be put on documentation of the fighting and entrance into sensitive sites (hospitals, mosques, schools). In the course of the operation, successes should be shown and reported as swiftly as possible to Israeli and international audiences . . . in order that the operation not be interpreted as retaliatory action.[43]

Out of the ashes of the hasbara failures of the second intifada—Al-Durrah and Jenin—came military visions for a solution to its media crisis. The solution lay in volume, territorial spread, and speed: namely, greater numbers of military cameras, with greater spatial distribution, delivering "successes . . . as swiftly as possible" to global audiences. Only a media program at this scale would solve the military's media woes, avoiding future viral scandals. It would take years for this vision to take hold. But in the ensuing decade, the military would eventually turn these speculative proposals into policy blueprints.

THE PROBLEM OF TIME

Military media efforts were also constrained by time. More pointedly, as analysts repeatedly lamented, by belatedness: military-generated images and documentation from operational theaters often arrived too late, long after enemy content had been circulated to global audiences. This problem had compounded as their enemies' facility with social media and mobile digital technologies had grown—and, it seemed to the military, at exponential rates. Israeli analysts understood the reason why. A longstanding military policy stipulated the review of all military-generated data prior to its circulation. Thus "pictures or information in real time" was effectively an operational impossibility.[44] This belabored process for verification and circulation had long been deemed a security necessity. But after Jenin, such security-driven procedures and protocols came under new-found scrutiny from Israeli analysts:

> The IDF's public relations department is often torn between the need to react quickly to events and its commitment to a high standard of verification. Such verification requires thorough investigation, including interviewing officers in the field, and [it] takes time. . . . For these reasons, the IDF's publication of information regarding the battle and casualties in Jenin in April 2002 was significantly delayed, unintentionally spawning rumors and uncertainty throughout the country.[45]

This tension between "credibility versus speed," as it would be framed, remained acute and unsolved in the decade following the second Palestinian intifada.[46] In 2010, a military spokesperson described the associated challenges to me this way: "one of the reasons we lose the media battle in so many cases is because *we are not fast enough*—because we try to verify things." It was a crucial point of contrast with their Palestinian enemies who were not, he noted with sarcasm, similarly encumbered ("does Hamas verify?"). Some Israeli analysts placed the blame more squarely on the spokespersons' office: "I just don't think that they completely understand what real time means," I would be told by a senior military correspondent—strictly off the record, he said—in 2010:

> I get reports that there are clashes with Palestinians and the IDF is there. So, I call up the IDF spokesman: "What's going on?" "We're looking into it," they say. What do you mean, you're looking into it? The media has evolved. I need

my information now. Everything is instant. You have to create real-time capability. And I don't think they've done it.

In that window of lag, he argued, the enemy usually gained the media advantage.

In 2010, the Israeli military would suffer another damning hasbara failure on
the scale of Jenin, or thus it would be perceived within Israel. Again, the issue
of timeliness was at its core. The event in question concerned a naval convoy—
named the Freedom Flotilla, or *Mavi Marmara*—that had traveled from Turkey
to the Gaza Strip, carrying humanitarian supplies and hundreds of international
activists who aimed to break Israel's blockade of the Gaza Strip. The Israeli
forces attempted to divert its course, charging the activists with violating its
naval blockade. When the vessels refused, they were forcibly raided by Israeli
commandos. A confrontation broke out and commandos opened fire, killing
nine passengers. International condemnation was immediate and widespread,
including a United Nations report denouncing Israel for unlawful and "excessive use of force."[47] The event would generate years of crisis in Israel–Turkey
diplomatic relations.[48]

Within Israel, the event would be read as another PR disaster "of strategic
proportions."[49] Again, Israelis focused their ire on the documentation gap. Unlike
the military, the *Mavi Marmara* activists were fluent social media users. A quar-
ter of a million people watched their livestream from the flotilla, while many
more consumed their footage on Twitter and television—including footage of
Israeli security forces beating *Marmara* passengers. All these media efforts
had continued, successfully, despite the Israeli navy's efforts to jam communications.

The failures of the military's media strategy would be dissected in the Israeli
media in months that followed. Although the military had dispatched a media
crew with the commando operation, they lacked the satellite technologies necessary for livestream, having planned to physically transport the footage back to
Israel by helicopter. But the raid didn't go as planned—"we didn't expect a lynch,"
I was told by a military spokesperson—and these helicopters were needed to
transport injured commandos.[50] As military spokespersons noted later, the ensuing confusion in military headquarters on the night of the raid was considerable:
"When the incident began, I was in the operations room and I'm saying: *Where
is the helicopter?* I need the pictures. They tell me: No, we need the helicopter to

evacuate the wounded."[51] While activists were livestreaming the commando raid, the military's footage was delayed in transit.[52]

In 2014, I spoke with a former high-ranking military spokesperson about the *Mavi Marmara* incident and he described the numerous hurdles involved where their media operation was concerned. First, he said, there were the problems associated with the physical transport of the footage. Then, they faced the belabored terms of their standard verification protocol:

> Just imagine that that footage comes in, and it takes a couple of hours to get it out back to like Tel Aviv headquarters . . . [with] a combination of helicopter and motorcycles . . . but [it takes a while to reach] the right office in the navy. The head of navy says no, so it goes back down to the navy spokesperson. That spokesperson speaks to the IDF spokesperson's central unit, goes to the top of the spokesperson's unit, and that guy calls up the head of the navy . . .. You can see it taking a long time. . . . The IDF is Israel's largest organization, so it's going to take a while for things to get through.

The time lag was considerable. The commando raid occurred at 4:30 AM. At the time, Al Jazeera was already broadcasting live from the naval convoy. The military would not publish its video until 3:00 PM the following day.[53] In this crucial window of media delay, this spokesperson argued, they lost the "battle for hearts and minds." Israeli analysts were quick to note the irony: "For a country so technologically advanced and with such acute public diplomacy challenges, to fail so miserably at preparing a communications offensive over new media is a failure of strategic proportions."[54]

What emerged from the ashes of the flotilla fiasco, as some Israeli journalists called it, was a newfound military embrace of the real-time image, an understanding of its strategic military value. The policy and protocol implications were considerable, requiring a wholesale shift in the ways that the military moved, processed, and distributed their media from operational contexts. In 2014, military spokesperson Peter Lerner spoke to me about the paradigm shift required to operationalize a livestream:

> The images were always understood to be core in the media effort of the IDF, but *what happened in 2010 was the time element,* where we could not counter the claims that were coming off the *Marmara* boat with alternate footage. Because our plan of action was to fly the footage off of the boat and bring it to coast to be edited, rather than have it broadcasted. It's not

that the technology wasn't harnessed within the military at the time. But it just wasn't a plan of action for the IDF spokesperson's unit. That realization initiated a shift in the spokesperson unit about the types of capabilities that were required—including the capability to stream live footage from the field to the headquarters, and the ability to actually edit it within, I'd say, *the golden hour* so that we can distribute it as soon as possible.

For the military, the imagined solution lay in a range of military innovations and technological upgrades in their digital infrastructures, camera technologies, and media action plans. And herein lay a fantasy that would endure for years to come. If only the Israeli military could get the time right, the rest would follow. If only they could deliver their images in the so-called the golden hour, beating their enemy to global audiences, Israel could win the PR war.

EXPERIMENTS IN SOCIAL MEDIA

The military's work with social media as a hasbara platform, an effort centralized in the office of the spokesperson, began improvisationally. In the early days of Israel's 2008–2009 incursion into the Gaza Strip (code-named Operation Cast Lead), several soldiers launched a YouTube channel to showcase footage of the aerial bombardment of Gaza, filmed from the vantage point of the Israeli weapon. Their experimental efforts had been wildly successful, drawing thousands of viewers to their footage and effectively controlling the global media story about the war. The results cemented the importance of social media within the military's PR efforts. The internet was "another war zone," the military spokesperson would boldly conclude in the war's aftermath. "We have to be relevant here."[55]

In March 2011, I paid my first visit to the military's social media team, housed in a nondescript West Jerusalem office building, full of young, uniformed soldiers bent over their desktop computers. Despite their earlier successes, the project remained in its nascency, just beginning to take shape as a vital branch of the spokesperson's division. Nonetheless, a paradigm shift was afoot. Senior spokespersons were becoming active on social media, using Twitter and Facebook on behalf of the military, and some were beginning to publicly embrace "the digital medium as a strategic weapon."[56] But privately, many were still struggling to understand social media's PR potential and even its appropriateness as a tool of state. Within these offices, the labor required to make the adjustment was considerable.

Indeed, it involved a wholesale reorientation in military protocols and practices. "This isn't what armies normally do," I was repeatedly told.

The team overseeing the military's social media output was small, and their operation remained somewhat improvisational. I was meeting with the head of this team, Aliza Landes, who worked on a laptop in a windowless corner office, adorned by a single postcard. Landes was the first to hold this position, a result of her instrumental role during the 2008–2009 Gaza incursion. It was something of a family affair. Her father, Richard Landes, was already consulting with the military's media team on the matter of Palestinian media fakery, as he put it.[57] They were complementary roles: he sought to manage the damning visuals being produced by their Palestinian enemies through hoax detection and denunciation, while she sought to improve the military's social media output. Both were committed to enhanced military hasbara.

During the course of our interview, Landes received calls and SMS updates from military personnel in the field. Some were about the aftermath of that day's bombing incident in West Jerusalem's central bus station (an explosive had been placed in a suitcase), and some were about the rockets being fired concurrently from the Gaza Strip into southern Israel, a response to Israeli air attacks on Gaza in the week prior. Once verified and cleared, much of this information would be posted to the military's official blog and Twitter feed. Breaking news about incoming rockets interrupted our interview, as Landes called in her young associate. "Can we tweet this, Tal?" The news came back a minute later. No, the details in the report were still unconfirmed. For the military, the social media buck stopped with her. She was responsible for their Twitter and YouTube accounts, as well as their blog, then thought to rival social media in PR efficacy.[58] Their Facebook account was still being programmed. It would launch a few months later.[59]

Like others at the new media headquarters, Landes was young, in her early 20s, having assumed the position a mere four years after her immigration to Israel from the United States. She was the perfect candidate for the job, her superiors told me, as her native English, youth, and digital fluency were deemed crucial to the position. Despite her official uniform, there was a casual air about her—with hair in a ponytail and an unceremonious mode of address. This posture of informality was at the core of the military's work on social media—an effort to conjoin the hierarchical and highly regulated work of the army with the idiom of casual intimacy required of online engagement.

"There's something fundamentally antithetical about social media and any major institution," Landes put it, "especially the military. Half of my time is spent trying to explain and convince other military personal that it's something that we have to learn to deal with." This sense of an antithesis was something I would hear repeated from many senior spokespersons during that 2011 visit:

> They [social media] are contradictory to the military institution. Any army is a closed organization, and usually it keeps its secrets and operational details inside. And new media works in the opposite way. Also, the language is different. Military language is very strict, with a lot of abbreviations and very specific intonations. The new media are exactly the opposite: a lot of emotions, a lot of questions . . . informality. So, it's a bit difficult to teach the military how new media is really an asset, but we've been doing it for the past two years.

As Landes conceded, many in higher military echelons had yet to embrace the paradigm shift. "Facebook has a tabloid-y look to it," I was told by one such high-ranking official. "And we are, after all, a serious organization." Landes explained this as a cultural gap that inflected the military throughout: "In 2008, the IDF still communicated with the world through faxes and beepers," she noted, and "the website looked like it had walked out of 1995." The labor required to come up to digital speed was considerable.

Landes had four soldiers working under her command. And although they were tasked with distributing online content about unfolding events, they were still navigating the parameters of their engagement, still developing best practices for military usage of these platforms. The question of how to manage "inflammatory stuff" remained a live issue. Landes provided the example of the military's YouTube page. Although the comments section had been open to the public on its first day live, it would be shut down a mere 24 hours later following a torrent of "hate comments," the volume and tenor of which had taken the team by surprise.

Other Israeli state actors and institutions were also experimenting with social media in these years and facing similar challenges. Such was the experience of the Israeli Foreign Ministry, celebrated as a leader in the emerging field of digital diplomacy, a mode of stagecraft pioneered in Washington, DC, where government 2.0 was being pioneered.[60] In the spring of 2011, I visited with the handful of employees working in the ministry's social media division, responsible for managing the online Brand Israel campaign.[61] A few months prior, in the aftermath of the popular revolutions in Tunisia and Egypt, they had described their sense of optimism about social media's potential as a regional bridge "between Israel and its Arab neighbors."[62] Now, faced with a growing volume of anti-Israel trolls, they were having doubts. I spent a morning with the only full-time administrator of the Foreign Ministry's Arabic Twitter and Facebook accounts. She was, she confessed, perpetually overwhelmed. Due to budgetary constraints, their Facebook page could only be surveyed during working hours and thus, she said, something was always missed. As a result, commentary deemed inflammatory could be assured a Facebook life of several hours when posted in the evening, only to be hastily removed in the morning. "We don't have the possibility to have people monitor the page 24 hours a day," another staff member explained during our interview. "People come to work, they do their job, they go home in the evening, and that's it." When she arrived in morning, she had to clean it up.

The military had taken note. At the time of my visit, they were actively programming its Facebook page—it would launch a few months later—and still developing a set of guidelines for its administration. The Foreign Ministry's strategy, deleting inflammatory posts the next morning, was not deemed a viable option: "We are going to need specific night shifts in relation to the [Facebook] wall," Landes explained. But she conceded that the funding for these additional personnel had not yet been secured.

Much had changed within the social media division when I returned for interviews a few months later. Landes had been replaced by a digital marketer from the private sector, the military's Facebook page had been launched in English and Arabic, and four soldiers were tweeting in the military's name. Now, the social media team was preparing Twitter content in advance—like, infographics about their humanitarian assistance to Gaza—anticipating military incursions to come and the associated PR needs. The potential threat of social media in enemy hands was also increasingly apparent within the spokesperson division, as they noted to the Israeli press: "one cell phone camera can harm a regime more than any intelligence agency's operations."[63]

Their approach to online detractors had also changed. Now, they were letting criticism stand on Facebook, rather than rushing to delete. "We're not responsible," said a senior spokesperson, "and I think that people understand that." Of course, there were limits: "Like, if somebody sprays graffiti on the front door of the IDF [military] headquarters in Tel Aviv—like, 'Zionist pigs'—nobody would assume that we spray painted that. But we're sure not gonna leave that." It was all a moving target, he conceded. In this new media environment, the "rules were being made up as you go . . ."

For the division of the military spokesperson, the labor of coming up to digital speed took considerable time and effort. In the years chronicled here, the use of social media as a military tool was new, requiring numerous changes to internal military practice.[64] At issue was a wholesale paradigm shift, a radical departure from the traditional norms governing military media. The learning curve was steep and uneven, and the margin of error high, as the social media division labored to bring the military in line with global shifts in media ecosystems.

THE PICTURES LOOK BAD

This history of military hasbara failures includes the story of Israeli officer Shalom Eisner, caught on camera beating an unarmed protestor. The events in question occurred on 14 April 2012. A group of approximately 200 anti-occupation activists, including Palestinians and internationals, attempted a protest bike ride through the West Bank. Israeli security forces, led by commanding officer Shalom Eisner, intercepted the group. One of the activists filmed Eisner striking a Danish protestor, Andreas Ayas, in the face with the butt of his M-16. Within a few hours, the footage had gone viral.[65] Israeli leaders and top military officials responded with a "storm of condemnation."[66] Eisner would be suspended following the findings of a military investigation, only to be reinstated in 2019 following an organized Israeli solidarity campaign.[67] Right-wing communities praised his work in "defending our country against the terrorists," and some parliamentarians proposed him for "man of the year."[68]

Israeli media coverage of the Eisner affair was voluminous. As one commentator noted, it was no less than a public obsession. Images of the beating appeared on newspaper front pages and dominated the evening television news programs, with commentators "showing the images over and over again like a snuff video."[69] Most Israelis embraced Eisner as hero, using social media to express their solidarity.[70] Military spokespersons, drawing on a familiar storyline, insisted that Eisner was a military aberration, having abandoned "the moral values that we teach our soldiers and commanders."[71] In the halls of parliament, government ministers sided with Eisner and warned of the dangers posed by "letting [foreign] activists roam freely."[72] The charge of media manipulation was prevalent: "The talented creator of the video . . . made sure not to show the part where the soldier

[Eisner] was attacked. The guy who shot the video did so with one goal, to mislead and incite world leaders . . . apparently a well-edited video can also confuse our own leaders."[73] It was a common storyline: "Why the hysteria? Yes it's wrong to hit someone like that, but we only saw a six-second long video, we don't know what happened. We already know they edit these things to make us look bad."[74] Critics from the Israeli left, including former members of parliament, attempted to redirect national eyes to the broader context of military occupation:

> But what if he is not an anomaly? What if there is more than one Eisner? In that case, this incident can actually be an opportunity—to examine and correct our behavior towards protesters who disagree with us, and to make a change beyond one single punishment.[75]

Throughout the course of the Eisner media event, the proxy logic reigned supreme, as voices from the left would note: "The prevalent argument . . . has to do with the PR angle: How foolish it was for the senior officer to act this way in front of the cameras . . . "[76]

Israeli left and right concurred on one point: Eisner's failure to understand the media environment of the digital age. "[H]ad it been up to me, I would send him packing for stupidity alone," wrote one Israeli journalist. He continued:

> In the 21st century *any IDF officer, regardless of rank or post, must take as a given the fact that cameras are everywhere* and that many people and organizations seek to tarnish the IDF's image. Under such [a] state of affairs, with every image making its way to thousands of television stations worldwide, one needs no more than a moderate IQ to realize that any unusual action by an IDF officer would resonate across the world and cause grave damage to the State of Israel's reputation and image.[77]

Many commentators agreed. Eisner had failed to understand that "in every confrontation like this there is a camera."[78] He had been "clumsy enough to be photograph[ed] in the act."[79] The oversight was grave, ceding a victory to Israel's enemies in the "media war":

> After the Arabs gave up on battlefield victories through operational maneuvers, they succeeded in *turning the battlefield into a set of photographs* with the aim of garnering as many likes and shares as possible. And here Eisner was baffled . . . failing to understand the mission.[80]

Yuli Edelstein, Israeli minister of public diplomacy, made the case more concretely: "The moment these people [the activists] are out of control, running around and creating trouble, their dream is to be hit by an officer and get it on camera."[81] The implication was clear: Israel's enemies were lying in wait with their cameras, eager for any opportunity to defame Israel, risking even their life for a media opportunity.

The Eisner affair also generated considerable debate within the military about media preparedness. Some suggested better internal education: "Officers in the field should be taking courses in diplomacy, they should speak with Israel's ambassadors, and be exposed to sources of global opinion" to avoid future PR plunders.[82] One prominent military correspondent minced few words in his critique of the military's wholesale "fail[ure] to grasp digital media":

> Besides raising questions about the IDF's ethical values, the Shalom Eisner affair *casts doubt on whether the military fully understands the new digital battlefield* that Israel faces today and will face to an even larger degree in a future war. . . . Watching the video though shows other clear mistakes such as the failure by Eisner and the other officers who were with him . . . to understand the power of the camera, or in this case cameras, which were filming the demonstration on Road 90 that day. The fact that *the officers did not understand that a video camera is like a weapon* in such a scenario is in itself a failure.[83]

As a result of military media incompetence, he wrote, Israel's detractors has secured the "winning propaganda photo." He continued:

> Another question that needs to be asked is: Where were the IDF cameras which should have been there to document the demonstration so that Israel would have proof to back up its claims if needed? A unit—called Combat Camera—was established exactly for this purpose.[84]

Here, again, the incident was recast as a problem of image management. Had the military's digital literacy been more advanced, the damning event could have been avoided. Eisner's public statements also hued closely to this logic: "[It] could have been a professional mistake," he would later concede, "to use a weapon in front of the cameras."[85] The answer to the correspondent's question—"where were the IDF cameras"—would be explained in subsequent national reporting: "One of Eisner's soldier's was supposed to record the incident, but the battery in his camera died before the flare-up began."[86] This detail about a quotidian military misstep received little media attention.

THE INCITING CAMERA

As digital technologies spread across the West Bank, Israeli military spokesperson Barak Raz looked on with concern. Camera numbers, internet connectivity, and social media usage were growing. The military had come to expect Palestinian civilians and international activists armed with cameras at every demonstration, as he noted to me in 2013:

> Today we're talking about people with their iPhones, or their GoPros, or whatever else. If he has something, he'll usually put it up to YouTube and if it's good enough, it'll go viral on the internet and possibly affect the news cycle as a whole.

Some Palestinian communities were perceived as particularly dangerous media actors. The West Bank village of Nabi Saleh was chief among them. In a small conference room in the military's Jerusalem offices, with the assistance of a whiteboard, Raz sketched a map of the village—delineating, in rough strokes of the pen, the village's relationship to the neighboring settlement of Halamish, demarcating the road that snakes between them—"this is route 465, here." With this schema as his guide, he walked me slowly through the challenges of "riot containment" in this dense landscape, with attention to military management of the village's weekly anti-occupation demonstrations, populated by Palestinian and international activists, Israeli journalists and human rights workers. All were armed with cameras and all posed a perceived threat.

In Raz's estimation, the threat of the Palestinian camera was paramount. Their forces routinely encountered Palestinian photographers who "get in the way" of their routine operations, considered particularly dangerous "when you have some sort of clash or riot." In these instances, Raz said, the border police or soldier would approach them "and say 'you need to move back fast because right now, you're interfering.'" Typically, he said, the photographer wouldn't comply. "You may not even be making a request: *I'm not asking, I'm telling, you need to move that way.*'" Raz claimed a passing familiarity with many of the veteran Palestinian videographers working in Nabi Saleh, including those affiliated with B'Tselem, citing frequent problems with their most seasoned videographer, Bilal Tamimi:

IMAGE 23. Soldier employing his personal smartphone as a tool of intimidation. A military crackdown on demonstrators would follow. Nabi Saleh. 30 March 2015. Source: Haim Schwarczenberg.

"Week after week after week, Tamimi will ignore the soldiers who say, 'listen, *you've got to move back.*'"

Other Palestinian cameras posed a different kind of threat. Raz repeated a storyline that I would hear numerous times in these offices: the story of the enemy camera whose function was to provoke or incite under the guise of documentation. Nabi Saleh was the locus of these inciting cameras, chiefly in the hands of its youth population. Raz described youth lying in wait for the military with their cameras, then tormenting the Israeli forces with verbal and sometimes physical aggression in hopes of a violent response on camera, determined to capture an image when military tempers were high. The challenge for soldiers in the field was "how not to fall victim to provocations when there's a camera." For Israeli listeners, this story would immediately conjure the figure of Nabi Saleh resident Ahed Tamimi—12 years old at the time of my interview with Raz—whose emboldened confrontations with Israeli authorities, often caught on camera, were frequently dissected on the Israeli evening news by so-called experts in Arab affairs. Tamimi's activist renown would peak in 2017, following another such confrontation with the occupying forces that had been livestreamed on Facebook, culminating in her arrest by Israeli soldiers on charges of incitement. In mainstream Israeli imaginations, Tamimi epitomized the danger of this new landscape of proliferating cameras.[87]

Raz had witnessed these incidents personally. He described a similar scene in Hebron from a few months prior, a "kind of verbal clash" between settlers and Palestinians, with security forces present to "break it up and keep things calm." It was then that the attempted provocation began:

> I saw this girl—she was probably about 15 years old—come up to one of the soldiers. And she was kind of cursing at him, and he was kind of ignoring her. . . . At one point he turns around to move towards her, I guess to contain her . . . he didn't even touch her, just walk towards her. . . . And then I saw her spit at him—a really fat piece of spit that I could see from about five meters away. The second she did that, all of a sudden, *she pulled a camera out from behind her back.*

Much to his dismay, his own camera was not live at the time: "I had my iPhone in my hand, and I cursed the moment that I didn't film this." So common are such scenes, Raz said, that they are now the focus of internal military education for recruits:

> We're like—listen, suck up the provocations. Because maybe you'll react in the proper way. Maybe the person will be arrested or you'll call the police authorities. . . . Or worse, you lose your cool and you do something you're not allowed or supposed to do. . . . It's enough for that one situation where they don't keep their cool...and all of a sudden it becomes a big status that is being shared on Facebook or YouTube.

In these years, the military was responding by increasing their own volume of military photographers in the West Bank, and Raz sometimes oversaw these media operations. As he conceded, they didn't always go as planned. A recent operation in Hebron—30 March 2013—was a case in point, as Raz would describe to me. They were targeting the Palestinian youth population of the city, whose daily stone throwing was, in the military's estimation, endangering the lives of settlers and soldiers. The military planned to respond with detentions and arrests of those responsible, accompanied by military photographers. "Rock throwing is common in Judea and Samaria," read an English-language post on the military's online blog, published a week prior to the operation. "And along with Molotov

Cocktails and booby-trapped tire throwing, [rock throwing] is a terror act that comes under the definition of 'popular terror.' These incidents happen daily, and are easily ignored by the mainstream media, because they don't seem that serious. But did you know that a simple rock can kill?"[88]

The office of the military spokesperson had dispatched a cameraman to film the operation as it unfolded, with the aim of making the footage rapidly available to media outlets—an effort, Raz explained, both to document the military's vantage and respond to enemy cameras in kind. Raz described their media calculation:

> We knew that Hebron is very heavily documented by individuals, B'Tselem, the journalists, and everyone else. So we said—okay, we're going to put a cameraman on the roof because we understand the questions that will arise. . . . We'll have him document it and he'll broadcast back so that we get that footage in real time.

The military operation resulted in the detention and arrest of twenty-seven Palestinian children.[89] As the military anticipated, the operation would be filmed by Palestinian residents and activists, including a set of B'Tselem photographers who released the footage the same day, alongside a vocal condemnation from the NGO regarding the mass arrests of minors.[90] B'Tselem footage showed images of school-age children and their parents struggling to avoid detention by the Israeli authorities, who were present in large numbers.

But the military's media operation did proceed as planned. Their rooftop filming unit captured the desired footage, but their transmitter had glitched during the operation, interrupting their upload from the field. Once back in military headquarters, it also emerged that something was wrong with the military's video file: "When we tried to bring it to a computer to adjust it, [we learned] that the file was corrupt . . . this was just a total snafu."

As the B'Tselem footage circulated, pressure rose within the office of the military spokesperson.[91] As Raz told me, Israeli and international journalists were calling his office and demanding a response to the mass arrests of children and he responded with the details of military protocol: "I told them, there's an identification process, kids who are under the age will be turned over and kids who are over the age will be arrested." But in the absence of explanatory footage—they were still dealing with the corrupted file shot by the military cameraman—his official response failed to persuade. He urged them to wait for the official military images:

I said: Keep in mind, we have this documented.... *I can't give you that pic-ture right now because of my own technological faults,* but make sure you are putting in that this isn't some random round up. These are kids who are throwing rocks every single day.... When [the military footage] is released, you can see it.... Right now, I'm having technological problems that I'm breaking my head over, but I have this footage and it can be expected in a few days.

The military footage finally reached the public on March 30, 10 days after the events in question: a set of blurry frames, 44 seconds in length, of stone-throw-ing children.[92] Scenes of the military's mass detention of dozens of Palestinian youth, some under the age of 10, had been omitted from these official frames. Raz would issue an accompanying statement, stressing the children's "daily rock throwing at civilians," and endeavoring to explain the technological cir-cumstances that had slowed their official messaging: "Unfortunately, we experi-enced technical difficulties that morning with retrieving the footage."

In Raz's estimation, this public relations damage was considerable. "I'm not naive. I know how the media works. A few days late is too late." In this window of delay, the human rights image had been codified as the story of the event. I asked Raz if the event reflected a continued learning curve, within the military, where new technologies were concerned:

Everything is a learning curve ... and everything is constantly changing. You constantly have to conduct what we call a "rolling situational assess-ment." You're analyzing everything that can affect the overall situation, how you deal with it, and how you implement lessons learned, ranging from how we use tear gas properly, to how we use cameras properly.

It was but a minor incident, paling in comparison to what the military deemed their larger media failures (Al-Durrah, Jenin, *Mavi Marmara*). But from where Raz sat, in the Jerusalem office of the military spokesperson, these everyday blunders were consequential: the glitch in the transmitter, the corrupted file, the delay in image transmission. These ordinary lapses in media functionality were what stood between the military and media success on any given day. In this window of delay, the enemy had won the media war, again.

THE VICTORY IMAGE

A decade after its founding during the first Palestinian uprising, the military's program for so-called photographer-warriors, or embedded military camera operators, continued to falter. Military analysts cited the project's persistent shortcomings: inadequate technology, poor training, belated images. In 2011, the military's professional journal, *Maarachot,* dedicated its cover story to the program's legacy of failures, authored by a former military spokesperson. Entitled "The Victory Image" (*tamunat nitzahon*), a reference to the desired PR outcome that had eluded the military heretofore, the article outlined proposals to correct "[t]he gap between the documentation abilities of the enemy and those of IDF."[93] The threat, the author stressed, was considerable: "Through false information from the battlefield, Israel's enemies attempt to undermine its legitimacy and restrict the IDF. The answer is building a unit for operational documentation [*tiyud mivtza'i*] to expose the enemy lies."[94] New staffing protocols were necessary, including "train[ing] 'soldier photographers' who will be an organic part of their units and will be prepared to document in war zones."[95] Although the military had "purchased cameras and distributed them to the warriors in the field," they lacked knowledge of "how to operate the equipment or what to shoot." Nor had the military solved the recurrent challenge of rapid image delivery and circulation: "[I]n practice, images shot rarely left the battlefield," or were "delivered to IDF [military] spokesmen in cars."[96] Then, after their "arrival [at headquarters] it takes a long time to edit and distribute." Encumbered by these numerous problems, the project had consistently failed to deliver "the victory image."[97]

This illusive photograph—the victory image—was the very heart of the military's hasbara blueprint. Namely, a photograph capable of securing a decisive PR victory: indeed a performative image, installing the outcome ("victory") it depicted. The magazine's accompanying illustration—a military camera crew with tripod-mounted camera—was suggestive of the considerable gap that remained between military media protocols, tethered to technologies of an earlier age, and the digital proficiencies of their foes (see Image 24). This gap in media literacy would persist for years.

The spokesperson's division unveiled its Combat Camera project later that year (2011), borrowing a name employed by a comparable US military program from which Israel received training.[98] The aim of the upgraded project was "better visuals": namely, greater numbers of military camera operators on the front lines of unfolding combat situations, equipped with better technology and training,

IMAGE 24. Cover of *Maarachot*, journal of the Israeli military, including feature article on combat photography. December 2011. Source: http://maarachot.idf.il/

"giv[ing] us an influx of visuals constantly, whether we are at war or combat or when nothing is going on," as a military spokesperson would explain to me in 2011. A shift in training protocols was at the core of the redesign:

> Now, they pull somebody out of their existing unit, train them [in photography], and throw them back in. So, you have people who know the battlefield *and* can carry a camera—instead of sending out an IDF greenhorn who's not really sure what's going on there.

The military envisioned photographer-warriors distributed across military theaters, in every operational context, as a spokesperson noted to the Israeli press:

"The idea is that just as each infantry company has a trained medic, a radio operator, and a heavy machine gun specialist, so too would it have a trained cameraman, from within its rank-and-file."[99]

The timing of the redesign was crucial, as Israeli headlines noted: "IDF
Soldiers May Take Cameras to War to Stave Off International Criticism."[100] At
the time of the project's 2011 launch, the military continued to suffer from the
widespread condemnation that followed their 2008–2009 bloody assault on the
Gaza Strip, including accusations of war crimes and the threat of prosecution
at the International Criminal Court.[101] The military hoped that a growing body
of images from military theaters would function as crucial tools in both media
and legal contexts. The project was ready for its first wartime operationalization
during the 2014 Israeli incursion into the Gaza Strip (code-named Operation
Protective Edge).

But Combat Camera, alone, was not enough to secure the desired media victory." During the 2014 Gaza incursion, the military also operationalized what
they called a "visual operations room" or "visual command center," designed to
centralize the full range of military visuals within a single, physical locale.[102] In
the process, their teams could expedite the labor of image selection, verification,
and processing, as a military spokesperson would explain to me: "The idea is
that one room can get video feeds from a number of different arenas—whether
coming from border cameras, coming from live crews out in the field, coming
from drones . . . [whatever] has a short loop."

The associated labor was considerable. The incoming footage had to be culled,
verified, and curated by soldiers—those sitting at computers in the operations
room, watching a set of simultaneous screens—before its dissemination.[103] A
senior spokesperson described the work this way:

> Stein: What are you looking for when you are in the [visual operations]
> room?
>
> IDF: It depends. . . . It could be all different types of things that serve to am-
> plify visually the message we are trying to send, to describe the mission we
> are carrying out, the type of enemy that we are facing. We need to fine-tune
> those images so that they serve that understanding.
>
> Stein: . . . By fine-tuning, you mean captioning, editing, that kind of thing?
>
> IDF: I wouldn't say editing it or manipulating it. . . . We put in titles and

freeze it so people can see the launch because that [only] takes a second. We freeze it to when you see the launch happening, put a circle around it to draw the attention to it. Otherwise you might miss it. . . . It shows why this is a legitimate target.

This work was also highly attuned to the social media field, as the Israeli media would report:

During an incident, when the rumors start to fly on WhatsApp and reporters and editors are jamming the phone lines with urgent demands for information, the NCOs [non-commissioned officers] in the operations room review the materials they have received, do an initial edit on them—mainly adding subtitles and selecting various angles—and send them to all the editorial desks with the flick of a finger.[104]

The curatorial work involved—the labor of assessment, verification, and editing—was not new. But the military's project of image centralization had changed their media work in both kind and degree. Most of the cameras that fed into the visual operations room were not new, including a broad range of surveillance technologies already operative in the field, but the project had given them new kinds of media applications (see Image 25). Senior military spokesperson Peter Lerner detailed the range and scope of military cameras on which the project drew:

[I]t could be surveillance drones, it could be towers that have video footage . . . special ops that had its own helmets—GoPro-type things—naval surveillance, lookout towers with field intelligence. . . . If it's somebody that is in field intelligence that also has cameras capabilities, that's also good. If we can utilize a visual intelligence post which also has camera footage—sometimes video, sometimes grainy sometimes from a distance, sometimes very high definition—that's also good. So, *it's utilizing everything which is visual* to its full scope to convey the Israeli point-of-view of what's happening.

Lerner's "everything which is visual" was broad and capacious. The project drew on the extensive range of military cameras and optical technologies already operating in the field, as the Israeli media would describe:

The NCOs [non-commissioned officers] in the [visual] operations room are able to connect to any lookout's camera in the relevant sector, and film what is happening in the field. So, it is possible to see video footage of soldiers fir-

IMAGE 25. Military infographic released during Israel's 2014 assault on the Gaza Strip, Operation Protective Edge, shot from suveillance drones. Source: IDF Spokesperson.

ing from behind a tree at an unseen enemy, or entry into a booby-trapped house in Gaza. Altogether, about 90 percent of the visual material filmed by the IDF comes into the operations room.[105]

Most of the military technologies feeding into the operations room had lacked a prior PR designation. Most were conventional surveillance technologies of various kinds. The visual operations room, with its capacity to harness "any lookout's camera," had remade them all as potential hasbara tools. The contours of military PR was shifting: that is, the designation of what constituted, for media purposes, a useable photographic technology. Smart fences and border technologies, lookout towers and observation balloons, cameras mounted on naval vessels: all were being integrated into the hasbara machinery (see Image 26).

In the process, the division of the military spokesperson was rescaling its visual field. It was the maturation of a process of that had begun during the

IMAGE 26. The IDF's Field Intelligence Corps using their tracking system for the Gaza border. This system fed into the visual operations room. 3 March 2010. Source: IDF Spokesperson.

2008–2009 Israeli incursion into the Gaza Strip, when the military's nascent social media team had retooled aerial images of the bombardment, shot from the vantage of the Israeli bombardier, as YouTube hasbara.[106] But the process had been highly improvisational. In the intervening years, this rescaling of hasbara visuality would be gradually institutionalized. Now, it reached from the lens of the embedded military photographer to the eye of the drone. If the chief ambition of the Combat Camera project had been the capacity to master time, the visual operations room had endeavored to master space and scale. A military dream was being concretized: that of a total hasbara camera.

THE CAMERA OF THE FUTURE

Within the Israeli military, over the course of the first two decades of the twenty-first century, the need for enhanced media production grew ever more acute. Officials watched with concern as digital cameras proliferated in the hands of their enemies in the occupied Palestinian territories. As years progressed, the volume of incendiary images grew. In 2008–2009, the time of the first Israeli ground incursion into the Gaza Strip of this period (Operation Cast Lead), Palestinians living in Gaza had lacked widespread social media literacy, internet connectivity, and access to mobile technologies—lacking, that is, the means to produce a digital archive at a scale substantial enough to counter the military message. By 2014, during Israeli Operation Protective Edge, social media literacy and tools had become widespread within the Gaza population. Now, the global social media field of the wartime period was saturated with the images and footage Gazans had produced—scenes of infrastructural devastation and death, shot from mobile devices, and often uploaded in the very midst of a lethal Israeli attack.[107]

The military responded to these changes in Palestinian media ecosystems with new media protocols and policies for embedded photographers, upgraded digital infrastructures, new educational programs concerning the enemy camera. Within the offices of the military spokesperson, the associated daily labor was considerable as officials struggled to incorporate these new protocols into their hasbara toolbox. Many Israeli analysts bemoaned the slow pace and scale of such innovations, lamenting that military operations continued to be plagued by recurrent missteps and miscalculations. In the wake of each media mishap, and ensuing public lament, the military would commit to remaking its media policy, again: promising more cameras, better infrastructures, faster verification.

I have read these recurrent laments, and episodes of policy reevaluation, as proxy operations, whereby the violence of state was replaced by the violence of the camera. Each chorus of lament drew national eyes away from the scene of Israeli militarism toward the scene of injurious images. The structure of victimhood was thereby inverted, with Israel figured as the chief casualty, wounded by the cameras of their foes. The disconnect with international responses—to Jenin, *Mavi Marmara*, Eisner—was stark. While Israeli military analysts bemoaned the media war being waged against the state of Israel, international human rights organizations accused Israel of wanton military aggression and, in the case of Jenin, "war crimes."[108] Such condemnations made the proxy discourse necessary. The story of the bad image performed a vital vanishing act at these moments of political crisis, removing the dead or injured Palestinian victims of military aggression from the mainstream Israeli discursive field.

While the lament was repetitive, the imagined military solutions were more variable, evolving alongside the changing media ecosystem. In 2002, the military proposed greater camera volume and geographic reach, envisioning military photographers at "all clashes and friction points." In 2010, the military focused its policy proposals on the digital infrastructures for real time and live feed, bent on overcoming a history of temporal belatedness. In 2014, the military's media solution had shifted from a chiefly temporal to a spatial template. Now, they envisioned total PR penetration within military theaters with every surveillance camera doing double duty as a hasbara technology, dreaming of a multi-scalar view of Israeli military rule without blindspots.[109] However varied these media visions, each worked within the logic of "technological solutionism": more cameras, better infrastructure, enhanced photographic vision, and so on.[110] In this recurrent storyline, the problem of the Israeli political present, the problem of Israeli state violence and its deadly effects, was rendered as a mere technological challenge that the right innovation could fix.

Some military officials spoke in a different idiom. In 2012, I sat with senior military spokesman Peter Lerner in his Jerusalem office for an interview about media developments. Lerner was feeling confident. Work on the visual command center was underway, and they had scored a recent hasbara victory in the Gaza Strip (Operation Pillar of Defense), praised in the global media for innovative digital warcraft.[111] He described the military's media future this way:

> And you know what, *I don't know if it'll ever be fully developed* . . . but before too long, sometime in the future, there's going to be 3D cameras or whatever. I already know that there are still-cameras where you don't need to select a field of depth when you're filming. You just take a picture of a wide area and it gets *the entire field of light,* and you can . . . just focus on specific parts of the picture and refocus to see them. When you have *the entire field of depth,* that changes how you're photographing things. And you know, the future is inevitably going to lead to total documentation.

Lerner's account breaks with the dominant framework of technological solutionism. He articulates his vision of mediatization in a highly speculative idiom, gesturing toward a photographic future that may never arrive: "I don't know if it'll ever be fully developed." His dream of total military seeing—enabled by "3D cameras or whatever"—surpassed existing military media blueprints, exceeding the visual operations center with its ability to capture total space and scale. Lerner's camera-of-the-future, by contrast, captures "the entire field of light . . . the entire field of depth." The temporality of this vision is crucial. This is not a military camera of the here and now. This is a camera to come.

This was more than a dream of total documentation. The military nearly had it within its grasp, thanks to its ever-expanding surveillance infrastructure. Rather, Lerner's phantasmatic vision exposed the dream at the heart of military media operations. It was audible at each moment of lament, undergirding two decades of military efforts to upgrade, enhance, and innovate in media arenas. With the more perfect camera of the future, it was hoped, military cameras would finally align with their hasbara mandate. Through the viewfinder of these future cameras, there would be no more military occupation, as activists insisted, only Judea and Samaria, as per preferred military terminology. These fantasy cameras would dispense with images of both Palestinian victims and Israeli perpetrators. With the camera to come, Israel would finally be redeemed. If only they could get the technology right.

Coda

BROKEN BONES, BROKEN DREAMS

The Politics of Failure

ON 26 FEBRUARY 1988, A FEW MONTHS AFTER THE OUTBREAK OF THE
first Palestinian intifada (1987–1991), a cameraman for CBS television news filmed
a group of Israeli soldiers assaulting two bound and blindfolded Palestinian youths
on a Nablus hillside.[1] The timing was telling. Several months prior, Israel's Minister
of Defense Yitzhak Rabin had directed troops to quell the intifada with "might,
power, and beatings."[2] "Break their bones," he was quoted as saying.[3] Widespread
military assaults on Palestinian demonstrators and bystanders had followed.[4]
Rabin's order had given troops "license to beat indiscriminately."[5]

Although Israeli and international television coverage of the intifada was
prolific, only this video from Nablus would achieve viral status. The footage was
blurry, filmed by the photojournalist at a distance, using a long-distance lens as a
protective strategy against potential military retribution. The Palestinian youths
at its center—cousins Wa'al and Usama Joudeh—are seen seated, their arms tied
behind their back, as a group of four soldiers kick and beat them, endeavoring
to break their bones with rocks. The attack was protracted and meticulous. "The
soldiers do not seem to be in any danger," an Israeli reporter would note later,
"nor do they seem disturbed by the events. They are utterly focused on meting
out the beating."[6]

Personal video cameras were scarce in occupied territories in these years. The production of images was centralized in the hands of the professional photo-journalists and correspondents who had arrived en masse to cover the uprising.[7] Official military orders stipulated that "the area [occupied territories] is open to the media, and members of the press are not to be prevented from moving or operating freely . . . in no case is violence to be used against media staff."[8] Conditions on the ground were otherwise. Journalists and camera operators were frequently obstructed by Israeli troops, often by force.[9] The video from Nablus had been filmed amid these difficult press conditions.

The entirety of the footage—some thirty minutes in length—was never screened on Israeli television. Only a portion would be aired on the evening news following orders from the head of the Israeli Broadcasting Authority (IBA). The damage would be too substantial, he argued, should Israeli viewers see it all.[10] The video quickly circulated within international media outlets, and massive outcry followed: "the incident aroused a storm of protest, and Israeli embassies in Washington, London, Paris, and Amsterdam were flooded with angry calls. In some countries the incident sparked anti-Israel demonstrations."[11] In Nicosia, a mob attacked the Israeli embassy, barely restrained by the police. In an interview with an Israeli newspaper, Elie Wiesel would note that "I have never seen such intense hatred for Israel in the world."[12]

The Israeli national conversation about the footage focused on questions of military strategy and soldier practice. Within the pages of the press, and on the floor of the Israeli parliament, debates ensued concerning best "methods for acting successfully against the Arab rioters."[13] Some parliamentarians proposed a journalist ban from the occupied territories: "it has become apparent that the rioters in Judea and Samaria and Gaza are staging disturbances because of the media presence."[14] The military responded by tightening press access. The four soldiers involved were given brief custodial sentences and eventually returned to their units. The Israeli parliament declined to investigate Rabin's role.[15]

Within the collective memory and mythology of the Israeli left, media representation of the first intifada has been marked as a crucial juncture in the Israeli relationship to its military occupation. Many Israeli leftists, reflecting on the moment, would speak in the language of political awakenings and exposures about the visual field of this moment, this in the context of a national media from which images of Palestinian life under occupation had been largely missing.[16] "[S]eeing the Israeli soldier pointing his gun at the violent, yet unarmed, Palestinian youths on TV that night felt like such a turning point," Yaron Ezrahi would write. "Can we, I asked myself, envision an album of images of our extended family which includes that picture?"[17] Einat Wilf, former Israeli member of parliament for the Labor Party, rehearsed a variant of this narrative:

> The first Palestinian intifada . . . created an appalling "reversal of images" that deeply unsettled the sense of moral rightness Israelis had held dear since the country's birth out of the ashes of the Holocaust. "The Palestinians were wielding the slingshot and the Israelis were in tanks," she remembered. *"It upended the Israeli founding myth."*[18]

In Wilf's account, this so-called reversal of images had shattered a set of sacred national myths. But other myths were being reconsolidated in the process: namely, the fiction of a benevolent Israeli national project that had only been corrupted in 1967 with the onset of military occupation. The Israeli NGO B'Tselem would emerge at precisely this historical juncture (1988), and would also invest in the dream of political exposure, as one of its founders noted thirty years hence: "We believed that the Israeli public just had to know what was being done in its name."[19]

The era of these political dreams was relatively short-lived, collapsing in 2000 with the end of the so-called Middle East Peace Process.[20] But a new variant would soon appear, tethered to the emerging digital landscape. By the century's second decade, mobile technologies were beginning to proliferate in the West Bank and Gaza Strip. Soon, the global social media field was saturated with footage produced by Palestinians living under occupation, sometimes filmed in the very midst of their bombardment by the Israeli military. The scene of Israeli state violence was now visible from new vantage points—both from the vertical eye of the drone and from the horizontal perspective of its Palestinian targets. Now, with the aid of new digital technologies, distant witnesses could watch the Israeli soldier shoot and the Palestinian body fall in something close to real time. The enhanced technological capacities of the bystander camera were generating eyewitness datasets that were bigger than ever before, making Israeli state violence visible at the scale of the pixel.[21] Amid these changes in the Palestinian media ecosystem, another set of political hopes and dreams reconsolidated among anti-occupation activists and scholars. The "widespread use of cameras by people around the world . . . [was] opening new possibilities of political action," some argued, new forms of justice and accountability.[22]

There was nothing new about these media dreams linking visual exposure to political rupture, as the first intifada reminds us. Nor were they unique to Israel and Palestine. Rather, this moment saw the reemergence of a recurrent fantasy that is reinvigorated when visual media technologies arrive, in new degrees or forms, on the scene of war or violent conflict: for example, the Vietnam War, the Bosnian genocide, the Syrian civil war.[23] Equally recurrent, as Sharon Sliwinski has written, is the lament that follows when these new media fail "to secure the practical social and political effects they are asked to procure . . . the dream of bringing the world's suffering to an end."[24]

Screen Shots has chronicled this dialectic of political dreams and breakdowns as tied to digital photography but has lingered on the latter: on what comes in the wake of these dreams. I have employed an analytic of failure—one focused on breakdowns, glitches, and interruptions in photographic processes—as a way of considering the wide range of media disillusionments that crosscut the political landscape of military rule in the first two decades of the twenty-first century. Failure took very different forms, born of different histories, across the political institutions and communities studied here. For Palestinian video-activists and human rights workers, failure was the result of repressive military policy—in the form of closures and curfews and capricious soldier vengeance—enacted on photographers and cameras. For Israeli human rights workers, failure coalesced in the almost impossible work of successfully mediating Palestinian videography of Israeli state violence to a national audience moving ever rightward. For the military, failure took shape in hasbara efforts that kept faltering, as their enemies kept "winning the media war." Across these vast political divides, digital photography offered no political guarantees.

In the same decades, in Palestine and Israel, other political dreams were faltering. The Israeli Jewish left continued to mourn its dwindling numbers, as they had since the outbreak of the second intifada.[25] While the two-state solution had long been a political dead letter, obstructed by Israeli territorial maximalism, the political fantasy remained.[26] By the end of these decades, even those on the Zionist left were accepting its demise.[27] The same period would see the "rise and fall" of a popular Palestinian investment in the transnational human rights industry, as Lori Allen has written, as its "long years of failure to protect Palestinians" became spectacularly evident.[28] Some Israeli human rights institutions were reaching the same conclusions. In 2016, B'Tselem would formally cease cooperation with the military law enforcement system, arguing that internal military probes had "failed

IMAGE 27. Israeli and Palestinian protestors demonstrating against the Israeli government, in solidarity with Black Lives Matter. Tel Aviv. 6 June 2020. Source: Oren Ziv/Activestills.

to deliver justice."[29] Many in the organization were also abandoning the exposure logic: "We believed that the Israeli public just had to know what was being done in its name. How wrong we were."[30] Failure, as an analytic lens, allows me to grapple with these concurrent political breakdowns for which discourses about cameras and photography often functioned as proxies. This framework allows me to consider a historical moment in which prior political blueprints and mythologies were coming to crisis, particularly so for Jewish publics and institutions on the Israeli left, even as alternative political futures were increasingly difficult to imagine.

As this book goes into production, the global political landscape is being powerfully transformed by an event of state violence, caught on camera: namely, the execution of George Floyd by a Minneapolis police officer. In the unprecedented swell of popular protest that this murder catalyzed, protestors across the globe are boldly insisting on transnational linkages between histories of police brutality, structural racism and colonialism. As I write, Palestinian flags are flying in Black Lives Matter demonstrations in Europe, even as demonstrators in Bethlehem and Tel Aviv are forging connections between Minneapolis and Jerusalem: "Palestinian Lives Matter!" "We can't breathe since 1948!" (see Image 27).[31]

This moment of global mobilization has also revived a popular investment in the power of photographic exposure as an engine of social justice— a hope that had waned for many activists in the prior decade amidst the growth of surveillance states. The imprint of this new global movement on Israel and Palestine remains to be seen, as do the political consequences of the popular reinvestment in visual exposure.

In this time of renewed global hope in the power of the bystander camera, what can the analytic of failure provide? I propose that it shares a commitment to combatting colonial logics. Since its inception, the Zionist project has been bolstered by claims about technological modernity, as my introduction notes. In the textual archive of Zionism, histories of violence and dispossession are subject to a disappearing act, obfuscated by the gleam of settler technology. So, too, in the twenty-first century, when this colonial storyline would be upgraded as a tale of digital innovation. If the narrative of technological modernity signals the endurance of the Israeli colonial project, then stories of military breakdown and belatedness might signal the inverse. It is my hope that such scenes of failure, with the Israeli state and its technologies out of synch, can provide a modest means of unsettling the colonial present. Perhaps in such failures, other political futures can become visible.

Notes

INTRODUCTION

1. B'Tselem, "Video: Soldier Executes Palestinian Lying Injured on Ground After the Latter Stabbed a Soldier in Hebron"; Roth-Rowland, "Nobody Should Be Shocked at the Hebron Execution." For an analysis of this case within a critical legal context, see Diamond, "Killing on Camera."

2. The photographer was Imad Abu Shamsiya. He would experience abuse and intimidation after the footage aired. Marom, "The Camera That Made Elor Azaria 'Man of the Year.'"

3. Galdi, "Everyone's Favorite Murderer."

4. Bob, "IDF Finds Ambulance Driver Tampered with Knife After Shooting of Hebron Attacker." On the legal history of this exculpatory military narrative, see Diamond, "Killing on Camera."

5. Cohen, "Hebron Shooter Elor Azaria Sentenced to 1.5 Years for Shooting Wounded Palestinian Attacker"; Kershner, "Israeli Soldier Who Shot Wounded Palestinian Assailant Is Convicted"; Omer-Man, "Nearly Half of Israeli Jews Support Extrajudicial Killings, Poll Finds."

6. Cohen et al., "Thousands Rally for Soldier Who Shot Palestinian Assailant."

7. Marom, "The Camera That Made Elor Azaria 'Man of the Year.'"

8. Cook, "Elor Azaria Case"; Kubovich and Landau, "Elor Azaria, Israeli Soldier Convicted of Killing a Wounded Palestinian Terrorist, Set Free After Nine Months"; Omer-Man, "Extrajudicial Killing with Near Impunity."

9. Konrad, "Elor Azaria and the Army of the Periphery."

10. Harkov, "Likud Deputy Minister Enlists Elor Azaria in Primary Campaign"; Livio and Afriat, "Politicised Celebrity in a Conflict-Ridden Society."

11. Marom, "The Camera That Made Elor Azaria 'Man of the Year.'"

12. Gregory, *The Colonial Present*.

13. Behdad, *Camera Orientalis*, Nassar *Photographing Jerusalem;* Sela, *Made Public;* Sheehi, *The Arab Imago;* Silver-Brody, *Documenters of the Dream*.

14. Della Ratta, *Shooting a Revolution;* Richardson, *Bearing Witness While Black;* Tufekci, *Twitter and Tear Gas;* Wall, *Citizen Journalism*; Wessels, *Documenting Syria*.

15. Scholarship under these headers would also proliferate in the 1990s and early 2000s. See, for example, Akrivopoulou and Garipidis, *Digital Democracy and the Impact of Technology on Governance and Politics*; Ziccardi, *Resistance, Liberation Technology and Human Rights in the Digital Age*. Adi Kuntsman and I discuss this in greater detail in *Digital Militarism*.

16. Adams, "March 3, 1991: Rodney King Beating Caught on Video."

17. Sontag, "Regarding the Torture of Others."

18. The Israeli organization Machsom Watch and the joint Israeli–Palestinian organization Ta'ayush were also early adopters of cameras as activist anti-occupation tools. Guy Butavia, interview with author, Jerusalem, 5 May 2013. Also see Ginsburg, *And You Will Serve as Eyes for Us*, and "Taking Pictures Over Soldiers' Shoulders."

19. Maimon and Grinbaum, *Activestills*. While the collective was formed in 2005, many of the photographers were part of the anti-occupation protests of previous years.

20. Bishara, *Back Stories*.

21. 5 *Broken Cameras* is a firsthand documentary about the experience of Palestinian activist photographer Emad Burnat from the West Bank city of Bi'ilin. The title of the film refers to numerous retributive attacks by the Israeli authorities.

22. Junka-Aikio, "Late Modern Subjects of Colonial Occupation"; Aouragh, *Palestine Online;* Tawil-Souri, "Digital Occupation." Also see Tawil-Souri and Aouragh, "Intifada 3.0?"

23. Hammami, "Precarious Politics," 181.

24. Maimon and Grinbaum, *Activestills*.

25. On the politics of human rights work in Israel during this period, including its tactical deployment by the Israeli right, see Perugini and Gordon, *The Human Right to Dominate*. On the "cynical" politics of transnational human rights in Palestine during the same period, see Allen, *The Rise and Fall of Human Rights*.

26. This global project would be led by the NGO WITNESS. See Diamond, "Killing

on Camera"; Gregory, "Ubiquitous Witnesses"; Ristovska, "The Rise of Eyewitness Video and Its Implications for Human Rights."

27. Shavit, *Media Strategy and Military Operations in the 21st Century.*

28. Ibid., 57, ch. 2.

29. For a review of the Israeli state crackdown on Palestinian online content, see 7amleh, *Hashtag Palestine 2018.*

30. Stein, "'Fake News!'"

31. This portion of my analysis builds on my collaborative work with Adi Kuntsman on "digital suspicion." See Kuntsman and Stein, *Digital Militarism* and "Digital Suspicion, Politics, and the Middle East."

32. On Israeli colonial surveillance, now and historically, see Gordon, "Israel's Emergence as a Homeland Security Capital"; Gordon, *The Political Economy of Israel's Homeland Security Industry*; Gregory, *The Colonial Present*; Handel and Dayan, "Multilayered Surveillance in Israel/Palestine"; Shalhoub-Kevorkian, *Security Theology, Surveillance and the Politics of Fear*; WhoProfits, *"Big Brother" in Jerusalem's Old City*; Zureik, "Colonialism as Surveillance"; Zureik et al., *Surveillance and Control in Israel/ Palestine.*

33. Gregory, *The Colonial Present*; Tawil-Souri and Aouragh, "Intifada 3.0?"; Weizman, *Hollow Land.*

34. WhoProfits, *"Big Brother" in Jerusalem's Old City.*

35. Gordon, "Israel's Emergence as a Homeland Security Capital," 158. Also see Kane, "How Israel Became a Hub for Surveillance Technology."

36. In these years, Israel was the leading global exporter of drones, fed by Tel Aviv's "drone startup" sector. Cohen, "Israel's New Ambiguity"; Rubin, "Israel's Drone Industry Angry over Draconian Defense Export Restrictions"; Sherwood, "Israel Is World's Largest Drone Exporter."

37. Gordon, "Israel's Emergence as a Homeland Security Capital"; Lee, *Commodified (In)Security.*

38. Hoffman, "57% of Israelis Have Smartphones"; Russell, "Israelis Are Now the World's Biggest Social Network Addicts, Says New Report"; Senor and Singer, *Start-Up Nation*; Shamah, "Digital World: Israel, the Telecom 'Continent.'"

39. Gordon, "Israel's Emergence as a Homeland Security Capital"; Swed and Butler, "Military Capital in the Israeli Hi-Tech Industry." For a celebratory rendering of this history of technology transfers, see Katz and Bohbot, *The Weapon Wizards;* Senor and Singer, *Start-Up Nation.*

40. Beinin and Stein, "Histories and Futures of a Failed Peace."

41. Levy, "Israel Does Not Want Peace." On the Oslo Process, see Khalidi, *Brokers of Deceit*; Said, *Peace and Its Discontents*; Said, *The End of the Peace Process*.

42. Rapoport, "The Israeli Right Stopped Talking About Occupation, and That Will Hurt It at the Polls."

43. Matar, "The Most Critical Issues Israelis Won't Be Voting on in the Next Election."

44. Gross, *The Writing on the Wall*.

45. Weiss, "Immigration and West Bank Settlement Normalization."

46. Nadera Shalhoub-Kevorkian calls this a "security theology": *Security Theology, Surveillance and the Politics of Fear*.

47. Jabareen and Bishara, "The Jewish Nation-State Law."

48. Eglash and Booth, "Israeli NGOs Decry 'Deeply Anti-Democratic Move' as New Law Approved."

49. Omer-Man, "Israel's Knesset Just Voted on a Very Dangerous Law for Democracy."

50. Gordon, "Human Rights as a Security Threat." Also see Perugini and Gordon, *The Human Right to Dominate*.

51. Matar, "Bit by Bit, Coverage of Occupation Disappears from Israeli News."

52. Stein, "Impossible Witness."

53. Hochberg writes: "For Israeli drivers who pass through Highway 6 . . . the enclosed Palestinian cities of Tulkarm and Qalqilya are hardly visible. . . . In other sections on the Israeli side, the wall is decorated . . . with landscape paintings capturing biblical scenes . . . devoid of Palestinians and free of security fences, gates, and walls." Hochberg, *Visual Occupations*, 18–20.

54. Ibid. On colonial epistemologies of vision, see Jay and Ramaswamy, *Empires of Vision*; Mirzoeff, *The Right to Look*; Pratt, *Imperial Eyes*.

55. Crary, *Techniques of the Observer*; Mirzoeff, *How to See the World*.

56. Cohen, "Elor Azarya, King of Israel."

57. Sontag, *On Photography*; Sontag, *Regarding the Pain of Others*, 24.

58. Scholarship on the politics and aesthetics of human rights and humanitarian witnessing, a literature that has proliferated in the last decade, includes the following: Boltanski, *Distant Suffering*; Kennedy and Patrick, *The Violence of the Image*; Kozol, *Distant Wars Visible*; Linfield, *The Cruel Radiance*; McLagan and McKee, *Sensible Politics*; Rangan, *Immediations;* Ristovka and Price, *Visual Imagery and Human Rights*; Sliwinski, *Human Rights in Camera*. On the interplay between violence and visual media, see Browne, *Dark Matters*; Jay and Ramaswamy, *Empires of Vision*; Kaplan,

Aerial Aftermaths; MacDonald et al., *Observant States*; Malkowski, *Dying in Full Detail*; Mirzoeff, *How to See the World* and *The Right to Look*. On the relationship between war and media, see Derian, *Virtuous War*; Feldman, *Archives of the Insensible*; Stahl, *Militainment, Inc.,* and *Through the Crosshairs*; Virilio, *War and Cinema*.

59. Azoulay, *Potential History*; *The Civil Contract of Photography* and *Civil Imagination*; Hochberg, *Visual Occupations*; Weizman, *Forensic Architecture* and *Hollow Land*. Additional examples include Allen, "Martyr Bodies in the Media"; Faulkner and Reeb, *Between States;* Ginsburg, *And You Will Serve as Eyes for Us;* Hatoum, "Framing Visual Politics"; Roei, *Civic Aesthetics*; Wigoder, "The Blocked Gaze."

60. Examples include Gürsel, *Image Brokers*; Morris, *Photographies East*; Spyer and Steedly, *Images That Move*; Strassler, *Demanding Images* and *Refracted Visions*.

61. This line of questioning is akin to Azoulay's discussion of "untaken photographs." See Azoulay, *Potential History, 239*.

62. Gitelman and Pingree, *New Media, 1740–1915*, vii.

63. On the politics of failure, see Graham, *Disrupted Cities*; Halberstam and Halberstam, *The Queer Art of Failure*; Larkin, *Signal and Noise*. Scholars of photography and visual culture have also considered this theme: Hochberg, *Visual Occupations*, 139–162; Sliwinski, *Human Rights in Camera*, 134–38.

64. Hochman, *Savage Preservation*; Larkin, *Signal and Noise*; Ryan, *Picturing Empire*; Tofighian, "Watching the Astonishment of the Native."

65. Larkin, *Signal and Noise*.

CHAPTER 1

1. At the bequest of many individuals included in this study, and due to the political sensitivity of the material, I have employed pseudonyms throughout, including when quoting from archival documents and collections. Exceptions have been made when the subject or interviewee is a public figure or when the incident in question was widely publicized.

2. Morris, *Believing Is Seeing*; Struk, *Private Pictures*.

3. Kennedy, "Soldier Photography"; Whitty, "Soldier Photography of Detainee Abuse in Iraq."

4. Sontag, "Regarding the Torture of Others."

5. Grundberg, *Point and Shoot*.

6. Ibid.

7. Rumsfeld, quoted in Sontag, "Regarding the Torture of Others."

8. Ibid.

9. The second intifada (2000–2005) was a popular Palestinian response to the collapse and political failures of the Oslo Process, or the so-called Middle East Peace Process. The military crackdown began shortly after the uprising broke out. By 2002, in response to a wave of Palestinian suicide bombings inside Israel, the crackdown, supported by the Jewish Israeli public, would escalate into the largest Israeli military operation since the 1982 invasion of Lebanon. See Hammami and Tamari, "The Second Uprising" and "Anatomy of Another Rebellion." Beinin and I discuss this history here: Beinin and Stein, *The Struggle for Sovereignty*, ch. 2. While there is some disagreement about the intifada's periodization, most scholars mark its end in 2005, following the death of Yasser Arafat in 2004. Thrall, *The Only Language They Understand*, 197.

10. Michaels, "Cellphones Put to 'Unnerving' Use in Gaza."

11. For scholarly discussion of Israeli soldier photography in the midst of military occupation or war, see Grassiani and Verweij, "The Disciplinary Gaze of the Camera's Eye"; Hochberg, "Soldiers as Filmmakers" and *Visual Occupations*; Kuntsman and Stein, *Digital Militarism*; Nathansohn, "Shooting Occupation" and "Soldier-Photographer and the Double Bind of Photographic Practice."

12. Scholarly writing on Breaking the Silence includes Grassiani, *Soldiering Under Occupation;* Handel, "Beyond Good and Evil—the Syndrome"; Helman, "Challenging the Israeli Occupation Through Testimony and Confession"; Katriel, "Accounts and Rebuttals in an Israeli Discourse of Dissent" and "Showing and Telling"; Katriel and Shavit, "Between Moral Activism and Archival Memory"; Morag, "Perpetrator Trauma and Current Israeli Documentary Cinema"; Nathansohn, "Shooting Occupation"; Pliskin et al., "Speaking out and Breaking the Silence"; Weiss, "Struggling with Complicity." On the everyday culture of soldiering in the Israeli military, see Grassiani, Soldiering Under Occupation.

13. From the organization's website: https://www.breakingthesilence.org.il/about/organization

14. On the militarization of everyday life, see Kaplan, "Precision Targets"; Lee, *Commodified (In)Security:* Stahl, *Militainment, Inc.* On technology transfers between the Israeli military and Israeli high-tech sector, see Gordon, *The Political Economy of Israel's Homeland Security Industry.*

15. Behdad, *Camera Orientalis;* Behdad and Gartlan, *Photography's Orientalism.* On the broader colonial history of cameras and photographic practices, see Chaudhary, *Afterimage of Empire*; Morris, *Photographies East*; Rizzo, *Photography and History in Colonial Southern Africa.*

16. Buzard, *The Beaten Track.*

17. Gavish, "An Account of an Unrealized Aerial Cadastral Survey in Palestine Under the British Mandate"; Fischbach, "British and Zionist Data Gathering on Palestinian Arab Landowners and Population During the Mandate"; Kaplan, *Aerial Aftermaths*.

18. Sela, *Made Public* and *Photography in Palestine/Eretz Israel in the Thirties and Forties*; Silver-Brody, *Documentors of the Dream*; Talmon and Peleg, *Israeli Cinema*.

19. Behdad, *Camera Orientalis*.

20. Khalidi, *All That Remains*; Nassar, "Familial Snapshots" and *Photographing Jerusalem*; Sheehi, *The Arab Imago*. On colonial archives as tools of dispossession, see Stoler, *Along the Archival Grain*.

21. Sela, "Rethinking National Archives in Colonial Countries and Zones of Conflict Dissonant Archives." Also see Sela, *Made Public* and "Present-Absent Palestinian Villages."

22. Sela, "Rethinking National Archives in Colonial Countries and Zones of Conflict Dissonant Archives," 87.

23. Sela, "Scouting Palestinian Territory, 1940–1948," 42. On colonial politics of early Zionist travel, also see Stein, "Travelling Zion."

24. From the instructional manual: "Photography for Scouts," Archive of the History of the Haganah, file 34/209, 10. Quoted in Sela, "The Genealogy of Colonial Plunder and Erasure," 41.

25. This photograph—Image 6—was first published here: Sela, *Made Public*, 97. For a detailed discussion of the field squads (Chayalot Hasadeh) pictured in the image and their intelligence-gathering operations in the guise of tourists, see Sela, *Made Public*, 47–48. My thanks to Rona Sela for assisting in the acquisition and identification of this image.

26. For a different conception of "military photography" as a rubric: Azoulay, "The Imperial Condition of Photography in Palestine" and *Potential History*.

27. *BaMahane* photographers produced both fictional and documentary films about the armed forces. See Zilber, *Military Photographer*.

28. Memo from Yigael Yadin, Commander of Operations to "Battlefronts, Brigades, Corps, Services," 3 October 1948, IDF Archives, 600137-1951.

29. Ibid. The military's film unit was initially established as a subdivision of the Mapping and Photography Service (MPS). Yadin's memo stipulated that the "above-mentioned [photographic] products will only be developed and printed at the labs of the MPS." For additional details, including Yadin's role in this area, see Sela, "Scouting Palestinian Territory."

30. On the colonial function of Israeli military photographic archives, see Azoulay,

"Declaring the State of Israel" and *Potential History*; Sela, "The Genealogy of Colonial Plunder and Erasure." On the role of colonial archives as tools of dispossession, see Stoler, *Along the Archival Grain.*

31. Shohat, *Israeli Cinema*, 260. The film was released in English under the title *Ricochet.* Also see Benziman, "'Mom, I'm Home'" and Gertz, "The Medium That Mistook Itself for War." For additional discussion of Israeli filmic renderings of this exculpatory narrative ("shooting and crying") that gained national prominence after Israel's 1967 military victory, see Hochberg, *Visual Occupations,* ch. 6.

32. Yariv Horowitz, interview by author, Tel Aviv, 14 December 2014; Anderman, "For 'Rock the Casbah' Helmer, a Director's Chair Became a Therapist's Couch."

33. Horowitz' experience would become the basis of his subsequent film, *Aftershock* (2002).

34. Bat Haim, "Lost in the Old City"; "Western Wall Area Cleared." Also see Stein, "Souvenirs of Conquest." On the role of Rubinger in Israeli state mythology, including a collection of his most iconic images, see Rubinger, *Israel Through My Lens.*

35. Israel Defense Forces, *A Rare Documentation.*

36. Stein, "Souvenirs of Conquest." This trope also appears in *Waltz with Bashir* about the 1982 Israeli invasion of Lebanon. See Hochberg, *Visual Occupations.*

37. On the military operation of this period, see Beinin and Stein, "Histories and Futures of a Failed Peace."

38. Permanent checkpoints would only emerge in 1993, after the signing of the Oslo Accords. Areas A, B, and C would be designated as discrete territorial units in 1995 with the signing of Oslo II, but the "prohibition on the entry of Israeli citizens into Area A . . . [would only be] enforced since the beginning of the second Intifada in September 2000." OCHA, *The Humanitarian Monitor.*

39. For discussion of the soldier experience of these military practices, see Breaking the Silence, *Our Harsh Logic*; Grassiani, *Soldiering Under Occupation.*

40. For a discussion of this recurrent visual trope, see Ginsburg, *And You Will Serve as Eyes for Us.*

41. Nathansohn, *Shooting Occupation*, 117–118. The soldiers would all become members of Breaking the Silence, and their photographs shown in the 2004 exhibit.

42. Ibid.,118.

43. Azoulay, "Getting Rid of the Distinction Between the Aesthetic and the Political," 240.

44. On the "personal documentaries" made during the intifada by Israeli reserve soldiers, see Duvdevani, "How I Shot the War," 284–285. Also see Morag, "Radical Con-

textuality." Nathansohn argues that soldier cameras functioned as "conscience-cleansing device[s] . . . purging the gun's immorality though an act of photography." Nathansohn, "Soldier-Photographer and the Double Bind of Photographic Practice," 439.

45. Morag, "Perpetrator Trauma and Current Israeli Documentary Cinema." On the history of this genre, and its manifestation during the 2006 Lebanon war, see Hochberg, *Visual Occupations*, ch. 6.

46. *JustVision*, "Yehuda Shaul."

47. There is a large scholarship on Israeli media coverage of the second intifada. See, for example: Dor, *Intifada Hits the Headlines*; Liebes and Kampf, "Black and White and Shades of Gray"; Wolfsfeld, "The News Media and the Second Intifada"; Wolfsfeld et al., "Covering Death in Conflicts."

48. On Israeli public secrecy, see Kuntsman and Stein, *Digital Militarism,* 14–15.

49. Urquhart, "Army Fury at Hebron Soldiers' Brutality Exhibition."

50. Maariv, "Breaking the Silence."

51. Urquhart, "Army Fury at Hebron Soldiers' Brutality Exhibition."

52. Lis, "IDF Questions Reservists Who Organized Hebron Photo Exhibit"; Urquhart, "Army Fury at Hebron Soldiers' Brutality Exhibition."

53. Orpaz, "Robots, and Not Humans, Can React to Sabotages."

54. On the use of aerial and satellite imaging as tools of military rule, see Gordon, *Israel's Occupation*; Weizman, *Hollow Land*; Zureik, Lyon and Abu-Lahan, *Surveillance and Control in Israel/Palestine.*

55. "Filming on Military Bases," 15 January 1986, General Staff Directive 21.0210, IDF. According to the directive, a military commander may grant permission for filming on military facilities provided photographers follow military orders regarding sensitive information.

56. Ibid., 3–4. Here is an excerpt from the directive: "(6) A soldier shall not possess a still or video camera, or any other filming device, while in a military facility or with a military unit unless he was given a permission to do so by the facility's commander or the commands' security officer. (7) A soldier shall not film a military facility, or other soldiers performing their duty, without first receiving a permit to do so from the facility's commander or from the command's security officer. (8) A soldier shall prevent any civilian from filming a military facility, equipment or soldiers fulfilling their duty (including inside a military vehicle, vessel or aircraft) unless the civilian holds a permit to do so provided by the command or the corps' security officer or by the Intelligence Branch's information security department."

57. "Filming on Military Bases" [Amended], 12 March 2007, General Staff Directive 21.0210, IDF.

58. Greenberg, "Soldiers Were Beaten by Their Commanders Like 'Ducks in a Firing Range.'"

59. Israel proudly celebrated its history as an "early adopter" of cellular technologies. See Senor and Singer, *Start-Up Nation*. Schejter and Cohen, "Israel: Chutzpah and Chatter in the Holy Land." Also see Cohen et al., *The Wonder Phone in the Land of Miracles*.

60. Levin, "The End of Male Fraternity?"

61. Schejter and Cohen, "Israel: Chutzpah and Chatter in the Holy Land," 38.

62. On the collaboration between the military and high-tech sector, see Gordon, "Israel's Emergence as a Homeland Security Capital" and *The Political Economy of Israel's Homeland Security Industry*.

63. Also see Levin, "The End of Male Fraternity?"

64. In 2004, the military would issue a new set of regulations regarding the usage of cellular technologies, stipulating that "[s]oldiers may not bring mobile phones to the front, military facility, or a location where an exercise, experiment, or operational activity is taking place." Such directives fell short of a categorical ban, as enforcement was left in the hands of the local command structure: "The unit commander . . . may order a soldier to refrain from carrying a mobile phone during military activity or may order the phone to be turned off and its battery removed for operational security considerations." Levin, "The End of Male Fraternity?" 91.

65. Military Ordinance 21.0113 (2004) cited in Cohen et al., *The Wonder Phone in the Land of Miracles*, 91.

66. Levin, "The End of Male Fraternity?" 203.

67. Also see Schejter and Cohen, "Mobile Phone Usage as an Indicator of Solidarity."

68. Ibid.

69. Caldwell et al., "Learning to Leverage New Media." Also see Darom, "Meet the Biggest PR Firm in the Middle East."

70. Rettig Gur, "Coordination Is Putting Israel Ahead in the Media War."

71. See Kuntsman and Stein, *Digital Militarism*.

72. Breiner, "Cellular Phone with a Camera?"

73. Ibid. Also see Schechter, "The IDF Requires Soldiers to Pay for Taking Cameras out of Their Phones."

74. Breiner, "Cellular Phone with a Camera?"

75. Ben-Hamo, "A Few Words About the IDF's Decision to Prohibit Cellular Phones with Cameras"; Breiner, "Cellular Phone with a Camera?"

76. Ben-Hamo, "A Few Words About the IDF's decision to Prohibit Cellular Phones with Cameras."

77. Dayagi, "The IDF's Exposure in the Media During the Second Lebanese War and Operation Cast Lead"; Schechter, "The IDF Requires Soldiers to Pay for Taking Cameras out of Their Phones."

78. Greenberg, "Top Officer."

79. Breaking the Silence, *Soldiers' Testimonies from Operation Cast Lead, Gaza 2009.*

80. Amnesty International, Operation "Cast Lead" and Tawil-Souri, "Digital Occupation." On "knock on the roof," see Weizman, "Lawfare in Gaza."

81. Fitsanakis and Allen, *Cell Wars*; Katz and Bohbot, *The Weapon Wizards*, 185; Krauthammer, "Israel's Moral Clarity in Gaza."

82. Kennedy, *Of War and Law,* cited in Weizman, "Lawfare in Gaza," 3. On the Israeli military's use of law to condition the battlefield, see Jones, "Frames of Law" and "Traveling Law." The military's legal division argued that "our goal is not to tie down the army, but to give it the tools to win in a way that is legal." Blau and Feldman, "How IDF Legal Experts Legitimized Strikes Involving Gaza Civilians."

83. Breaking the Silence, *Soldiers' Testimonies from Operation Cast Lead*, Gaza 2009. Emphasis added.

84. Ibid. Emphasis added.

85. The Association for Civil Rights in Israel (ACRI) defines mapping as "logging and documentation of the rooms of the house" and argues that it is an illegal military practice. Their 2008 report notes that the organization only "recently . . . learned about the existence of [these] patterns of activity," thanks to soldier testimonies. Association for Civil Rights in Israel, *Residential Searches ("Mapping").* For discussion of this term within military rubrics, see Manekin, *Waging War Among Civilians,* 233. For soldier testimonies on mapping, see Breaking the Silence, *Our Harsh Logic,* 213–217. Also see Yesh Din et al., *A Life Exposed*; Grassiani, "Militarizing the Enemy's home, Israel/Palestine"; Huss, "Mapping the Occupation."

86. Breaking the Silence, "They're Familiar with It as Mapping, Because It's Done All the Time."

87. Breaking the Silence, *Our Harsh Logic;* Huss, "Mapping the Occupation:"

88. Breaking the Silence, *Our Harsh Logic,* 29–30.

89. Hagar Kotef and Merav Amir make a related argument about military checkpoints, arguing that they "are part of a network of corrective technologies that are meant to fail." Kotef and Amir, "Between Imaginary Lines Violence and Its Justifications at the Military Checkpoints in Occupied Palestine," 21–22.

90. Nathansohn, *Shooting Occupation*, 115.

91. Breaking the Silence, *Our Harsh Logic*, 29–30.

92. On dual use, see Kaplan, "Precision Targets"; Stahl, *Militainment, Inc.*

CHAPTER 2

1. For a discussion of the harsh conditions of military occupation in Hebron during the second intifada period, see B'Tselem's report: Feuerstein, *Ghost Town*. Note that *Ghost Town* was written on the basis of research conducted in Hebron by Musa Abu Hashhash (with 'Issa 'Amru).

2. Scholarly discussion of the B'Tselem camera project includes Alexandrowicz, "50 Years of Documentation"; Berdugo, *The Weaponized Camera in the Middle East*; Ginsburg; *And You Will Serve as Eyes for Us*, "Emancipation and Collaboration" and "Gendered Visual Activism."

3. B'Tselem, "The Occupation's Fig Leaf." Also see Yesh Din, *Mock Enforcement*.

4. Allen, *The Rise and Fall of Human Rights*.

5. On the permit regime, see Berda, "The Bureaucracy of the Occupation" and *Living Emergency*.

6. Recent scholarship on the politics of infrastructure in the occupied Palestinian territories includes Alimahomed-Wilson and Potiker, "The Logistics of Occupation"; Salamanca, "Assembling the Fabric of Life"; Stamatopoulou-Robbins, *Waste Siege*; Zawawi et al., "Public Spaces in the Occupied Palestinian Territories." On the legacy of Israeli de-development, see United Nations Conference on Trade and Development, *Report on UNCTAD Assistance to the Palestinian People*.

7. For an additional example, see *5 Broken Cameras*.

8. "Slow violence" is Rob Nixon's term for environmental violence: Nixon, *Slow Violence and the Environmentalism of the Poor*. For a rendering of "slow violence" as infrastructural neglect in Palestine, see Stamatopoulou-Robbins, *Waste Siege*. Also see Ophir and Azoulay on the difference between "eruptive" and "withheld" violence in the context of Israeli military rule: Azoulay and Ophir, *The One-State Condition*.

9. Bishara has written the definitive study of Palestinian journalism under military occupation, with a focus on the second intifada period. See Bishara, *Back Stories* and "The Geopolitics of Press Freedoms in the Israeli-Palestinian Context."

10. Bishara, "The Geopolitics of Press Freedoms in the Israeli-Palestinian Context," 169–170.

11. Palestinian Center for Human Rights, *Silencing the Press*.

12. Ibid.

13. Committee to Protect Journalists, *CPJ Names World's Worst Places to be a Journalist*. Cited in Bishara, *Back Stories,* 73.

14. Committee to Protect Journalists, *At Risk.*

15. Ibid. Cited in Bishara, *Back Stories,* 94.

16. This incident took place in Hebron on 18 April 2006. Fuerstein and Shulman, *Ghost Town,* 56.

17. Palestinian Center for Human Rights, *Silencing the Press,* 6–7. Emphasis added.

18. Feuerstein, *Ghost Town.*

19. Levy, "Twilight Zone, Mean Streets."

20. For a fuller study of this footage, see Ginsburg, "Gendered Visual Activism."

21. Derfner, "Image Makers."

22. Dayan, "Two Tales of One City."

23. Asheri, "Power Play/Disappointing Finale."

24. Jerusalem Post Staff, "Virtual Existence."

25. Asheri, "Power Play/Disappointing Finale." Also see Sofer, "Olmert on the Violence in Hebron."

26. B'Tselem, *Ghost Town,* 42. The prime minister made these comments at a cabinet meeting.

27. Also see Ginsburg, "Gendered Visual Activism."

28. For further discussion of the Nabi Saleh protest movement, see Alazzeh, *Non-Violent Popular Resistance in the West Bank*; Al Haq, *Repression of Non-Violent Protest in the Occupied Palestinian Territory*; B'Tselem, *Show of Force*; Ehrenreich, *The Way to the Spring.*

29. Alazzeh, *Non-Violent Popular Resistance in the West Bank;* Al Haq, *Repression of Non-Violent Protest in the Occupied Palestinian Territory.*

30. Ziv, "IDF Falsely Arrested Photographers During Palestinian Protest, Court Rules."

31. The political legacy of both the Tamimi family and the popular struggle in Nabi Saleh have been heavily chronicled. The most prominent example is Ehrenreich, *The Way to the Spring.* On Tamimi's work as an activist videographer, see Faulkner, "On Israel/Palestine and the Politics of Visibility" and Ginsburg, "Emancipation and Collaboration." For a discussion of the role of photography in the Nabi Saleh protests, see Maimon and Grinbaum, *Activestills.*

32. Tamimi's photographic work would also be supported by the Popular Struggle Coordination Committee of Nabi Saleh.

33. Nabi Saleh activist Mustafa Tamimi was killed by the Israeli authorities on 9 December 2011, and the event was caught on film. It was one of the first such killings

to be captured on camera, as registered by a headline in the Israeli media: "Mustafa Tamimi: A Murder Captured on Camera." The soldier responsible would not be indicted. Matar, "Mustafa Tamimi."

34. For a chronicle of another celebrated media activist from Nabi Saleh, Nariman Tamimi, mother of Palestinian teen activist Ahed Tamimi, see B'Tselem, *Show of Force*; Ehrenreich, *The Way to the Spring*; Maimon and Grinbaum, *Activestills*, 94–95.

35. Bilal's footage from this demonstration can be seen here: B'Tselem, "Investigation into Border Police Violence Against Protesters in a-Nabi Saleh."

36. Ziv, "IDF Falsely Arrested Photographers During Palestinian protest, Court Rules."

37. "Middle of the Night in a-Nabi Saleh." For additional discussion of mapping practices, see Chapter 1.

38. Sherwood, "Palestinian Children Woken in Night to Be Photographed by Soldiers."

39. Mackey, "Palestinians Record West Bank Protests with Cameras Supplied by Israelis."

40. This was one of three night raids on Nabi Saleh during that month alone, all of which Bilal filmed. Dana, "14 Year Old Child Arrested in Night Raid in Nabi Saleh."

41. The declaration of a "closed military zone" was a frequent military strategy to prevent Palestinian access and quash protest. Human Rights Watch has noted that "the Israeli army, between July 1, 2014 and June 30, 2019, prosecuted 4,590 Palestinians for entering a 'closed military zone,' a designation it frequently attaches on the spot to protest sites." See Shakir, *Born Without Civil Rights*, 3.

42. This portion of my study draws on B'Tselem correspondence with a range of bodies within the Israeli security services, but chiefly Central Command (*Pikud Merkaz*), the military branch responsible for its activities in the West Bank. I focus on memos written to B'Tselem, and the lawyers with whom they worked, in response to B'Tselem complaints and inquiries regarding the treatment of their Palestinian photographers. B'Tselem's original letters of complaint are not part of this analysis. Due to political sensitivity, documents have been anonymized. For a discussion of the regularized communications process between Israeli human rights organizations and branches of the Israeli state, see Grinberg, "Facsimileing the State." For background on the relationship between Israeli human rights institutions and the Israeli state, see Perugini and Gordon, *The Human Right to Dominate*.

43. B'Tselem, "The Occupation's Fig Leaf," 30–31.

44. For a discussion of internal debates within B'Tselem and the broader Israeli

left regarding the NGO's work with the military law enforcement system, see Weiss, "Struggling with Complicity."

45. Berda, "The Bureaucracy of the Occupation," 12. Also see Berda, *Living Emergency: Israel's Permit Regime in the Occupied West Bank*; Gordon, *Israel's Occupation*.

46. Rotem, *The Case for Dismantling Israel's Human Rights Organizations*.

47. See Yesh Din, *Mock Enforcement* and Perugini and Gordon, *The Human Right to Dominate*. Also see Allen, *The Rise and Fall of Human Rights*.

48. B'Tselem, "The Occupation's Fig Leaf."

49. Cohen, "Citing IDF Failure to Bring Soldiers to Justice, B'Tselem Stops Filing Complaints on Abuse of Palestinians."

50. For background on this process, see Grinberg, "Facsimileing the State."

51. Memo from Central Command to B'Tselem. "The Treatment of Unusual Events Involving Photographers Opposing [*mul*] General Security Activity [*Batash*]: Operational Guidelines" [in Hebrew]. July 2008 [date unclear]. B'Tselem collection. Emphasis added.

52. Memo from Central Command to B'Tselem, "Your Inquiry Regarding Video Filming by B'Tselem's Employees and Volunteers [in Hebrew]." 26 August 2008. B'Tselem collection. Emphasis added.

53. Memo from Central Command to B'Tselem, "Harassment of B'Tselem Employees and Volunteers Taking Photos and a Suspicion of Violent Attacks Against Photographers [in Hebrew]." 8 January 2013. B'Tselem collection. Emphasis added.

54. Memo from Defense Establishment, Legal Advisor to B'Tselem, Legal Council, "Photographing at Checkpoints Administered by the Passages That Are Under the Ministry of Defense's Responsibility [in Hebrew]." 15 September 2010. B'Tselem collection. Later memos from the military to B'Tselem would refine the terms of this policy, noting that "on the basis of security considerations, there is a distinction in the checkpoint between areas where photography is allowed and areas when documentation might cause harm to the country's defense." Military guidelines for border police would be the subject of an additional exchange with the NGO: Memo from Border Police to B'Tselem, "Guidelines for Border Police Regarding Treatment of Photographers in the West Bank [in Hebrew]." 30 November 2010. B'Tselem collection.

55. Memo from Central Command to B'Tselem, "The Treatment of Unusual Events Involving Photographers Opposing [*mul*] General Security Activity [*Batash*]: Operational Guidelines" [in Hebrew]. July 2008 [date unclear]. B'Tselem collection.

56. Ibid.

57. Ibid.

58. Ibid. Emphasis in original.

59. For discussion of the Israeli military's tactical deployment of ethics, see Eastwood, *Ethics as a Weapon of War*.

60. On the infrastructure of the South Hebron hills during the period chronicled here, see Ashkar and Shulman, *Means of Expulsion*; B'Tselem, *Khirbet Susiya*.

61. B'Tselem, "Visual."

62. For a study of role of Palestinian women within the B'Tselem camera project, see Ginsburg, "Gendered Visual Activism."

63. B'Tselem, "Israeli Military Must Permit Video Documentation in Occupied Territories and Conduct Investigation of Attack on Photographers."

64. B'Tselem, "The Occupation's Fig Leaf."

65. On the permit regime, see Berda, "The Bureaucracy of the Occupation" and *Living Emergency*.

66. Allen, *The Rise and Fall of Human Rights*.

67. For discussions of "the cultural politics of time and waiting" in occupied Palestine, see Peteet, "Closure's Temporality" and *Space and Mobility in Palestine*.

68. For another such example, see *5 Broken Cameras*.

CHAPTER 3

1. For an overview of the incident, see B'Tselem, "The Army Must Internalize the Gravity of the Ni'lin Shooting Incident."

2. *In the Image*. On the role of Salaam Amira, also see Cook, "Israeli Amy Targets Family over Brutality Film" and Reese, "B'Tselem: Views to a Kill."

3. Breiner, "Ni'lin Shooting."

4. This analysis builds on my co-authored work with Adi Kuntsman on "digital suspicion—a mode of suspicion directed against the digital image and archive." Many of the concepts elaborated in this chapter have their roots in this collaborative work. See Kuntsman and Stein, *Digital Militarism* and "Digital Suspicion, Politics, and the Middle East."

5. On the "digital transformation of legal persuasion and judgment," see Feigenson and Spiesel, *Law on Display*.

6. On the legacy of the military law enforcement system in this regard, see B'Tselem, "The Occupation's Fig Leaf"; Yesh Din, *Mock Enforcement*. For a discussion of the legal status of Palestinian eye-witness footage within the Israeli military court system, see Diamond, "Killing on Camera."

7. Foundational scholarship includes Pratt, *Imperial Eyes*, and Said, *The Question of*

Palestine. I discuss this colonial logic in more details here: Stein, *Itineraries in Conflict* and "Travelling Zion."

8. Wolfe, "Settler Colonialism and the Elimination of the Native."

9. Fineman, *Faking It*; Mitchell, *The Reconfigured Eye*; Morris, *Believing Is Seeing*; Tucher, "'I Believe in Faking.'"

10. For additional discussion, see Kuntsman and Stein, *Digital Militarism.*

11. Ristovska, "The Rise of Eyewitness Video and Its Implications for Human Rights." On the longer history of film as legal evidence, see Schwartz, *Mechanical Witness.*

12. Stein, "'Fake News!'"

13. Analysis of the Al-Durrah case has been voluminous. For discussion of its ramifications within Israeli legal and state culture, see Diamond, "Law Trumps Hate?" Additional cites appear in the following notes.

14. Schwartz, "In the Footsteps of the al-Dura Controversy." For discussion of U.S. media coverage, see Ackerman, "Al-Aqsa Intifada and the U.S. Media."

15. Liebes and First, "Framing the Palestine–Israeli Conflict," 64.

16. Cook, *Martyrdom in Islam,* 156.

17. Much of the literature on the Al-Durrah affair reads the incident as an Israeli public relations failure: Gilboa, "Public Diplomacy"; Shai, *Hearts and Minds*; Shavit, *Media Strategy and Military Operations in the 21st Century.*

18. Schwartz, "In the Footsteps of the al-Dura Controversy"; Shavit, *Media Strategy and Military Operations in the 21st Century.*

19. Ibid.

20. BBC News, "Israel 'Sorry' for Killing Boy."

21. Seaman, "We Did Not Abandon Philippe Karsenty."

22. Seaman, "Palestinian Industry of Lies."

23. Quote from Israeli TV critic Yair Ettinger, cited in Marmari, "The Purity of Shame."

24. On Shahaf's "eccentric obsession" with Al-Durrah, see Ginsburg, "Nahum Shahaf's Relentless Muhammad Al-Dura Dissent." A decade earlier, Shahaf had supported conspiracy theories about the assassination of Israeli Prime Minister Yitzhak Rabin: Levy, "Mohammed al-Dura Lives On."

25. Landes, "The Muhammad Al-Dura Blood Libel." Emphasis added.

26. See Landes's blogs: http://www.seconddraft.org/; http://www.theaugeanstables.com/. Pallywood was the subject of Landes's 2005 video: "Pallywood: 'According to Palestinian Sources.'"

27. B'Tselem, "The Army Must Internalize the Gravity of the Ni'lin Shooting Incident."

28. For additional information on the Ni'ilin protests and Israeli military response, see Cook, "Israeli Army Targets Family over Brutality Film"; Frykberg, "Palestinian Village Takes on Israeli Military" and "West Bank: The Villagers Hemmed In."

29. Lazaroff and Lappin, "B'Tselem to Call for Ni'lin Death Probe."

30. For additional details about the shooting, including a spatial reconstruction of the scene, see SITU Research and Forensic Architecture, *Nil'in Report*.

31. Cook, "Israeli Army Targets Family over Brutality Film." Also see *In the Image*.

32. Dvory, "IDF Soldier Shot a Cuffed Palestinian from Zero Range"; It's All Talk, With Yaron Dekel." The latter was a radio interview with B'Tselem spokesperson Sarit Michaeli, who appeared on numerous Israeli radio and television programs after the footage's publication.

33. "The Day That Was." B'tselem, for its part, was concerned about the timing of the military investigation, noting that "[i]t was only after the footage was broadcast on a national news channel that the Military Police opened an investigation." B'Tselem, "The Army Must Internalize the Gravity of the Ni'lin Shooting Incident."

34. "Five in the Evening."

35. B'Tselem's dossier on the Ni'ilin trial, including the findings of the Israeli police criminal forensic unit, is available here (in Hebrew): https://www.btselem.org/heb/legal_documents/20101214_nilin_shooting_difs_report.pdf

36. The full quote reads: "Just this week, the Israeli Police's Criminal Forensic unit, a body that cannot under any circumstances be presented as biased towards B'Tselem, categorically disproved another allegation invented to malign B'Tselem. The unit's number one expert on digital photography examined the original videotape that captured the 2008 shooting of a bound, blindfolded Palestinian in Ni'ilin and determined that the tape was authentic and un-doctored." Montell, "B'Tselem Chief." For additional discussion of the police's findings, see Tchaikovsky, "An Expert's Opinion."

37. Shamir, "The Main Matter."

38. The initial indictment consisted of only one charge: conduct unbecoming. Abu-Rahma, along with several NGOs, filed a petition to Israel's High Court of Justice and requested that it order the Judge Advocate General (JAG) to amend the indictment to include more severe charges. The High Court of Justice, in a precedential decision, issued a mandamus and ordered the JAG to worsen the charges against Borberg and Correa. M 5/08 Chief Military Prosecutor v. Let. Col. Borberg and Sag. Correa; HCJ

7195/08 *Abu Rahma et al. v. the Judge Advocate General et al.* Also see Ben-Naftali and Zamir, "Whose 'Conduct Unbecoming'?"

39. Cohen-Friedman, "B'Tselem Hands Naalin Shooting Tape to Police." For additional discussion of Shahaf's role in the case, see Diamond, "Law Trumps Hate?"; Ginsburg, "Nahum Shahaf's Relentless Muhammad Al-Dura Dissent."

40. Baruch, "Dahoah Halevi—"B'Tselem's Video, The Open Questions."

41. Baruch, "Dahoah Halevi -- B'Tselem's Allegations Are Baseless." Emphasis added.

42. Fyler, "Physicist: Naalin Shooting Tape Doctored."

43. Ibid.

44. B'tselem noted: "[T]he special military court sentenced Lt. Col. Borberg [the officer involved] to a suspended jail sentence and determined that he will not be demoted.... Correa [the soldier involved] was sentenced to demotion from the rank of staff sergeant to the rank of private." B'Tselem, "The Army Must Internalize the Gravity of the Ni'ilin Shooting Incident." For detailed discussion of the trials and court rulings, see Ben-Naftali and Zamir, "Whose 'Conduct Unbecoming'?"; Diamond, "Law Trumps Hate?"; Miretski and Bachmann, "The Panopticon of International Law."

45. On the verdict, see Brainer, "Ni'ilin shooting"; Tchaikovsky, "An Expert's Opinion."

46. Breiner, "Ni'ilin Shooting."

47. Ibid.

48. Grinberg, "Ni'lin Shooting."

49. Kuntsman and Stein, *Digital Militarism.*

50. Landes's daughter, Aliza Landes, was the former head of the unit's social media division. See Chapter 5.

51. For background, see Bayoumi, *Midnight on the Mavi Marmara.* For additional discussion, see: Kuntsman and Stein, "Another War Zone."

52. The event in question was an Israeli mortar strike on 6 January 2009, resulting in the killing of over forty Palestinian civilians. See Harel, "UN Backtracks on Claim That Deadly IDF Strike Hit Gaza School." Landes credited right-wing conspiratorial blogs with successful media victories regarding the Gaza war of 2008–2009: ManagingTeam, "The Gaza War in Review."

53. Johnson, "More Death Cult Propaganda."

54. For discussion of the "cognitive warfare" concept as utilized by Landes, see Green, *Cognitive Warfare.*

55. Landes was referring to the state's belated media response to the *Mavi Marmara.*

56. Prime Minister's Office (Israel), *Publication of the Report of the Government Review Committee Regarding the France 2 Al-Durrah*; Caspit, "Muhammad Al-Dura."

57. Prime Minister's Office (Israel), *Publication of the Report of the Government Review Committee Regarding the France 2 Al-Durrah*. On the government report, also see Kerstein, "Discrepancies Raised, Inconsistencies Revealed"; Ravid, "Government Report"; Somfalvi, "Israeli Committee"; Tazna, "Government Committee."

58. Kuperwasser and Ya'alon, "The France 2 Al-Durrah Report, Its Consequences and Implications."

59. Somfalvi, "Israeli Committee."

60. Hirshfeld, "Video."

61. The organization's website provides additional background: http://www.tazpit.org.il/

62. Weizman, *Hollow Land*.

63. Silverman, "Evyatar Borovsky."

64. Also see Harrison, "Tazpit News Agency Founder Amotz Eyal Tells of Israelis' Fight for Balanced News Coverage in Judea and Samaria."

65. For an example of such accusations, regularly aired by the Israeli media, see Altman, "War of Stones—The Settlers' Version." Altman writes: "B'Tselem gives the Palestinians cameras and they create provocations, film the event from a particular angle, and edit it to make it look as though the settlers are abusing the poor Palestinians."

66. See Chapter 2 for additional discussion of this incident.

67. On NGO Monitor, see Gordon, "Human Rights as a Security Threat"; Perugini and Gordon, *The Human Right to Dominate*. For example, NGO Monitor said this about B'Tselem's camera project: "*Shooting Back* [project's early name] reinforces the false image of Israel as the world's major perpetrator of war crimes and a systematic violator of human rights . . . when the fact is that the vast majority of soldiers are the opposite, and we know that much of the army goes out of its way to avoid unnecessary civilian casualties, and does take human rights seriously." Derfner, "Image Makers."

68. Tepper, "IDF Officer Seen Head-Butting Palestinian Youth in B'Tselem Video."

69. B'Tselem, "B'Tselem's Initial Findings on Nakba Day Incident at Bitunya."

70. Sheizaf, "Beitunia Killings and the Media's Incredibly High Bar for Palestinian Stories."

71. Eishton, "Pallywood." For additional discussion of this case, see Forensic Architecture, "The Killing of Nadeem Nawara and Mohammed Abu Daher."

72. "UN Calls for Probe into Shooting of Palestinian Youths."

73. Human Rights Watch, "Israel: Killing of Children Apparent War Crime."

74. Rudoren, "Two Palestinians Killed in Clashes with Israeli Forces."

75. B'Tselem, "B'Tselem's Initial Findings on Nakba Day Incident at Bitunya."

76. Ibid.

77. B'Tselem, "Use of Live Ammunition Confirmed in Nawarah Shooting."

78. For a chronology of the case, including responses by military spokespersons, see Benziman, "A Trick and a Shtick."

79. "Ya'alon Says Troops in Nakba Day Killings Were in Danger, Acted as Needed."

80. Kahana, "Liberman."

81. Ibid.

82. Khoury and Levinson, "IDF Says Forgery Likely in Video Showing Palestinian Teens' Deaths"; Kahana, "Liberman."

83. The speaker was identified as Israeli ballistics expert Yosef Yekutiel, who was interviewed by Israel's Channel 2 evening news on 22 May 2014. See Hamo, "New Documentation Proves." Also see Benziman, "A Trick and a Shtick"; Eishton, "Pallywood"; Sharir, "Roni Daniel."

84. Tobin, "Was Nakba Shooting Another al-Dura Libel?"

85. Derfner, "Day of Catastrophe for 'Pallywood' Conspiracy Theorists."

86. Ibid.

87. Benziman, "A Trick and a Shtick." The speaker was Israeli military correspondent Roni Daniel. For a critique of the incident, see Sharir, "Roni Daniel."

88. "Of Course Nadim Nawara Was Killed by Live Fire—But Where?" Emphasis added.

89. CNN, "Outrage over Teens' Death Growing." Oren was elected to the Israeli parliament the subsequent year.

90. Benziman, "A Trick and a Shtick."

91. For an overview of the fraudulence accusation made in this case, see Derfner, "Day of Catastrophe for 'Pallywood' Conspiracy Theorists"; Eishton, "Making a Murderer . . . Only Criminally Negligent."

92. Zonshein, "Going to War with Cameras." Emphasis added.

93. Leifer, "'Nakba Day Killings.'" For full analysis of the legal proceedings, see Eishton, "Making a Murderer . . . Only Criminally Negligent."

94. Berger, "Border Policeman Gets Plea Deal After Admitting Negligence in Shooting Death of Palestinian Teen"; Brown, "IDF Soldiers Who Killed Armed Palestinian Set for Community Service."

95. Kershner, "Israeli Who Shot Palestinian Teenager Is Sentenced to 9 Months in Prison."

96. Netanyahu, "Netanyhu to CNN's Wolf Blitzer."

97. Eishton, "Pallywood." Also see Eishton, "Making a Murderer . . . Only Criminally Negligent."

98. On "forensic aesthetics," see Keenan and Weizman, *Mengele's Skull*.

99. Diamond, "Killing on Camera" and "Law Trumps Hate?"

100. Diamond, "Law Trumps Hate," 32. Emphasis added.

101. Ibid., 49.

102. Kuperwasser and Ya'alon, "The France 2 Al-Durrah Report, Its Consequences and Implications," 5. Emphasis added.

103. Ibid., 6.

CHAPTER 4

1. B'Tselem, "Investigation into Border Police Violence Against Protesters in a-Nabi Saleh."

2. B'Tselem, "Israeli Soldiers Continue Firing Tear Gas Canisters Directly at Human Targets, Despite the Army's Denials."

3. Hassen, "Palestinian Dies After Hit by Tear Gas Canister."

4. B'Tselem, "Israeli Soldiers Continue Firing Tear Gas Canisters Directly at Human Targets, Despite the Army's Denials."

5. Bilal Tamimi and Nariman Tamimi filmed the footage for B'Tselem. Their footage can be screened here: B'Tselem, "Investigation into Border Police Violence Against Protesters in a-Nabi Saleh." Less than a month later, Palestinian activist Mustafa Tamimi from Nabi Saleh would be killed following injuries sustained by a tear gas canister shot by Israeli forces. See Rahman, "Nabi Saleh Protester Hit by Tear Gas Canister Dies from Wounds."

6. B'Tselem, "Three Appeals Submitted Regarding Closure of 3 Investigations of Police Officers."

7. For a review of scholarship on the B'Tselem camera project, see Chapter 2, note 2. For a review of recent scholarship on the visual politics of human rights, see Introduction, note 58.

8. Yesh Din, *Mock Enforcement*. See Chapter 2 for more discussion.

9. B'Tselem, "State-Backed Settler Violence."

10. Padania, et al, "Cameras Everywhere," 12. Also see Gregory, "Ubiquitous Witnesses" and Ristovska, "The Rise of Eyewitness Video and Its Implications for Human Rights."

11. For more elaboration on this concept, see Stein, "Impossible Witness."

12. B'Tselem, "The Occupation's Fig Leaf," 30–31.

13. Gürsel, *Image Brokers*, 2.

14. On the demographics of the Israeli left, see Weiss, *Conscientious Objectors in Israel*.

15. Note that Israeli law stipulates that Israeli passport holders are not permitted to enter Palestinian cities in the West Bank, classified as Area A. Amir, "The Making of a Void Sovereignty," 239.

16. For an example of unattributed footage, see B'Tselem, "Video Footage Shows the Army Failed in Its Duty to Protect Palestinians from Settler Attacks."

17. See Chapter 3 for additional discussion of this incident.

18. Eishton, "Pallywood."

19. See Chapter 3 for a study of such fraudulence accusations.

20. B'Tselem, "Two Settlers Arrested on Suspicion of Attack on Palestinian Shepherds."

21. Derfner, "Image Makers." This incident is also discussed in Chapter 2.

22. The Israeli satiric program *Eretz Nehederet* did a spoof of this footage.

23. Shalhoub-Kevorkian, *Security Theology, Surveillance and the Politics of Fear*; Shalhoub-Kevorkian and David, "Is the Violence of Tag Mehir a State Crime?"

24. B'Tselem, "Settlers Vandalize Property as Revenge for Stone Throwing—Police Do Not Detain Them."

25. B'Tselem has also taken advantage of this idiom to produce self-satirizing materials: B'Tselem, "Who Is B'Tselem?"

26. See Chapter 3 for a study of such fraudulence accusations.

27. Zonszein, "Violence Is a Cruel Reminder of a Reality That Is Neither Calm nor Stable."

28. Kershner, "Mosque Set on Fire in Northern Israel." Also see Shalhoub-Kevorkian and David, "Is the Violence of Tag Mehir a State Crime?"

29. Footage of these attacks can be seen here: B'Tselem, "Video Footage Shows the Army Failed in Its Duty to Protect Palestinians from Settler Attacks." Also see: International Solidarity Movement, "Villages of Urif, Burin and Asira Violently Attacked by Settlers."

30. B'Tselem, "Video Footage Shows the Army Failed in Its Duty to Protect Palestinians from Settler Attacks."

31. Peteet, "Closure's Temporality." I discuss these issues in Chapter 2.

32. See B'Tselem, "State-Backed Settler Violence."

33. On the legal impunity that settlers enjoy, see Al Haq, *Institutionalised Impunity*.

34. The video can be seen here: B'Tselem, "Video Provided by B'Tselem Leads to Indictment of Three Settlers for Property Damage and Threats in a-Lubban a-Sharqiyah." Also see Levinson, "IDF Soldier Linked to 'Price Tag' Attack in West Bank Palestinian Village."

35. On settlement normalization, see Weiss, "Homeowners in Israel" and "Immigration and West Bank Settlement Normalization."

36. B'Tselem, "The Film *Smile, and the World Will Smile Back* Won the Best Short Film Award at the Milano Film Festival."

37. Diamond, "Killing on Camera" and Yesh Din, *Mock Enforcement.* See Chapter 2 for further discussion.

38. Montell, "Learning from What Works." In 2016, B'tselem ceased cooperation with the Israeli Military Law Enforcement System: B'Tselem, "The Occupation's Fig Leaf." See Chapter 2 for additional discussion.

39. See, for example, Arkadi Zaides's dance performance *Archive* (2014), based on footage shot by Palestinian videographers working with B'Tselem: Kruschkova, "Disappearing Dance, Dancing Disappearance."

CHAPTER 5

1. On the Israeli military deployment of selfies as a tool of military occupation, see Kuntsman and Stein, *Digital Militarism.*

2. Fleishman, "Soldiers: Our Hands Are Being Tied." Emphasis added.

3. Shavit, *Media Strategy and Military Operations in the 21st Century,* 57.

4. Shavit, "The Victory Image," 57. Emphasis added.

5. Ibid., 56.

6. Note that as late as 1998, the term "operational documentation" did not yet appear within the *Dictionary of IDF Terminology.* Shai, *Hearts and Minds,* 91.

7. Shavit, *Media Strategy and Military Operations in the 21st Century,* 155. Emphasis added. Also see Sheafer and Shenhav, "Mediated Public Diplomacy in a New Era of Warfare."

8. Shavit, *Media Strategy and Military Operations in the 21st Century.*

9. Israel Defense Forces, "IDF Spokesperson's Unit."

10. Ibid.

11. "Aliza Landes Talks About the IDF Spokesperson Unit."

12. Darom, "Meet the Biggest PR Firm in the Middle East." Also see Omer-Man, "The Israeli Army's War on Consciousness."

13. Scholarly examples include: Gilboa, "Public Diplomacy" and Shoval, "Why Israel Lost the Hasbara War."

14. The 2006 Israeli war on Hezbollah was also included within the military's own list of media failures in a wartime context. See Chapter 2 for discussion.

15. Kuntsman and Stein, *Digital Militarism,* 15.

16. Beinin and Stein, "Histories and Futures of a Failed Peace."

17. B'Tselem, *Operation Defensive Shield.*

18. Amnesty International, *Shielded from Scrutiny*; Human Rights Watch, "Jenin: IDF Military Operations" and "Jenin War Crimes Investigation Needed."

19. B'Tselem, *Operation Defensive Shield.*

20. Amnesty International, *Shielded from Scrutiny;* Human Rights Watch, "Jenin: IDF Military Operations."

21. Human Rights Watch, "Jenin: IDF Military Operations."

22. See, for example, Shai, *Hearts and Minds.*

23. Steele, "The Tragedy of Jenin."

24. Har'el and Hass, cited in Reinhart, "Jenin—the Propoganda War."

25. King, "Israeli Court Lifts Ban on Film."

26. Bresheeth, "The Nakba Projected."

27. In 2013, a bill would be introduced in the Israeli parliament—the so-called Jenin-Jenin law—allowing Israeli soldiers to sue Palestinian activists for libel. The bill failed to make headway in 2013 but would advance in 2017. Kremnitzer and Fuchs, "The Jenin-Jenin Law." Also see Koron, "The Israelis 'Fighting to the Last Drop of Blood' Against Palestinian Documentary."

28. Reinhart, "Jenin—The Propaganda War"; Hadari and Turgeman, "Chaos Is the Message," 396. On Israel's hasbara legacy in the context of the military occupation, see Aouragh, "Hasbara 2.0"; Goodman, "Explaining the Occupation." For a review of hasbara strategies from the vantage of a former Israeli military spokesperson, see Shai, *Hearts and Minds.*

29. Diker, *Why Are Israel's Public Relations So Poor?*

30. Weimann, "The Media's Stance Towards the IDF," 159.

31. Shavit, *Media Strategy and Military Operations in the 21st Century*, 39; Nevo and Shur, *The IDF and the Press During Hostilities*, 26.

32. Reinhart, "Jenin— The Propaganda War."

33. Landsberg, "Who Is Afraid of Cameras?"

34. Hadari and Turgeman, "Chaos Is the Message," 396.

35. Nevo and Shur, *The IDF and the Press During Hostilities*, 26.

36. On the ten-year anniversary of Jenin, Israeli journalists returned to consider the event: Sheff, "A Decade Since the Battle of Jenin, 'The Myth of Jeningrad.'"

37. Ya'ari made these remarks at an academic symposium entitled *The IDF and the Press During Hostilities*, held on 4 June 2002 at the Israel Democracy Institute (Jerusalem), cosponsored by the Israeli military. As the publication notes, "[a] number of senior IDF officers participated, including the chief of staff." Nevo and Shur, *The IDF and the Press During Hostilities*, 26. Also see Goodman and Cummings, *The Battle of Jenin.*

38. Nevo and Shur, *The IDF and the Press During Hostilities*, 26.

39. Landsberg, "Who Is Afraid of Cameras?"

40. Shavit, *Media Strategy and Military Operations in the 21st Century*, 41.

41. Shavit notes that in this period, "operational documentation . . . wavered between the belief that the army should train combat solders to photograph operations designed for media needs and the view that photography specialists from the Spokesperson's Division should be embedded with fighting forces." Shavit, *Media Strategy and Military Operations in the 21st Century,* 41.

42. Ibid., 41–42.

43. Spokesperson's Division, Information and Hasbara, "Implementation of Conclusions," 12 May 2002 (distributed to the Spokesperson's Commanders Forum) (in Hebrew). Cited in Shavit, *Media Strategy and Military Operations in the 21st Century*, 49.

44. Reinhart, "Jenin—The Propaganda War."

45. Nevo and Shur, *The IDF and the Press During Hostilities*, 12

46. Ibid.

47. United Nations, *Report of the International Fact-Finding Mission to Investigate Violations of International Law* . . .

48. The Israeli assault on the *Mavi Marmara* has been heavily chronicled by scholars. See Allan and Brown, "The *Mavi Marmara* at the Frontlines of Web 2.0"; Bayoumi, *Midnight on the* Mavi Marmara; Blumenthal, *Goliath.* Adi Kuntsman and I discuss it in more detail in Kuntsman and Stein, *Another War Zone.*

49. "How *Free* Explains Israel's Flotilla Fail."

50. Harel et al., "Israel Navy Commandos."

51. Darom, "Meet the Biggest PR Firm in the Middle East."

52. For additional discussion, see Stein, "GoPro Occupation."

53. Darom, "Meet the Biggest PR Firm in the Middle East."

54. "How *Free* Explains Israel's Flotilla Fail."

55. Kuntsman and Stein, "Another War Zone."

56. Fyler, "IDF Says Enlisting Hackers."

57. See Chapter 3 for a discussion of these issues.

58. On Aliza Landes's role in this project, see Ahren, "My IDF Contact."

59. Their Facebook page would launch in August 2011. See Stein, "Inside Israel's Twitter War Room."

60. Lichtenstein, "Digital Diplomacy." Also see Stein, "The Other Wall."

61. Hadari and Turgeman, "Chaos Is the Message."

62. Stein, "StateTube."

63. Fyler, "IDF Says Enlisting Hackers."

64. Kuntsman and Stein, *Digital Militarism.*

65. For a chronicle of the day's events, see Joseph and Emiliano, "Palestinians and Internationals Attacked During Biking Trip in Jordan Valley."

66. Mackey, "Israeli Anger at Foreign 'Provocateurs' Boils Over."

67. Cohen, "IDF Chief Dismisses Officer Who Hit Danish Activist with Rifle."

68. Sharon, "The Officer Who Beat a Left-Wing Activist Will Return to the Post from Which He Was Removed"; Kaufman, "MK Ben-Ari: My Man of the Year Is 'Rifle Butting' Col. Shalom Eisner."

69. Ziv, "Severe Images."

70. Benari, "Israelis Believe Eisner's Dismissal Unjustified."

71. Flower, "Israel Dismisses Officer Videotaped Striking Activist."

72. Associated Press, "Video Captures Israeli Soldier's Attack on Danish Protester with Rifle."

73. Lavi, "The Anarchist Photographer Who Beat Israel."

74. Noybach, "Ben Dror Yemini Commentary of the Brigade Commander Incident."

75. Pines-Paz, "Suspending Officer Who Hit Danish Protester Isn't Enough." The author is a former member of the Israeli parliament from the Labor Party.

76. Ziv, "Severe Images."

77. Haber, "Guilty of Stupidity." Emphasis added.

78. Tausig, "Persistent Commitment."

79. Segal, "Don't Dismiss Eisner."

80. Yifrach, "Lieutenant Colonel Shalom Eisner and the Video War." Emphasis added.

81. Segal, "Don't Dismiss Eisner."

82. Pines-Paz, "Suspending Officer Who Hit Danish Protester Isn't Enough."

83. Katz, "Analysis of Eisner." Emphasis added.

84. Ibid.

85. Cohen, "IDF Chief Dismisses Officer Who Hit Danish Activist with Rifle."

86. Zeiger and Zaken, "Officer Blasts Top Brass."

87. Yemini, "The Blue-Eyed Poster Girl of Palestinian Propaganda."

88. Israel Defense Forces, "Rocks Can Kill."

89. "IDF Arrest 7 Children for Throwing Stones in Hebron."

90. B'Tselem, "Mass Arrest of Palestinian Children on Their Way to School in Hebron—at Least 5 Under the Age of Criminal Responsibility."

91. Ibid.

92. Levick, "What the Guardian Didn't Tell You About Palestinian Youths Arrested in Hebron."

93. Shavit, "The Victory Image," 56.

94. Ibid.

95. Ibid., 59.

96. Ibid.

97. Ibid,

98. Shavit, *Media Strategy and Military Operations in the 21st Century,* 41.

99. Associated Press. "IDF Soldiers May Take Cameras to War to Stave Off International Criticism."

100. Ibid.

101. Ibid.

102. Also see Darom, "Meet the Biggest PR Firm in the Middle East"; Kampinsky, "IDF Spokesperson"; Shavit, *Media Strategy and Military Operations in the 21st Century.*

103. Darom, "Meet the Biggest PR Firm in the Middle East."

104. Ibid. As the article notes, the story of a "flick of a finger" was belied by the numerous slow-downs that occurred within the operations room of the Gaza 2014 operation: "During the operation, the computer nearly crashed from a material's overload."

105. Darom, "Meet the Biggest PR Firm in the Middle East."

106. Kuntsman and Stein, *Digital Militarism*; Stein, "StateTube."

107. Kuntsman and Stein, *Digital Militarism.*

108. Landsberg, "Who Is Afraid of Cameras?"

109. Chamayou, *A Theory of the Drone.*

110. Morozov, *To Save Everything, Click Here.*

111. Stein, "Inside Israel's Twitter War Room."

CODA

1. For background, see Lockman and Beinin, *Intifada.*

2. Peretz, *Intifada,* 46-47, 50–52.

3. Schiff and Yaari, *Intifada,* 149, 159.

4. Al Haq, *Punishing a Nation.*

5. Al-Shaybani Society of International Law, *The Palestine Yearbook of International Law 1987–1988,* 144.

6. Fogelman, "Freeze Frame."

7. Schiff and Yaari, *Intifada,* 159. On IDF policy towards journalists and during the intifada, see ibid., 160–161.

8. Ibid., 160.

9. Ido Sela, interview with author, Tel Aviv, 22 September 2016.

10. Ibid.

11. Peretz, *Intifada*, 51.

12. Fogelman, "Freeze Frame."

13. Ibid.

14. Ibid.

15. "Israel Declines to Study Rabin Tie to Beatings."

16. *Hadashot* newspaper was an exception, particularly the work of Israeli photographers Miki Kratsman and Alex Levac. Miki Kratsman, interview with author, Jerusalem, 30 April 2013. Also see Azoulay, *Civil Contract of Photography*, 10–11, 393; Sela, "Genealogy of an Image in Public Consciousness."

17. Ezrahi, *Rubber Bullets*, 4.

18. Fairbanks, "The Battle to be Israel's Conscience." Emphasis added.

19. Galon, "We Thought the Israeli Public Should Know About the Occupation." When B'Tselem twenty years later launched its camera project in 2007, it would also speak in the language of exposure: "[W]hat I hope to achieve [is] a feeling that everything is being filmed, nothing is being done in the dark." *Internet and Democracy Blog*, "'Shooting Back' Project Empowers Palestinian Citizen Journalism."

20. Beinin and Stein, "Histories and Futures of a Failed Peace."

21. Weizman, *Forensic Architecture*.

22. Azoulay, *The Civil Contract of Photography*, 24.

23. See Keenan, "Publicity and Indifference."

24. Sliwinski, *Human Rights in Camera*, 135–136.

25. See, for example, Friedman, "The Last Remnants of the Israeli Left."

26. See, for example, Sheizaf, "We Are All One Staters Now."

27. See, for example, Beinart, "I No Longer Believe in a Jewish State."

28. Allen, *The Rise and Fall of Human Rights*.

29. B'Tselem, "The Occupation's Fig Leaf."

30. Galon, "We Thought the Israeli Public Should Know About the Occupation."

31. On the history of these connections, see Fischbach, *Black Power and Palestine*.

Bibliography

Abramson, Larry. "A West Bank Story, Told Through Palestinian Eyes." *All Things Considered: NPR* (20 February 2013). https://www.npr.org/2013/02/20/172505481/a-west-bank-story-told-through-palestinian-eyes

Abunimah, Ali. "'It's a Shame They Didn't Kill Him': Israelis React to Video of Soldiers Kicking Palestinian Child." *Electronic Intifada* (2 July 2012). http://electronicinti-fada.net/blogs/ali-abunimah/its-shame-they-didnt-kill-him-israelis-react-vid-eo-soldiers-kicking-palestinian?utm_source=EI+readers&utm_campaign=dofa611

AbuShanab, Anan. *Connection Interrupted: Israel's Control of the Palestinian ICT Infrastructure and Its Impact on Digital Rights.* 7amleh- The Arab Center for the Advancement of Social Media (2018). https://7amleh.org/wp-content/uploads/2019/01/Report_7amleh_English_final.pdf

Ackerman, Seth. "Al-Aqsa Intifada and the U.S. Media." *Journal of Palestine Studies* 30, no. 2 (2001): 61–74.

Adams, Cydney, "March 3, 1991: Rodney King Beating Caught on Video." *CBS News* (3 March 2016). https://www.cbsnews.com/news/march-3rd-1991-rodney-king-lapd-beating-caught-on-video/

Ahren, Raphael. "My IDF Contact." *Haaretz.com* (18 June 2010). https://www.haaretz.com/1.5135961

Akrivopoulou, Christina, and Nicolaos Garipidis. *Digital Democracy and the Impact of Technology on Governance and Politics: New Globalized Practices.* Hershey, PA: IGI Global, 2013.

Alazzeh, Ala. *Non-Violent Popular Resistance in the West Bank: The Case of the Popular Struggle Committees.* International Institute for Nonviolent Action, Birzeit University, February 2011.

Alexandrowicz, Ra'anan. "50 Years of Documentation: A Brief History of the Audio-Visual Documentation of the Israeli Occupation." In *Visual Imagery and Human Rights Practice* (pp. 15–34), edited by Sandra Ristovska and Monroe Price. Cham: Palgrave, 2018.

Al Haq. *Institutionalised Impunity: Israel's Failure to Combat Settler Violence in the Occupied Palestinian Territory* (26 November 2013). https://www.alhaq.org/publications/8072.html

———. *Punishing a Nation: Human Rights Violations During the Palestinian Uprising, December 1987–December 1988* (11 July 2011). https://www.alhaq.org/publications/8171.html

———. *Repression of Non-Violent Protest in the Occupied Palestinian Territory: Case Study on the Village of Al-Nabi Saleh* (10 December 2011). https://www.alhaq.org/publications/8078.html

Alimahomed-Wilson, Jake, and Spencer Louis Potiker. "The Logistics of Occupation: Israel's Colonial Suppression of Palestine's Goods Movement Infrastructure." *Journal of Labor and Society* 20, no. 4 (2017): 427–447.

"Aliza Landes Talks About the IDF Spokesperson Unit." *YouTube* (12 December 2009). https://www.youtube.com/watch?v=Dlgr2e_97cU

Allan, Diana, and Curtis Brown. "The *Mavi Marmara* at the Frontlines of Web 2.0." *Journal of Palestine Studies* 40, no. 1 (Autumn 2010): 63–77.

Allen, Lori. *The Rise and Fall of Human Rights: Cynicism and Politics in Occupied Palestine.* Stanford, CA: Stanford University Press, 2013.

———. "Martyr Bodies in the Media: Human Rights, Aesthetics, and the Politics of Immediation in the Palestinian Intifada." *American Ethnologist* 36, no. 1 (2009): 161–180.

Al-Shaybani Society of International Law. *The Palestine Yearbook of International Law 1987–1988*, edited by Anis F. Kassim. Netherlands: Kluwer Law International, 1988.

Altman, Yair. "War of Stones—the Settlers' Version." *Ynetnews.com* (1 April 2011). https://www.ynetnews.com/articles/0,7340,L-4009065,00.html

Amir, Meirav. "The Making of a Void Sovereignty: Political Implications of the Military Checkpoints in the West Bank." *Environment and Planning D: Society and Space* 1, no. 2 (2013): 227–244.

Amnesty International. *Operation "Cast Lead": 22 Days of Death and Destruction.*

London: Amnesty International Publications, 2009. https://www.amnesty.org/download/Documents/48000/mde150152009en.pdf

———. *Shielded from Scrutiny: IDF Violations in Jenin and Nablus* (4 November 2002). https://www.amnesty.org/en/documents/MDE15/143/2002/en/

Anderman, Nirit. "For 'Rock the Casbah' Helmer, a Director's Chair Became a Therapist's Couch." *Haaretz.com* (25 February 2013). https://www.haaretz.com/israel-news/culture/.premium-getting-therapy-in-the-director-s-chair-1.5231422

Aouragh, Miriyam. "Hasbara 2.0: Israel's Public Diplomacy in the Digital Age." *Middle East Critique* 25, no. 3 (2016): 271–297.

———. *Palestine Online: Transnationalism, the Internet and the Construction of Identity.* New York: I. B. Tauris, 2011.

Asheri, Ehud. "Power Play/Disappointing Finale." *Haaretz.com* (18 January 2007). https://www.haaretz.com/1.4951549

Ashkar, Antigona, and Zvi Shulman. *Means of Expulsion: Violence, Harassment and Lawlessness Against Palestinians in the Southern Hebron Hills.* Jerusalem: B'Tselem, 2005. https://www.btselem.org/download/200507_south_mount_hebron_eng.pdf

Associated Press. "IDF Soldiers May Take Cameras to War to Stave Off International Criticism." *Haaretz.com* (11 April 2011). https://www.haaretz.com/1.5150307

———. "Video Captures Israeli Soldier's Attack on Danish Protester with Rifle." *The Australian* (17 April 2012). https://www.theaustralian.com.au/news/world/video-captures-israeli-soldiers-attack-on-danish-protester-with-rifle/news-story/1090825ca5dd76ce6c478e8938b608d0

Association for Civil Rights in Israel. *Residential Searches ("Mapping"): An Illegal Pattern of Operations in the Occupied Territories* [in Hebrew] (25 February 2008).

Azoulay, Ariella. *The Civil Contract of Photography.* New York: Zone Books, 2008.

———. *Civil Imagination: A Political Ontology of Photography.* London and New York: Verso, 2012.

———. "Declaring the State of Israel: Declaring a State of War." *Critical Inquiry* 37, no. 2 (2011): 265–285. http://www.jstor.org/stable/10.1086/657293

———. "Getting Rid of the Distinction Between the Aesthetic and the Political." *Theory, Culture & Society* 27, no. 7–8 (2010): 239–262. https://doi.org/10.1177/0263276410384750

———. "The Imperial Condition of Photography in Palestine: Archives, Looting, and the Figure of the Infiltrator." *Visual Anthropology Review* 33, no. 1 (2017): 5–17.

———. *Potential History: Unthinking Imperialism.* London: Verso, 2019.

Azoulay, Ariella, and Adi Ophir. *The One-State Condition: Occupation and Democracy in Israel/Palestine.* Stanford, CA: Stanford University Press, 2012.

Baruch, Uzi. "Dahoah Halevi—B'Tselem's Allegations Are Baseless [in Hebrew]." *Channel 7* (21 July 2008). https://www.inn.co.il/News/News.aspx/177597

———. "Dahoah Halevi—B'Tselem's Video: The Open Questions [in Hebrew]." *News1: First Class* (25 July 2008).

Bat Haim, Hadassah. "Lost in the Old City." *Jerusalem Post* (11 June 1967).

Bayoumi, Moustafa, ed. *Midnight on the* Mavi Marmara: *The Attack on the Gaza Freedom Flotilla and How It Changed the Course of the Israel/Palestine Conflict.* New York: O/R Books, 2010.

BBC News. "Israel 'Sorry' for Killing Boy." *BBC News* (3 October 2000). http://news.bbc.co.uk/2/hi/world/middle_east/954703.stm

Behdad, Ali. *Camera Orientalis: Reflections on Photography of the Middle East.* Chicago: University of Chicago Press, 2016.

Behdad, Ali, and Luke Gartlan, eds. *Photography's Orientalism: New Essays on Colonial Representation.* Los Angeles: Getty Research Institute, 2013.

Beinart, Peter. "I No Longer Believe in a Jewish State." *New York Times* (8 July 2010). https://www.nytimes.com/2020/07/08/opinion/israel-annexation-two-state-solution.html

Beinin, Joel, and Rebecca L. Stein. "Histories and Futures of a Failed Peace." In *The Struggle for Sovereignty: Palestine and Israel, 1993–2005* (pp. 1–26), edited by Joel Beinin and Rebecca L. Stein. Stanford, CA: Stanford University Press, 2006.

———. *The Struggle for Sovereignty: Palestine and Israel, 1993–2005.* Stanford, CA: Stanford University Press, 2006.

Benari, Elad. "Israelis Believe Eisner's Dismissal Unjustified." *Israeli National News* (22 April 2012). http://www.israelnationalnews.com/News/News.aspx/154980#.T5PGutnrVRU

Ben-Hamo, Chetz. "A Few Words About the IDF's Decision to Prohibit Cellular Phones with Cameras [in Hebrew]." *Parshan* (23 July 2008). http://www.parshan.co.il/index2.php?id=2126&lang=HE

Ben-Naftali, Orna, and Noam Zamir. "Whose 'Conduct Unbecoming'?: The Shooting of a Handcuffed, Blindfolded Palestinian Demonstrator." *Journal of International Criminal Justice* 7, no. 1 (2009): 155–175.

Benziman, Uzi. "A Trick and a Shtick [in Hebrew]." *The Seventh Eye* (29 May 2014). https://www.the7eye.org.il/110932

Benziman, Yuval. "'Mom, I'm Home': Israeli Lebanon-War Films as Inadvertent Preservers of the National Narrative." *Israel Studies* 18, no. 3 (2013): 112–132.

Berda, Yael. "The Bureaucracy of the Occupation: An Introduction to the Permit Regime." Unpublished manuscript, 2012.

———. *Living Emergency: Israel's Permit Regime in the Occupied West Bank.* Stanford, CA: Stanford University Press, 2017.

Berdugo, Liat. *The Weaponized Camera in the Middle East: Videography, Aesthetics and Politics in Israel and Palestine.* London: I. B. Tauris, 2021.

Berger, Yotam. "Border Policeman Gets Plea Deal After Admitting Negligence in Shooting Death of Palestinian Teen." *Haaretz.com* (30 January 2017). http://www.haaretz.com/israel-news/.premium-1.768580. Haaretz

Bishara, Amahl A. *Back Stories: U.S. News Production and Palestinian Politics.* Stanford, CA: Stanford University Press, 2013.

———. "The Geopolitics of Press Freedoms in the Israeli-Palestinian Context." In *Media and Political Contestation in the Contemporary Arab World: A Decade of Change* (pp. 161–186), edited by Lena Jayyusi and Anne-Sofie Roald. New York: Palgrave Macmillan, 2015.

Blau, Uri, and Yotam Feldman. "How IDF Legal Experts Legitimized Strikes Involving Gaza Civilians." *Haaretz.com* (22 January 2009). https://www.haaretz.com/1.5065810

Blumenthal, Max. *Goliath: Life and Loathing in Greater Israel.* New York: Nation Books, 2013.

Bob, Yonah Jeremy. "IDF Finds Ambulance Driver Tampered with Knife After Shooting of Hebron Attacker." *Jerusalem Post* (1 June 2016). https://www.jpost.com/Arab-Israeli-Conflict/IDF-finds-ambulance-driver-moved-knife-closer-to-Hebron-attacker-after-shooting-455675

Boltanski, Luc. *Distant Suffering: Morality, Media and Politics.* Cambridge, UK: Cambridge University Press, 1999.

Bornstein, Avram. *Crossing the Green Line: Between the West Bank and Israel.* Philadelphia: University of Pennsylvania Press, 2002.

Breaking the Silence. *Our Harsh Logic: Israeli Soldiers' Testimonies from the Occupied Territories, 2000–2010.* New York: Henry Holt, 2012.

———. *Soldiers' Testimonies from Operation Cast Lead, Gaza 2009.* Jerusalem: Breaking the Silence, 2009.

———. "They're Familiar with It as Mapping, Because It's Done All the Time" (2013). https://www.breakingthesilence.org.il/testimonies/database/227393

Breiner, Josh. "Cellular Phone with a Camera? Not at Our Base [in Hebrew]." *Walla News* (21 July 2008). http://news.walla.co.il/?w=/9/1316618

———. "Forensics: Documentation of the Ni'lin Protestor Authentic [in Hebrew]." *Walla News* (6 January 2011). https://news.walla.co.il/item/1776914

———. "Ni'lin Shooting: The Battalion Commander Will Not Lose His Ranks [in Hebrew]." *Walla News* (27 January 2011). https://news.walla.co.il/item/1785582

Bresheeth, Haim. "The Nakba Projected: Recent Palestinian Cinema." *Third Text* 20, no. 3–4 (2006): 499–509.

Brown, John. "IDF Soldiers Who Killed Armed Palestinian Set for Community Service." *+972 Magazine* (19 December 2016). https://972mag.com/idf-soldiers-who-killed-un-armed-palestinian-set-for-community-service/123801/

B'Tselem. "The Army Must Internalize the Gravity of the Ni'lin Shooting Incident" (27 January 2011). https://www.btselem.org/firearms/20110127_nilin_shooting_sentence#Background

———. *B'Tselem Annual Activity Report: 2007* (May 2007). https://www.btselem.org/download/2007_activity_report_eng.pdf

———. "B'Tselem's Initial Findings on Nakba Day Incident at Bitunya: Grave Suspicion That Forces Willfully Killed Two Palestinians, Injured Two Others" (20 May 2014). https://www.btselem.org/releases/20140520_bitunya_killings_on_nakba_day

———. "The Film *Smile, and the World Will Smile Back* Won the Best Short Film Award at the Milano Film Festival" (15 September 2014). https://www.btselem.org/press_releases/20140915_btselem_documentary_wins_at_milano_film_festival

———. "Investigation into Border Police Violence Against Protesters in a-Nabi Saleh" (15 May 2011). https://www.btselem.org/video/20110513_border_police_violence_against_protesters_abi_saleh

———. "Israeli Military Must Permit Video Documentation in Occupied Territories and Conduct Investigation of Attack on Photographers" (18 December 2012). https://www.btselem.org/press_releases/20121218_allow_video_documentation

———. "Israeli Soldiers Continue Firing Tear Gas Canisters Directly at Human Targets, Despite the Army's Denials" (22 April 2012). https://www.btselem.org/firearms/20120422_direct_firing_of_tear_gas_continues

———. "Khirbet Susiya—a Village Under Threat of Demolition" (19 August 2012). https://www.btselem.org/south_hebron_hills/susiya

———. "Mass Arrest of Palestinian Children on Their Way to School in Hebron—at Least 5 Under the Age of Criminal Responsibility" (20 March 2013). https://www.btselem.org/press_releases/20130320_minors_detained_in_hebron

———. "The Occupation's Fig Leaf: Israel's Military Law Enforcement System as a

Whitewash Mechanism" (May 2016). https://www.btselem.org/publications/sum-maries/201605_occupations_fig_leaf

———. *Operation Defensive Shield: Soldiers' Testimonies, Palestinian Testimonies* (2002). https://www.btselem.org/download/200207_defensive_shield_eng.pdf

———. "Settlers Vandalize Property as Revenge for Stone Throwing—Police Do Not Detain Them" (8 December 2014). https://www.btselem.org/press_re-leases/20141208_settlers_throwing_stones_in_hebron

———. "Show of Force: Israeli Military Conduct in Weekly Demonstrations in a-Nabi Saleh" (September 2011). https://www.btselem.org/publications/summa-ries/201109_show_of_force

———. "State-Backed Settler Violence" (11 November 2017). https://www.btselem.org/settler_violence

———. "Three Appeals Submitted Regarding Closure of 3 Investigations of Police Officers" (28 December 2014). https://www.btselem.org/accountability/20120605_appeals_on_closing_of_files

———. "Two Settlers Arrested on Suspicion of Attack on Palestinian Shepherds" (8 June 2008). https://www.btselem.org/settler_violence/20080608_settler_as-sault_shepherd_in_khirbet_susiya

———. "Use of Live Ammunition Confirmed in Nawarah Shooting" (12 June 2014). https://www.btselem.org/ota/142096

———. "Video Footage Shows the Army Failed in Its Duty to Protect Palestinians from Settler Attacks" (2 May 2013). https://www.btselem.org/settler_violence/20130502_military_not_protecting_palestinians_from_vengeful_settler

———. "Video Provided by B'Tselem Leads to Indictment of Three Settlers for Prop-erty Damage and Threats in a-Lubban a-Sharqiyah" (28 February 2012). https://www.btselem.org/settler_violence/20120228_settlers_charged_with_vandaliz-ing_property

———. "Video: Soldier Executes Palestinian Lying Injured on Ground After the Latter Stabbed a Soldier in Hebron" (24 March 2016). https://www.btselem.org/video/20160324_soldier_executes_palestinian_attacker_in_hebron

———. "Visual: Settlers Attack Palestinian Shepherds." *YouTube* (15 June 2008). https://www.youtube.com/watch?v=XHhECvN2kQI

———. "Who Is B'Tselem? [in Hebrew]." *YouTube* (22 November 2009). https://www.youtube.com/watch?v=YSd_3E18oWo&feature=relmfu

Browne, Simone. *Dark Matters: On the Surveillance of Blackness*. Durham, NC: Duke University Press, 2015

Buzard, James. *The Beaten Track: European Tourism, Literature, and the Ways to "Culture," 1800–1918.* Oxford and New York: Oxford University Press, 1993.

Caldwell, William B., IV, Dennis M. Murphy, and Anton Menning. "Learning to Leverage New Media: The Israeli Forces in Recent Conflicts." *Military Review* 89, no. 3 (May–June 2009): 2–10.

Caspit, Ben. "Muhammad Al-Dura: The Boy Who Wasn't Really Killed." *Jerusalem Post* (12 May 2013). https://www.jpost.com/Middle-East/Muhammad-Al-Dura-The-boy-who-was-not-really-killed-312930

Chamayou, Gregoire. *A Theory of the Drone,* translated by Janet Lloyd. New York: The New Press, 2015.

Chaudhary, Zahid R. *Afterimage of Empire: Photography in Nineteenth-Century India.* Minneapolis: University of Minnesota Press, 2012.

CNN. "Outrage over Teens' Death Growing." Transcript. CNN.com (22 May 2014). http://transcripts.cnn.com/TRANSCRIPTS/1405/22/wolf.02.html

Cohen, Akiba A., Dafna Lemish, and Amit Schejter. *The Wonder Phone in the Land of Miracles: Mobile Telephony in Israel.* New York: Hampton Press, 2008.

Cohen, Dan. "Elor Azarya, King of Israel." *Mondoweiss* (4 May 2016). https://mondoweiss.net/2016/05/azarya-king-israel/

Cohen, Gili. "Citing IDF Failure to Bring Soldiers to Justice, B'Tselem Stops Filing Complaints on Abuse of Palestinians." *Haaretz.com* (25 May 2016). https://www.haaretz.com/israel-news/.premium-btselem-gives-up-on-idf-justice-1.5387167

———. "Hebron Shooter Elor Azaria Sentenced to 1.5 Years for Shooting Wounded Palestinian Attacker." *Haaretz.com* (21 February 2017). https://www.haaretz.com/israel-news/hebron-shooter-sentenced-for-shooting-wounded-palestinian-attacker-1.5489979

———. "IDF Chief Dismisses Officer Who Hit Danish Activist with Rifle." *Haaretz.com* (18 April 2012). https://www.haaretz.com/1.5215082

———. "Israel's New Ambiguity: Where Are Its Drones Headed?" *Haaretz.com* (22 October 2016). https://www.haaretz.com/israel-news/.premium-israel-s-new-ambiguity-where-are-its-drones-headed-1.5451883

Cohen, Gili, Barak Ravid, and Jonathan Lis. "Thousands Rally for Soldier Who Shot Palestinian Assailant; Netanyahu Urges Calm." *Haaretz.com* (19 April 2016). https://www.haaretz.com/israel-news/.premium-thousands-rally-for-soldier-who-shot-palestinian-assailant-1.5436631

Cohen-Friedman, Naama. "B'Tselem Hands Naalin Shooting Tape to Police." *Ynetnews.*

com (28 November 2010). https://www.ynetnews.com/articles/0,7340,L-3991122,00. html

Committee to Protect Journalists. *At Risk: Covering the Intifada* (26 June 2001). https:// cpj.org/reports/2001/06/israeljun01.php

———. *CPJ Names World's Worst Places to Be a Journalist* (3 May 2002). https://ifex. org/cpj-names-worlds-worst-places-to-be-a-journalist/

Cook, David. *Martyrdom in Islam.* Cambridge, UK: Cambridge University Press, 2007.

Cook, Jonathan. "Elor Azaria Case: 'No Hope of Equality Before the Law.'" *Al-Jazeera* (5 January 2017). https://www.aljazeera.com/indepth/features/2017/01/elor-azaria-case-hope-equality-law-170105070408594.html

———. "Israeli Army Targets Family over Brutality Film." *Jonathan-Cook.net* (2008). http://www.jonathan-cook.net/2008–09–02/israeli-army-targets-family-over-brutality-film/

Crary, Jonathan. *Techniques of the Observer: On Vision and Modernity in the Nineteenth Century.* Cambridge, MA: MIT Press, 1992.

Dana, Joseph. "14 Year Old Child Arrested in Night Raid in Nabi Saleh." *+972 Magazine* (23 January 2011). https://www.972mag.com/child-arrested-in-night-raid-in-nabi-saleh/

Darom, Naomi. "Meet the Biggest PR Firm in the Middle East: IDF Spokesman's Unit." *Haaretz.com* (31 December 2014). https://www.haaretz.com/.premium-idf-the-world-s-largest-pr-agency-not-the-best-1.5330072

"The Day That Was [in Hebrew]." Channel 10 (10 May 2011). Television broadcast.

Dayagi, Yoav. "The IDF's Exposure in the Media During the Second Lebanese War and Operation Cast Lead [in Hebrew]." *Machbash* (14 March 2012). http://machbash. co.il

Dayan, Aryeh. "Two Tales of One City." *Haaretz.com* (17 January 2007). https://www. haaretz.com/1.4951516

Della Ratta, Donatella. *Shooting a Revolution: Visual Media and Warfare in Syria.* Digital Barricades: Interventions in Digital Culture and Politics. London: Pluto Press, 2018.

Derfner, Larry. "Day of Catastrophe for 'Pallywood' Conspiracy Theorists." *+972 Magazine* (13 November 2014). https://www.972mag.com/nakba-day-indeed-for-pallywood-conspiracy-freaks/98735/

———. "Image Makers." *Jerusalem Post* (2 October 2008). https://www.jpost.com/ Magazine/Features/Image-makers-116199

Derian, James Der. *Virtuous War: Mapping the Military-Industrial-Media-Entertainment Network.* New York: Routledge, 2009.

Diamond, Eitan. "Killing on Camera: Visual Evidence, Denial and Accountability in Armed Conflict." *London Review of International Law* 6, no. 3 (2018): 361–390.

———. "Law Trumps Hate? Enforcing Legal Constraints on Use of Force in Armed Conflict in the Face of Literal, Interpretive and Implicatory Denial." Unpublished manuscript, 2017.

Diker, Dan. *Why Are Israel's Public Relations So Poor?* Jerusalem Center for Public Affairs (15 October–1 November 2002). http://www.jcpa.org/jl/vp487.htm

Dor, Daniel. *Intifada Hits the Headlines: How the Israeli Press Misreported the Outbreak of the Second Palestinian Uprising.* Bloomington: Indiana University Press, 2004.

Duvdevani, Shmulik. "How I Shot the War—Ideology and Accountability in Personal Israeli War Documentaries." *Studies in Documentary Film* 7, no. 3 (2013): 279–294.

Dvory, Nir. "IDF Soldier Shot a Cuffed Palestinian from Zero Range [in Hebrew]." *Ynet. com* (20 July 2008). http://reshet.ynet.co.il/%D7%97%D7%93%D7%A9%D7%95%D7%AA/News/Politics/Security/Article,5260.aspx

Eastwood, James. *Ethics as a Weapon of War: Militarism and Morality in Israel.* London: Cambridge University Press, 2017.

Eder, Jens, and Charlotte Klonk, eds. *Image Operations: Visual Media and Political Conflict.* Manchester, UK: Manchester University Press, 2017.

Eglash, Ruth, and William Booth. "Israeli NGOs Decry 'Deeply Anti-Democratic Move' as New Law Approved." *Washington Post* (12 July 2016). https://www.washington-post.com/world/israeli-ngos-decry-deeply-anti-democratic-move-as-new-law-approved/2016/07/12/a07b1bdb-a431-4fce-b76d-d0a35dfca519_story.html

Ehrenreich, Ben. *The Way to the Spring: Life and Death in Palestine.* New York: Penguin Press, 2016.

Eishton. "Making a Murderer . . . Only Criminally Negligent: How Israel Turned a Serial Killer of Palestinians into a Clumsy Hero" *Eishton Abroad* (4 February 2017). https://eishtonabroad.wordpress.com/2017/02/04/making-a-murderer-only-crim-inally-negligent-how-israel-turned-a-serial-killer-of-palestinians-into-a-clum-sy-hero/#C7

———. "Pallywood: The Dark Matter of the Zionist Universe." *+972 Magazine* (17 February 2017). https://972mag.com/pallywood-the-dark-matter-of-the-zionist-universe/125274/

Ezrahi, Yaron. *Rubber Bullets: Power and Conscience in Modern Israel.* Berkeley: University of California Press, 1998.

Fairbanks, Eve. "The Battle to Be Israel's Conscience." *The Guardian* (12 March 2015).

Faulkner, Simon, and David Reeb. *Between States.* London: Black Dog Publishing, 2015.

———. "On Israel/Palestine and the Politics of Visibility." In *Immigrant Protest: Politics, Aesthetics, and Everyday Dissent* (pp. 147–168), edited by Katarzyna Marciniak and Imogen Tyler. Albany: State University of New York Press, 2014.

Feigenson, Neal, and Christina Spiesel. *Law on Display: The Digital Transformation of Legal Persuasion and Judgment.* New York: New York University Press, 2009.

Feldman, Allen. *Archives of the Insensible: Of War, Photopolitics, and Dead Memory.* Chicago: University of Chicago Press, 2015.

Feuerstein, Ofir. *Ghost Town: Israel's Separation Policy and Forced Eviction of Palestinians from the Center of Hebron.* B'Tselem and the Association for Civil Rights in Israel, 2007. https://www.btselem.org/download/200705_hebron_eng.pdf

Fineman, Mia. *Faking It: Manipulated Photography Before Photoshop.* New York: Metropolitan Museum of Art, 2012.

Fischbach, Michael R. *Black Power and Palestine: Transnational Countries of Color.* Stanford, CA: Stanford University Press, 2019.

———. "British and Zionist Data Gathering on Palestinian Arab Landowners and Population During the Mandate." In *Surveillance and Control in Israel/Palestine: Population, Territory, and Power* (pp. 297–312), edited by David Lyon, Elia Zureik, and Yasmeen Abu-Laban. London: Routledge, 2011.

Fitsanakis, Joseph, and Ian Allen. *Cell Wars: The Changing Landscape of Communications Intelligence.* Research Institute for European and American Studies (May 2009).

5 Broken Cameras. Directed and produced by Emad Burnat, Guy Davidi, et al. New York: Kino Lorber, 2012. Videorecording.

"Five in the Evening." Channel 10 (5 August, 2008). Television broadcast.

Fleishman, Itamar. "Soldiers: Our Hands Are Tied" (10 December 2012). https://www.ynetnews.com/articles/0,7340,L-4317755,00.html

Flower, Kevin. "Israel Dismisses Officer Videotaped Striking Activist." *CNN.com* (18 April 2012). https://www.cnn.com/2012/04/18/world/meast/israel-activist-video/index.html

Fogelman, Shay. "Freeze Frame." *Haaretz.com* (14 January 2011). https://www.haaretz.com/1.5108167

Forensic Architecture. "The Killing of Nadeem Nawara and Mohammed Abu Daher." *Forensic Architecture.org* (20 November 2014). https://forensic-architecture.org/investigation/the-killing-of-nadeem-nawara-and-mohammed-abu-daher

Friedman, Matti. "The Last Remnants of the Israeli Left." New York Times (27 April 2020). https://www.nytimes.com/2020/04/27/opinion/labor-likud-knesset-israel.html

Frykberg, Mel. "Palestinian Village Takes on Israeli Military." *Electronic Intifada* (8 July 2008). https://electronicintifada.net/content/palestinian-village-takes-is-raeli-military/7610

Fyler, Boaz. "IDF Says Enlisting Hackers." *Ynetnews.com* (2 August 2011). https://www.ynetnews.com/articles/0,7340,L-4025751,00.html

———. "Physicist: Naalin Shooting Tape Doctored." *Ynetnews.com* (1 June 2011). https://www.ynetnews.com/articles/0,7340,L-4010082,00.html

Galdi, David Sarna. "Everyone's Favorite Murderer: Looking at the Cases of OJ Simpson and Elor Azaria." *Jerusalem Post* (2 August 2017). https://www.jpost.com/Opinion/Everyones-favorite-murderer-501446

Galon, Zehava. "We Thought the Israeli Public Should Know About the Occupation. How Wrong Were We." *Haaretz.com* (10 December 2019). https://www.haaretz.com/israel-news/.premium-we-believed-it-was-enough-for-the-israeli-public-to-know-1.8252269

Gavish, Dov. "An Account of an Unrealized Aerial Cadastral Survey in Palestine Under the British Mandate." *Geographical Journal* 153, no. 1 (1987): 93–98.

Gertz, Nurith. "The Medium That Mistook Itself for War: 'Cherry Season' in Comparison with 'Ricochets' and 'Cup Final.'" *Israel Studies* 4, no. 1 (1999): 153–174.

Gilboa, Eytan. "Public Diplomacy: The Missing Component in Israel's Foreign Policy." *Israel Affairs* 12, no. 4 (2006): 715–747.

Ginsburg, Mitch. "Nahum Shahaf's Relentless Muhammad Al-Dura Dissent." *Times of Israel* (4 April 2013). https://www.timesofisrael.com/nahum-shahafs-relent-less-muhammad-al-dura-dissent/

Ginsburg, Ruthie. *And You Will Serve as Eyes for Us: Israeli Human Rights Organizations as Seen Through the Camera's Eye* [in Hebrew]. Tel Aviv: Resling Publishing House, 2014.

———. "Emancipation and Collaboration: A Critical Examination of Human Rights Video Advocacy." *Theory, Culture & Society* (2019).

———. "Gendered Visual Activism: Documenting Human Rights Abuse from the Private Sphere." *Current Sociology* 66, no. 1 (2018): 38–55.

———. *"Taking Pictures over Soldiers' Shoulders: Reporting on Human Rights Abuse from the Israeli Occupied Territories." Journal of Human Rights 10, no. 1 (2011): 17–33.*

Gitelman, Lisa, and Geoffrey B. Pingree. *New Media, 1740–1915.* Cambridge, MA: MIT Press, 2003.

Goodman, Giora. "Explaining the Occupation: Israeli Hasbara and the Occupied

Territories in the Aftermath of the June 1967 War." *Journal of Israeli History* 36, no. 1 (2017): 71–93.

Goodman, Hirsh, and Jonathan Cummings, eds. *The Battle of Jenin: A Case Study in Israel's Communications Strategy.* Tel Aviv: Jaffee Center for Strategic Studies, Tel Aviv University, 2003.

Gordon, Neve. "Human Rights as a Security Threat: Lawfare and the Campaign Against Human Rights NGOs." *Law & Society Review* 48, no. 2 (2014): 311–344.

———. "Israel's Emergence as a Homeland Security Capital." In *Surveillance and Control in Israel/Palestine: Population, Territory and Power* (pp. 199–218), edited by Elia Zureik, David Lyon, and Yasmeen Abu-Laban. London: Routledge, 2011.

———. *Israel's Occupation.* Berkeley and Los Angeles: University of California Press, 2008.

———. *The Political Economy of Israel's Homeland Security Industry.* The Surveillance Project, Queens University (28 April 2009). https://www.sscqueens.org/sites/sscqueens.org/files/The%20Political%20Economy%20of%20Israel%E2%80%99s%20Homeland%20Security.pdf

Graham, Stephen. *Disrupted Cities: When Infrastructure Fails.* New York and London: Routledge, 2010.

Grassiani, Erella. "Militarizing the Enemy's home, Israel/Palestine: A Photo Essay." *Critical Planning* (Summer 2012): 108–114.

———. *Soldiering Under Occupation: Processes of Numbing Among Israeli Soldiers in the Al-Aqsa Intifada.* New York: Berghahn Books, 2013.

Grassiani, Erella, and Desiree Verweij. "The Disciplinary Gaze of the Camera's Eye: Soldiers' Conscience and Moral Responsibility." *Journal of Military and Strategic Studies* 15, no. 3 (2014).

Green, Stuart A. *Cognitive Warfare.* Master's thesis, Joint Military Intelligence College, 2008. http://www.theaugeanstables.com/wp-content/uploads/2014/04/Green-Cognitive-Warfare.pdf

Greenberg, Hanan. "Soldiers Were Beaten by Their Commanders Like 'Ducks in a Firing Range' [in Hebrew]." *Ynet.com* (17 July 2009). http://www.ynet.co.il/articles/0,7340,L-3748132,00.html

———. "Top Officer: Activity Efficient for Limited Amount of Time." *Ynetnews.com* (13 January 2009). https://www.ynetnews.com/articles/0,7340,L-3655094,00.html

Gregory, Derek. *The Colonial Present: Afghanistan, Palestine, Iraq.* Oxford, UK: Blackwell Publishing, 2004.

Gregory, Sam. "Ubiquitous Witnesses: Who Creates the Evidence and the Live(D)

Experience of Human Rights Violations?" *Information, Communication & Society* 18, no. 11 (2015): 1378–1392.

Grinberg, Hanan. "Ni'lin Shooting: The Battalion Commander and the Soldier Were Convicted of Serious Offenses [in Hebrew]." *Ynet.com* (15 July 2010). https://www.ynet.co.il/articles/0,7340,L-3920174,00.html

Grinberg, Omri. "Facsimileing the State: The Bureaucracy of Document Transmission in Israeli Human Rights NGOs." *Anthropologica* 60, no. 1 (May 2018): 259–273.

Gross, Aeyal. *The Writing on the Wall: Rethinking the International Law of Occupation.* Cambridge, UK: Cambridge University Press, 2017.

Grundberg, Andy. "Point and Shoot: How the Abu Ghraib Images Redefine Photography." *The American Scholar* (1 December 2004). https://theamericanscholar.org/point-and-shoot/#.VsE_9JPEWRs

Gürsel, Zeynep Devrim. *Image Brokers: Visualizing World News in the Age of Digital Circulation.* Oakland: University of California Press, 2016.

Haber, Eitan. "Guilty of Stupidity." *Ynetnews.com* (17 April 2012). https://www.ynetnews.com/articles/0,7340,L-4217344,00.html.

Hadari, Gal, and Asaf Turgeman. "Chaos Is the Message: The Crisis of Israeli Public Diplomacy." *Israel Journal of Foreign Affairs* 10, no. 3 (2017): 393–404.

Halberstam, Judith, and Jack Halberstam. *The Queer Art of Failure.* Durham, NC: Duke University Press, 2011.

Hammami, Rema. "Destabilizing Mastery and the Machine: Palestinian Agency and Gendered Embodiment at Israeli Military Checkpoints." *Current Anthropology* 60 (2019): 87–97. https://www.journals.uchicago.edu/doi/abs/10.1086/699906

———. "Precarious Politics: The Activism of 'Bodies That Count' (Aligning with Those That Don't) in Palestine's Colonial Frontier." In *Vulnerability in Resistance* (pp. 167–190), edited by Judith Butler, Zeynep Gambetti, and Leticia Sabsay. Durham, NC: Duke University Press, 2016.

Hammami, Rema, and Salim Tamari. "The Second Uprising: End or New Beginning?" *Journal of Palestine Studies* 30, no. 2 (2001): 5–25.

Hamo, Ohed. "New Documentation Proves: Rubber Bullets in Beitunia [in Hebrew]." *Mako.co.* (22 May 2014). https://www.mako.co.il/news-military/security/Article-50bafcbe6f42641004.htm

Handel, Ariel. "Beyond Good and Evil—The Syndrome: Shame and Responsibility in Soldiers' Testimonies." *Theory and Criticism* 32 (2008): 45–69.

Handel, Ariel, and Hilla Dayan. "Multilayered Surveillance in Israel/Palestine: Dialectics of Inclusive Exclusion." *Surveillance and Society* 15, no. 3–4 (2017).

Harel, Amos. "UN Backtracks on Claim That Deadly IDF Strike Hit Gaza School." *Haaretz.com* (3 February 2009). https://www.haaretz.com/1.5070297

Harel, Amos, Avi Issacharoff, and Anshel Pfeffer. "Israel Navy Commandos: Gaza Flotilla Activists Tried to Lynch Us." *Haaretz.com* (31 May 2010). https://www.haaretz.com/1.5127050

Harkov, Lahav. "Likud Deputy Minister Enlists Elor Azaria in Primary Campaign." *Jerusalem Post* (23 January 2019). https://www.jpost.com/israel-elections/likud-deputy-minister-enlists-elor-azaria-in-primary-campaign-578417

Harrison, Donald H. "Tazpit News Agency Founder Amotz Eyal Tells of Israelis' Fight for Balanced News Coverage in Judea and Samaria." *San Diego Jewish World* (4 May 2014). http://www.sdjewishworld.com/2014/05/04/tazpit-news-agency-founder-amotz-eyal-tells-israelis-fight-balanced-news-coverage-judea-samaria/

Hassen, Nir. "Palestinian Dies After Hit by Tear Gas Canister." *Haaretz.com* (10 December 2011). https://www.haaretz.com/1.5218242

Hatoum, Nayrouz Abu. "Framing Visual Politics: Photography of the Wall in Palestine." *Visual Anthropology Review* 33, no. 1 (2017): 18–27.

Helman, Sara. "Challenging the Israeli Occupation Through Testimony and Confession: The Case of Anti-Denial SMOs Machsom Watch and Breaking the Silence." *International Journal of Politics, Culture, and Society* 28, no. 4 (2015): 377–394.

Hirshfeld, Rachel. "Video: National Victory, Blow to Arab Propaganda." *Arutz Sheva* (19 February 2012). http://www.israelnationalnews.com/News/News.aspx/152906

Hochberg, Gil. "Soldiers as Filmmakers: On the Prospect of 'Shooting War' and the Question of Ethical Spectatorship." *Screen* 54, no. 1 (2013): 44–61.

———. *Visual Occupations: Violence and Visibility in a Conflict Zone.* Durham, NC: Duke University Press, 2015.

Hochman, Brian. *Savage Preservation: The Ethnographic Origins of Modern Media Technology.* Minneapolis: University of Minnesota Press, 2014.

Hoffman, Tzahi. "57% of Israelis Have Smartphones." *Globes* (10 June 2013). http://www.globes.co.il/en/article-1000851195

"How *Free* Explains Israel's Flotilla Fail." *Wired* (2 June 2010). http://www.wired.com/2010/06/how-free-explains-israels-flotilla-fiasco/

Human Rights Watch. "Israel: Killing of Children Apparent War Crime" (9 June 2014). https://www.hrw.org/news/2014/06/09/israel-killing-children-apparent-war-crime

———. "Jenin: IDF Military Operations" (May 2002). https://www.hrw.org/reports/2002/israel3/israel0502.pdf

———. "Jenin War Crimes Investigation Needed" (2 May 2002). https://www.hrw.

org/news/2002/05/02/israel/occupied-territories-jenin-war-crimes-investiga-tion-needed

Huss, Michal. "Mapping the Occupation: Performativity and the Precarious Israeli Identity." *Geopolitics* 24, no. 3 (2019): 756.

"IDF Arrest 7 Children for Throwing Stones in Hebron." *Ynetnews.com* (20 March 2013). https://www.ynetnews.com/articles/0,7340,L-4359014,00.html

International Solidarity Movement. "Villages of Urif, Burin and Asira Violently Attacked by Settlers" (1 May 2013). https://palsolidarity.org/2013/05/villag-es-of-urif-burin-and-asira-violently-attacked-by-settlers/

Internet and Democracy Blog. "'Shooting Back' Project Empowers Palestinian Citizen Journalism" (6 August 2008). https://blogs.harvard.edu/idblog/2008/08/06/shoot-ing-back-project-empowers-palestinian-citizen-journalism/

In the Image: Palestinian Women Capture the Occupation. Directed by Judith Montell and Emmy Scharlatt. New York: Kino Lorber, 2016.

"Israel Declines to Study Rabin Tie to Beatings." *New York Times* (12 July 1990). https://www.nytimes.com/1990/07/12/world/israel-declines-to-study-rabin-tie-to-beat-ings.html

Israel Defense Forces. "IDF Spokesperson's Unit" (n.d.). https://idfspokesperson.word-press.com/about/idf-spokespersons-unit/

———. *A Rare Documentation: The Triumph of the Yom Kippur War Through a Camera Lens* (5 November 2014). https://www.idf.il/en/minisites/wars-and-operations/a-rare-documentation-the-triumph-of-the-yom-kippur-war-through-a-camera-lens/

———. "Rocks Can Kill" (n.d.). https://www.idfblog.com/2013/03/18/rocks-can-kill/

"It's All Talk, with Yaron Dekel [in Hebrew]." Reshet Beit (21 July 2008). Radio broadcast.

Jabareen, Hassan, and Suhad Bishara. "The Jewish Nation-State Law." *Journal of Pal-estine Studies* 48, no. 2 (2019): 43–57.

Jay, Martin, and Sumathi Ramaswamy, eds. *Empires of Vision: A Reader.* Durham, NC: Duke University Press, 2014.

Jerusalem Post Staff. "Virtual Existence." Jerusalem Post (25 January 2007). https://www.jpost.com/magazine/features/virtual-existence

Johnson, Charles. "More Death Cult Propaganda." *LittleGreenFootballs.com* (10 August 2006). http://littlegreenfootballs.com/article/22036_More_Death_Cult_Propa-ganda/comments/

Jones, Craig A. "Frames of Law: Targeting Advice and Operational Law in the Israeli Military." *Environment and Planning D: Society and Space* 33, no. 4 (2015): 676–696.

———. "Traveling Law: Targeted Killing, Lawfare, and the Deconstruction of the

Battlefield." In *American Studies Encounters the Middle East* (pp. 207–240), edited by Alex Lubin and Marwan Krady. Chapel Hill, NC: University of North Carolina Press, 2016.

Joseph and Emiliano. "Palestinians and Internationals Attacked During Biking Trip in Jordan Valley." *International Solidarity Movement* (15 April 2012). https://pal-solidarity.org/2012/04/palestinians-and-internationals-attacked-during-bik-ing-trip-in-jordan-valley/

Junka-Aikio, Laura. "Late Modern Subjects of Colonial Occupation: Mobile Phones and the Rise of Neoliberalism in Palestine." *New Formations* (2012): 93–115.

JustVision. "Yehuda Shaul" (2008). https://justvision.org/portrait/1391/interview

Kahana, Ariel. "Liberman: 'There Is No Need to Investigate Beitunia Incidents' [in Hebrew]." *NRG* (21 May 2014). https://www.makorrishon.co.il/nrg/online/1/ART2/580/502.html

Kampinsky, Yoni. ""IDF Spokesperson: More Combative, More Networked [in Hebrew]." *Channel 7* (15 October 2013). https://www.inn.co.il/News/News.aspx/263749

Kane, Alex. "How Israel Became a Hub for Surveillance Technology." *The Intercept* (17 October 2016). https://theintercept.com/2016/10/17/how-israel-be-came-a-hub-for-surveillance-technology/

Kaplan, Caren. *Aerial Aftermaths: Wartime from Above.* Durham, NC: Duke University Press, 2018.

———. "Precision Targets: GPS and the Militarization of U.S. Consumer Identity." *American Quarterly* 58, no. 3 (2006): 693–713.

Katriel, Tamar. "Accounts and Rebuttals in an Israeli Discourse of Dissent." *Journal of Multicultural Discourses* 13, no. 1 (2018): 1–16.

———. "Showing and Telling: Photography Exhibitions in Israeli Discourses of Dissent." In *Curating Difficult Knowledge* (pp. 109–127), edited by Erica Lehrer, Cynthia E. Milton, and Monica Eileen Patterson. London: Palgrave Macmillan, 2011.

Katriel, Tamar, and Nimrod Shavit. "Between Moral Activism and Archival Memory: The Testimonial Project of 'Breaking the Silence.'" In *On Media Memory* (pp. 77–87), edited by M. Neiger, O. Meyers, and E. Zandberg. London: Palgrave Macmillan, 2011.

Katz, Yaakov. "Analysis of Eisner: IDF Fails to Grasp Digital Media." *Jerusalem Post* (23 April 2012). https://www.jpost.com/Defense/Analysis-of-Eisner-IDF-fails-to-grasp-digital-media

Katz, Yaakov, and Amir Bohbot. *The Weapon Wizards: How Israel Became a High-Tech Military Superpower.* New York: St. Martin's Press, 2017.

Kaufman, Ami. "MK Ben-Ari: My Man of the Year Is 'Rifle Butting' Col. Shalom Eisner."

+972 *Magazine* (15 September 2012). https://www.972mag.com/mk-ben-ari-my-man-of-the-year-is-rifle-butting-col-shalom-eisner/

Keenan, Thomas. "Publicity and Indifference (Sarajevo on Television)." *PMLA* 117, no. 1 (2002): 104–116.

Kennedy, Liam. "Soldier Photography: Visualising the War in Iraq." *Review of International Studies* 35, no. 04 (2009): 817–833.

Kennedy, Liam, and Caitlin Patrick. *The Violence of the Image: Photography and International Conflict.* London: I. B. Tauris, 2014.

Kershner, Isabel. "Israeli Soldier Who Shot Wounded Palestinian Assailant Is Convicted." *New York Times* (4 January 2017). http://www.nytimes.com/2017/01/04/world/middleeast/elor-azaria-verdict-israel.html

———. "Israeli Who Shot Palestinian Teenager Is Sentenced to 9 Months in Prison." *New York Times* (25 April 2018). https://www.nytimes.com/2018/04/25/world/middleeast/israel-border-shooting-sentencing.html

———. "Mosque Set on Fire in Northern Israel." *New York Times* (3 October 2011). https://www.nytimes.com/2011/10/04/world/middleeast/mosque-set-on-fire-in-northern-israel.html

Kerstein, Benjamin. "Discrepancies Raised, Inconsistencies Revealed." *Jerusalem Post* (22 June 2013). https://www.jpost.com/opinion/op-ed-contributors/discrepancies-raised-inconsistencies-revealed-317391

Khalidi, Rashid. *Brokers of Deceit: How the U.S. Has Undermined Peace in the Middle East.* Boston: Beacon Press, 2013.

Khalidi, Walid. *All That Remains: The Palestinian Villages Occupied and Depopulated by Israel in 1948.* Washington, DC: Institute for Palestine Studies, 1992.

Khoury, Jack, and Chaim Levinson. "IDF Says Forgery Likely in Video Showing Palestinian Teens' Deaths." *Haaretz.com* (22 June 2014). https://www.jpost.com/opinion/op-ed-contributors/discrepancies-raised-inconsistencies-revealed-317391

Kiley, Sam. "Palestinians Shot Boy, Disputed Report Says." *The Times* (London) (11 November 2000). https://shib.oit.duke.edu/idp/authn/external?conversation=e2s1

King, Laura. "Israeli Court Lifts Ban on Film." *Latimes.com* (12 November 2003). https://www.latimes.com/archives/la-xpm-2003-nov-12-fg-jenin12-story.html

Konrad, Edo. "Elor Azaria and the Army of the Periphery." +972 *Magazine* (4 January 2017). https://972mag.com/elor-azaria-and-the-army-of-the-periphery/124155/

Koron, Doron. "The Israelis 'Fighting to the Last Drop of Blood' Against Palestinian Documentary." *Ha'aretz.com* (10 August 2020). https://www.haaretz.com/israel-news/.

premium.MAGAZINE-the-israelis-fighting-till-the-last-drop-of-blood-against-pal-estinian-documentary-1.9060806

Kotef, Hagar. *Movement and the Ordering of Freedom: On Liberal Governances of Mobility*. Durham, NC, and London: Duke University Press, 2015.

Kotef, Hagar, and Merav Amir. "Between Imaginary Lines Violence and Its Justifications at the Military Checkpoints in Occupied Palestine." *Theory, Culture & Society* 28, no. 1 (2011): 55–80.

Kozol, Wendy. *Distant Wars Visible: The Ambivalence of Witnessing*. Minneapolis: University of Minnesota Press, 2014.

Krauthammer, Charles. "Israel's Moral Clarity in Gaza." *Washington Post* (5 January 2009).

Kremnitzer, Mordechai, and Amir Fuchs. "The Jenin-Jenin Law: A Blessing or a Curse? [in Hebrew]." *Maariv* (11 June 2013). https://en.idi.org.il/articles/6907

Kruschkova, Krassimira. "Disappearing Dance, Dancing Disappearance: On Arkadi Zaides's Choreography Archive." *Performance Research: A Journal of the Performing Arts* 24, no. 7 (2020): 32–38.

Kubovich, Yaniv, and Noa Landau. "Elor Azaria, Israeli Soldier Convicted of Killing a Wounded Palestinian Terrorist, Set Free After Nine Months." *Haaretz.com* (8 May 2018). https://www.haaretz.com/israel-news/.premium-hebron-shooter-elor-azaria-released-from-prison-after-nine-months-1.6070371

Kuntsman, Adi, and Rebecca L. Stein. "Another War Zone." *Middle East Report* (September 2010). https://merip.org/2010/09/another-war-zone/

———. *Digital Militarism: Israel's Occupation in the Social Media Age*. Stanford, CA: Stanford University Press, 2015.

———. "Digital Suspicion, Politics, and the Middle East." *Critical Inquiry* (2011). https://criticalinquiry.uchicago.edu/digital_suspicion_politics_and_the_middle_east/

Kuperwasser, Yossi, and Moshe Ya'alon. "The France 2 Al-Durrah Report, Its Consequences and Implications." Report of the Government Review Committee (19 May 2013). http://aldurah.com/the-al-durah-incident/analysis/kuper-wasser-report/

Landes, Richard. "Faqs for Al Durah Case." *The Augean Stables* (n.d.). http://www.theaugeanstables.com/al-durah-affair-the-dossier/al-durah-faqs/

———. "The Muhammad Al-Dura Blood Libel: A Case Analysis." *Jerusalem Center for Public Affairs* (6 October 2008). http://jcpa.org/article/the-muhammad-al-dura-blood-libel-a-case-analysis/

———. "Pallywood: 'According to Palestinian Sources.'" *Vimeo.com*: Al Durah Project, 2013. https://vimeo.com/65294892

Landsberg, Itay. "Who Is Afraid of Cameras? [in Hebrew]." *Maarachot* (2000): 24–25.

Larkin, Brian. *Signal and Noise: Media, Infrastructure, and Urban Culture in Nigeria.* Durham, NC: Duke University Press, 2008.

Lavi, Israel. "The Anarchist Photographer Who Beat Israel [in Hebrew]." *Kikar haShabbat* (19 April 2012). https://mobile.kikar.co.il/article/94731

Lazaroff, Tovah, and Yaakov Lappin. "B'Tselem to Call for Ni'lin Death Probe." *Jerusalem Post* (4 August 2008). https://www.jpost.com/israel/btselem-to-call-for-nilin-death-probe

Lee, Shimrit. *Commodified (In)Security: Cultural Mediations of Violence in Israel, Palestine, and Beyond.* PhD dissertation, New York University, 2019.

Leifer, Joshua. "'Nakba Day Killings': Cop Gets 9 Months Prison for Killing Unarmed Teen." *+972 Magazine* (25 April 2018). https://www.972mag.com/nakba-day-killings-cop-gets-9-months-prison-for-killing-unarmed-teen/

Levick, Adam. "What the Guardian Didn't Tell You About Palestinian Youths Arrested in Hebron." *The Guardian* (31 March 2013). https://ukmediawatch.org/2013/03/31/what-the-guardian-didnt-tell-you-about-palestinian-youths-arrested-in-hebron/

Levin, David. "The End of Male Fraternity? The Mobile Phone and Reserve Military Duty." In *The Wonder Phone in the Land of Miracles: Mobile Telephony in Israel* (pp. 197–205), edited by Akiba A. Cohen, Dafna Lemish, and Amit Schejter. New York: Hampton Press, 2008.

Levinson, Chaim. "IDF Soldier Linked to 'Price Tag' Attack in West Bank Palestinian Village." *Haaretz.com* (10 February 2012). https://www.haaretz.com/1.5184155

———. "Nearly 100% of All Military Court Cases in West Bank End in Conviction, Haaretz Learns." *Haaretz.com* (28 November 2011). https://www.haaretz.com/1.5214377

Levy, Gideon. "Israel Does Not Want Peace." *Haaretz.com* (4 July 2014). http://www.haaretz.com/news/diplomacy-defense/israel-peace-conference/1.601112

———. "Mohammed Al-Dura Lives On." *Haaretz.com* (6 October 2007). https://www.haaretz.com/1.4982233

———. "Twilight Zone, Mean Streets." *Haaretz.com* (8 September 2005). https://www.haaretz.com/1.5128096

Lichtenstein, Jesse. "Digital Diplomacy." *New York Times Magazine* (16 July 2010). https://www.nytimes.com/2010/07/18/magazine/18web2-0-t.html

Liebes, Tamar, and Anat First. "Framing the Palestine–Israeli Conflict." In *Framing*

Terrorism: The News Media, the Government and the Public (pp. 59–74), edited by Pippa Norris, Montague Kern, and Marion Just. London: Routledge, 2003.

Liebes, Tamar, and Zohar Kampf. "Black and White and Shades of Gray: Palestinians in the Israeli Media During the 2nd Intifada." *International Journal of Press/Politics* 14, no. 4 (October 2009): 434–453.

Linfield, Susie. *The Cruel Radiance: Photography and Political Violence*. Chicago: University of Chicago Press, 2010.

Lis, Jonathan. "IDF Questions Reservists Who Organized Hebron Photo Exhibit." *Haaretz.com* (22 June 2004). https://web.archive.org/web/20090722010500/http://www.haaretz.com/hasen/pages/ShArt.jhtml?itemNo=442123

Livio, Oren, and Hagar Afriat. "Politicised Celebrity in a Conflict-Ridden Society: The Elor Azaria Case and Celebritisation Discourses in Israel." *Celebrity Studies* (May 2019).

Lockman, Zachary, and Joel Beinin, eds. *Intifada: The Palestinian Uprising Against Israeli Occupation*. Washington, DC: MERIP, South End Press, 1989.

Maariv. "Breaking the Silence: Soldiers' Photos." *Occupation Magazine* (29 March 2005). https://web.archive.org/web/20131202231757/http://www.kibush.co.il/show_file.asp?num=1318

MacDonald, Fraser, Rachel Hughes, and Klaus Dodds, eds. *Observant States: Geopolitics and Visual Culture*. London and New York: I. B. Tauris, 2010.

Mackey, Robert. "Israeli Anger at Foreign 'Provocateurs' Boils Over." *New York Times* (12 April 2012). https://thelede.blogs.nytimes.com/2012/04/16/israels-battle-with-foreign-activists/?mtrref=undefined&gwh=3FEBF7C2DDCA5AB291128007B-83D1385&gwt=pay&assetType=REGIWALL

———. "Palestinians Record West Bank Protests with Cameras Supplied by Israelis." *The Lede* (17 June 2011). https://thelede.blogs.nytimes.com/2011/06/17/palestinians-film-west-bank-protests-with-israeli-supplied-cameras/

Maimon, Vered, and Shiraz Grinbaum, eds. *Activestills: Photography as Protest in Palestine/Israel*. Chicago: University of Chicago Press, 2016.

Malkowski, Jennifer. *Dying in Full Detail: Mortality and Digital Documentary*. Durham, NC: Duke University Press, 2017.

ManagingTeam. "The Gaza War in Review." *Honest Reporting* (6 February 2009). https://honestreporting.com/the-gaza-war-in-review/

Manekin, Devorah Sarah. "Waging War Among Civilians: The Production and Restraint of Counterinsurgent Violence in the Second Intifada." PhD diss, UCLA.

Marmari, Hanoch. "The Purity of Shame [in Hebrew]." *The Seventh Eye* (10 December 2009). https://www.the7eye.org.il/41806

Marom, Yael. "The Camera That Made Elor Azaria 'Man of the Year.'" +972 *Magazine* (2 October 2016). https://972mag.com/the-camera-that-made-elor-azaria-man-of-the-year/122371/

Matar, Haggai. "Bit by Bit, Coverage of Occupation Disappears from Israeli News." +972 *Magazine* (19 January 2012). http://972mag.com/bit-by-bit-coverage-of-occupation-disappears-from-israeli-news/33397/

———. "The Most Critical Issues Israelis Won't Be Voting on in the Next Election." +972 *Magazine* (24 December 2018). https://972mag.com/the-most-critical-issue-israelis-wont-be-voting-on-in-the-next-election/139359/

———. "Mustafa Tamimi: A Murder Captured on Camera." +972 *Magazine* (11 December 2011). https://www.972mag.com/mustafa-tamimi-a-murder-captured-on-camera/

McLagan, Meg, and Yates McKee, eds. *Sensible Politics: The Visual Culture of Nongovernmental Activism.* New York: Zone Books, 2012.

Michaels, Jim. "Cellphones Put to 'Unnerving' Use in Gaza." *USA Today* (13 January 2009).

"Middle of the Night in a-Nabi Saleh." B'Tselem for *YouTube* (10 November 2011). https://www.youtube.com/watch?v=-jnb6z5HZ34&feature=emb_logo

Miretski, Pini Pavel, and Sascha Dov Bachmann. "The Panopticon of International Law: Human Rights Compliance in a Transnational Society." *Osgoode Hall Law Journal* 52, no. 1 (2015): 235–262.

Mirzoeff, Nicholas. *How to See the World.* London: Pelican, 2015.

———. *Watching Babylon: The War in Iraq and Global Visual Culture.* New York and London: Routledge, 2005.

Mirzoeff, Nicholas, and Duke University Press. *The Right to Look: A Counterhistory of Visuality.* Durham, NC: Duke University Press, 2011.

Mitchell, William J. *The Reconfigured Eye: Visual Truth in the Post-Photographic Era.* Cambridge, MA: MIT Press, 1992.

Montell, Jessica. "B'Tselem Chief: 'Caroline Glick a Hack Who Parrots Any Drivel.'" +972 *Magazine* (21 January 2011). https://972mag.com/btselem-chief-caroline-glick-is-a-hack-journalist-who-parrots-any-drivel/

———. "Learning from What Works: Strategic Analysis of the Achievements of the Israel–Palestine Human Rights Community." *Human Rights Quarterly* 38 (2016): 928–968.

Morag, Raya. "Perpetrator Trauma and Current Israeli Documentary Cinema." *Camera Obscura: Feminism, Culture, and Media Studies* 27, no. 2 (80) (2012): 93–133.

———. "Radical Contextuality: Major Trends in Israeli Documentary Second Intifada Cinema." *Studies in Documentary Film* 6, no. 3 (2012): 253–272.

Morozov, Evgeny. *To Save Everything, Click Here: The Folly of Technological Solutionism.* New York: Public Affairs, 2014.

Morris, Errol. *Believing Is Seeing: Observations on the Mysteries of Photography.* New York: Penguin Books, 2014.

Morris, Rosalind. *Photographies East: The Camera and Its Histories in East and Southeast Asia.* Durham, NC: Duke University Press, 2009.

Nassar, Issam. "Familial Snapshots: Representing Palestine in the Work of the First Local Photographers." *History & Memory* 18, no. 2 (2006): 139–155. https://muse.jhu.edu/article/208015

———. *Photographing Jerusalem: The Image of the City in Nineteenth-Century Photography.* East European Monographs. Boulder and New York: East European Monographs, 1997.

Nathansohn, Regev. "Shooting Occupation: Sociology of Visual Representation [in Hebrew]." *Theory and Criticism* 31 (2007): 127–154.

———. "Soldier-Photographer and the Double Bind of Photographic Practice." *Critical Asian Studies* 42, no. 3 (2010): 437–440.

Netanyahu, Benjamin. "Netanyhu to CNN's Wolf Blitzer: 'I Support Taking Whatever Action Is Necessary to Stop This Insane Situation . . .'" *State of the Union, CNN* (20 July 2014). http://cnnpressroom.blogs.cnn.com/2014/07/20/netanyahu-to-cnns-wolf-blitzer-i-support-taking-whatever-action-is-necessary-to-stop-this-insane-situation/

Nevo, Baruch, and Yael Shur, eds. *The IDF and the Press During Hostilities: The Army and Society Forum.* Israel Democracy Institute, Jerusalem (4 June 2002). Jerusalem: The Old City Press, 2003.

Nixon, Rob. *Slow Violence and the Environmentalism of the Poor.* Cambridge, MA: Harvard University Press, 2011.

Noybach, Seder Yom, with Keren. "Ben Dror Yemini Commentary on the Brigade Commander Incident [in Hebrew]." Reshet Beit (16 April 2012). Radio broadcast.

OCHA. *The Humanitarian Monitor.* United Nations: Office for the Coordination of Humanitarian Affairs, Occupied Palestinian Territory (2009). https://www.un.org/unispal/document/auto-insert-206938/

"Of Course Nadim Nawara Was Killed by Live Fire—But Where?" *Elder of Ziyon* (12 June 2014). http://elderofziyon.blogspot.com/2014/06/of-course-nadim-nawara-was-killed-by.html

Omer-Man, Emily Schaeffer. "Extrajudicial Killing with Near Impunity: Excessive Force by Israeli Law Enforcement Against Palestinians." *Boston University International Law Journal* 35, 115 (2017).

Omer-Man, Michael Schaeffer. "The Israeli Army's War on Consciousness." *+972 Magazine* (12 April 2018). https://www.972mag.com/israels-war-on-consciousness/134610/

———. "Israel's Knesset Just Voted on a Very Dangerous Law for Democracy." *+972 Magazine* (29 March 2016). https://972mag.com/israels-knesset-just-voted-on-a-very-dangerous-law/118227/

———. "Nearly Half of Israeli Jews Support Extrajudicial Killings, Poll Finds." *+972 Magazine* (14 September 2016). https://972mag.com/nearly-half-of-israeli-jews-support-extrajudicial-killings-poll-finds/121904/

Orpaz, Inbal. "Robots, and Not Humans, Can React to Sabotages [in Hebrew]." *The Marker* (9 September 2012).

Padania, Sameer, Sam Gregory, Yvette Thijm, and Bryan Nunez. *Cameras Everywhere: Current Challenges and Opportunities at the Intersection of Human Rights, Video and Technology* (2011).

Palestinian Center for Human Rights. *Silencing the Press: Report on Israeli Attacks Against Journalists* (2012). http://www.pchrgaza.org/files/Reports/English/pdf_press/silencing%20the%20press%2012.pdf

Peretz, Don. *Intifada: The Palestinian Uprising.* Boulder, CO: Westview, 1990.

Perugini, Nicola, and Neve Gordon. *The Human Right to Dominate.* New York: Oxford University Press, 2015.

Peteet, Julie. "Closure's Temporality: The Cultural Politics of Time and Waiting." *South Atlantic Quarterly* 117, no. 1 (2018): 43–64.

———. *Space and Mobility in Palestine.* Bloomington: Indiana University Press, 2017.

Pines-Paz, Ophir. "Suspending Officer Who Hit Danish Protester Isn't Enough." *+972 Magazine* (20 April 2012). https://972mag.com/suspending-officer-that-hit-danish-activist-isnt-enough/42628/

Pliskin, Ruthie, Amit Goldenberg, Efrat Ambar, and Daniel Bar-Tal. "Speaking out and Breaking the Silence." In *Self-Censorship in Contexts of Conflict: Theory and Research* (pp. 243–268), edited by Daniel Bar-Tal, Rafi Nets-Zehngut, and Keren Sharvit. Cham: Springer International Publishing, 2017.

Pratt, Mary Louise. *Imperial Eyes: Travel Writing and Transculturation,* 2nd edition. London and New York: Routledge, 2007.

Prime Minister's Office (Israel). *Publication of the Report of the Government Review*

Committee Regarding the France 2 Al-Durrah (19 May 2013). https://www.gov.il/en/departments/news/spokeadora190513

Rahman, Omar H. "Nabi Saleh Protester Hit by Tear Gas Canister Dies from Wounds." *+972 Magazine* (9 December 2011). https://www.972mag.com/nabi-saleh-palestinian-shot-in-head-with-tear-gas-canister/29317/

Rangan, Pooja. *Immediations: The Humanitarian Impulse in Documentary*. Durham, NC: Duke University Press, 2017

Rapoport, Meron. "The Israeli Right Stopped Talking About Occupation, and That Will Hurt It at the Polls." *+972 Magazine* (27 August 2019). https://972mag.com/occupation-religious-right-netanyahu/143066/

Ravid, Barak. "Government Report: Muhammad a-Dora Wasn't Hurt from the Netzarim Shooting [in Hebrew]." *Haaretz.com* (19 May 2013). https://www.haaretz.co.il/news/politics/1.2024027

Reese, Matt. "B'Tselem: Views to a Kill." *The Telegraph* (16 January 2009). https://www.telegraph.co.uk/culture/film/4270681/BTselem-views-to-a-kill.html

Reinhart, Tanya. "Jenin—the Propaganda War." *Utretch University Repository*, 2002.

Rettig Gur, Haviv. "Coordination Is Putting Israel Ahead in the Media War." *Jerusalem Post* (30 December 2008). https://www.jpost.com/international/coordination-is-putting-israel-ahead-in-the-media-war

Richardson, Allissa V. *Bearing Witness While Black: African Americans, Smartphones, and the New Protest #Journalism*. New York: Oxford University Press, 2019.

Ristovska, Sandra. "The Rise of Eyewitness Video and Its Implications for Human Rights: Conceptual and Methodological Approaches." *Journal of Human Rights* 15, no. 3 (2016): 347–360.

Ristovska, Sandra, and Monroe Price, eds. *Visual Imagery and Human Rights Practice*. Cham: Palgrave, 2018.

Rizzo, Lorena. *Photography and History in Colonial Southern Africa: Shades of Empire*. New York: Routledge, 2020.

Roei, Noa. *Civic Aesthetics: Militarism in Israeli Art and Visual Culture*. London: Bloomsbury Publishing, 2016.

Rosner, Shmuel. "Extreme Makeover, Israel." *New York Times* (8 January 2013). https://latitude.blogs.nytimes.com/2013/01/08/extreme-makeover-israel/

Rotem, Noam. "The Case for Dismantling Israel's Human Rights Organizations." *+972 Magazine* (18 July 2015). https://www.972mag.com/the-case-for-dismantling-israels-human-rights-organizations/

Roth-Rowland, Natasha. "Nobody Should Be Shocked at the Hebron Execution." *+972*

Magazine (26 March 2016). https://972mag.com/nobody-should-be-shocked-at-the-hebron-execution/118138/

Rubin, Eliran. "Israel's Drone Industry Angry over Draconian Defense Export Restrictions." *Haaretz.com* (29 November 2016). https://www.haaretz.com/.premium-drone-industry-angry-at-export-restrictions-1.5467737

Rubinger, David, and Ruth Corman. *Israel Through My Lens: Sixty Years as a Photojournalist.* New York: Abbeville Press, 2007.

Rudoren, Jodi. "Two Palestinians Killed in Clashes with Israeli Forces." *New York Times* (15 May 2014). https://www.nytimes.com/2014/05/16/world/middleeast/two-palestinians-killed-in-clashes-with-israeli-forces.html

Russell, Jon. "Israelis Are Now the World's Biggest Social Network Addicts, Says New Report." *The Next Web* (22 December 2011). http://thenextweb.com/socialmedia/2011/12/22/israelis-are-now-the-worlds-biggest-social-network-addicts-says-new-report/

Ryan, James R. *Picturing Empire: Photography and the Visualization of the British Empire.* Chicago: University of Chicago Press, 1998.

Said, Edward. *Peace and Its Discontents: Essays on Palestine in the Middle East Peace Process.* New York: Random House, 1996.

———. *The End of the Peace Process: Oslo and After.* New York: Pantheon Books, 2000.

———. *The Question of Palestine.* New York: Times Books, 1979.

Salamanca, Omar Jabary. "Assembling the Fabric of Life: When Settler Colonialism Becomes Development." *Journal of Palestine Studies* 45, no. 4 (2016): 64–80.

Schechter, Eran. "The IDF Requires Soldiers to Pay for Taking Cameras out of Their Phones [in Hebrew]." *SCOOP* (6 May 2008).

Schejter, Amit, and Akiba Cohen. "Israel: Chutzpah and Chatter in the Holy Land." In *Perpetual Contact: Mobile Communication, Private Talk, Public Performance* (pp. 30–41), edited by James E. Katz and Mark Aakhus. New York: Cambridge University Press, 2002.

Schejter, Amit M., and Akiba A. Cohen. "Mobile Phone Usage as an Indicator of Solidarity: Israelis at War in 2006 and 2009." *Mobile Media & Communication* 1, no. 2 (2013): 174–195.

Schiff, Zeev, and Ehud Yaari. *Intifada: The Palestinian Uprising, Israel's Third Front.* New York: Simon & Schuster, 1991.

Schwartz, Adi. "In the Footsteps of the al-Dura Controversy." *Haaretz.com* (31 October 2007). https://www.haaretz.com/1.4993146

Schwartz, Louis-George. *Mechanical Witness: A History of Motion Picture Evidence in U.S. Courts.* New York: Oxford University Press, 2009.

Seaman, Daniel. "We Did Not Abandon Philippe Karsenty." *Jerusalem Post* (25 June 2008). https://www.jpost.com/Opinion/Op-Ed-Contributors/We-did-not-abandon-Philippe-Karsenty

Seaman, Danny. "Palestinian Industry of Lies." *Ynetnews.com* (29 May 2008). https://www.ynetnews.com/articles/0,7340,L-3549532,00.html

Segal, Hagai. "Don't Dismiss Eisner." *Ynetnews.com* (17 April 2012). https://www.ynetnews.com/articles/0,7340,L-4217179,00.html

Sela, Rona. "The Genealogy of Colonial Plunder and Erasure—Israel's Control over Palestinian Archives." *Social Semiotics* (3 March 2017).

———. "Genealogy of an Image in Public Consciousness. From David Rubinger's Photograph of Paratroopers Beside the Western Wall to Alex Levak's Photograph of the Affair of Bus Line 300." In *Israel: The 1967 War and Its Impact on Culture and the Media* [Hebrew] (pp. 161–180), edited by Na'ama Sheffi and Tammy Razi. The Chaim Weizmann Institute for the Study of Zionism and Israel, 2008.

———. *Made Public: Palestinian Photographs in Military Archives in Israel* [in Hebrew]. Israel: Helena Publishing House, 2009.

———. *Photography in Palestine/Eretz Israel in the Thirties and Forties* [in Hebrew]. Tel Aviv: Helenah, 2009.

———. "Present-Absent Palestinian Villages [in Hebrew]." *Terminal 28* (2006): 22–25.

———. "Rethinking National Archives in Colonial Countries and Zones of Conflict Dissonant Archives." In *Dissonant Archives: Contemporary Visual Culture and Contested Narratives in the Middle East*, edited by A. Downey. London: I. B. Tauris, 2015.

———. "Scouting Palestinian Territory, 1940–1948: Haganah Village Files, Aerial Photos, and Surveys." *Jerusalem Quarterly* (2017).

Senor, Dan, and Saul Singer. *Start-Up Nation: The Story of Israel's Economic Miracle.* New York: Twelve, 2009.

7amleh: The Arab Center for the Advancement of Social Media. *Hashtag Palestine 2018: An Overview of Digital Rights Abuses of Palestinians* (March 2019). https://www.apc.org/sites/default/files/Hashtag_Palestine_English_digital_pages.pdf

Shai, Nachman. *Hearts and Minds: Israel and the Battle for Public Opinion.* Buffalo: State University of New York Press, 2018.

Shakir, Omar. *Civil Rights: Israel's Use of Draconian Military Orders to Repress Palestinians in the West Bank.* New York: Human Rights Watch, 2019.

Shalhoub-Kevorkian, Nadera. *Security Theology, Surveillance and the Politics of Fear.* Cambridge, UK: University of Cambridge, 2015.

Shalhoub-Kevorkian, Nadera, and Yossi David. "Is the Violence of Tag Mehir a State Crime?" *British Journal of Criminology* 56, no. 5 (2020): 835–856.

Shamah, David. "Digital World: Israel, the Telecom 'Continent.'" *Jerusalem Post* (18 October 2010). https://www.jpost.com/business/commentary/digital-world-israel-the-telecom-continent

Shamir, Gal. "The Main Matter [in Hebrew]." (21 July 2008).

Sharir, Moran. "Roni Daniel: The One Who Doesn't Know How to Ask [in Hebrew]." *Haaretz*.com (21 May 2014). https://www.haaretz.co.il/gallery/television/tv-review/.premium-1.2327148?=&ts=_1488994493519

Sharon, Roi. "The Officer Who Beat a Left-Wing Activist Will Return to the Post from Which He Was Removed [in Hebrew]." *Kan.org* (19 June 2019). https://www.kan.org.il/item/?itemid=53944

Shavit, Michal. *Media Strategy and Military Operations in the 21st Century: Mediatizing the Israel Defence Forces.* New York: Routledge, 2016.

Shavit, Shlomit. "The Victory Image [in Hebrew]." *Maarachot* 440 (December 2011): 56–61.

Sheafer, Tamir, and Shaul R. Shenhav. "Mediated Public Diplomacy in a New Era of Warfare." *Communication Review* 12, no. 3 (2009): 272–283.

Sheehi, Stephen. *The Arab Imago: A Social History of Portrait Photography, 1860–1910.* Princeton, NJ: Princeton University Press, 2016.

Sheff, Marcus. "A Decade Since the Battle of Jenin, 'the Myth of Jeningrad.'" *Jerusalem Post* (19 April 2012). https://www.jpost.com/opinion/columnists/a-decade-since-the-battle-of-jenin-the-myth-of-jeningrad

Sheizaf, Noam. "Beitunia Killings and the Media's Incredibly High Bar for Palestinian Stories." *+972 Magazine* (21 May 2014). https://972mag.com/beitunia-killings-and-the-medias-incredibly-high-bar-for-palestinian-stories/91166/

———. "We Are All One Staters Now." *+972 Magazine* (27 December 2019). https://www.972mag.com/one-state-annexation-decade/

Sherwood, Harriet. "Israel Is World's Largest Drone Exporter." *The Guardian* (20 May 2013). https://www.theguardian.com/world/2013/may/20/israel-worlds-largest-drone-exporter

———. "Palestinian Children Woken in Night to Be Photographed by Soldiers." *The Guardian* (28 September 2011). http://www.theguardian.com/world/view-from-jerusalem-with-harriet-sherwood/2011/sep/28/palestinian-territories-israel

Shehadeh, Raja. "'Look Where We've Got To—Defeated and Dominated': My Genera-
    tion's Failure to Liberate Palestine." *The Guardian* (8 August 2019).

Shohat, Ella. *Israeli Cinema: East/West and the Politics of Representation.* London and
    New York: I. B. Tauris, 1989.

Shoval, Zalman. "Why Israel Lost the Hasbara War." *Israeli Journal of Foreign Affairs*
    1, no. 2 (2015): 5–18.

Silver-Brody, Vivienne. *Documentors of the Dream: Pioneer Jewish Photographers in
    the Land of Israel, 1890–1933.* Jerusalem: Magnes Press, Hebrew University, 1998.

Silverman, Anav. "Evyatar Borovsky: A Settler with an Actor's Legacy." *HuffPost*
    (5 March 2013). https://www.huffpost.com/entry/evyatar-borovsky-a-set-
    tle_b_3207357?guccounter=1

SITU Research and Forensic Architecture. *Nil'in Report* (2010). https://situ.nyc/re-
    search/projects/nilln-report

Sliwinski, Sharon. *Human Rights in Camera.* Chicago and London: University of Chi-
    cago Press, 2011.

Sofer, Roni. "Olmert on the Violence in Hebron: I Saw it and was Ashamed." Ynetnews.
    com (14 January 2006).

Somfalvi, Attila. "Israeli Committee: Al-Dura Alive at End of Video." *Ynetnews.com* (20
    May 2013). http://www.ynetnews.com/articles/0,7340,L-4381574,00.html

Sontag, Susan. *On Photography.* New York: Dell Publishing Co., 1977.

———. *Regarding the Pain of Others.* New York: Farrar, Straus and Giroux, 2003.

———. "Regarding the Torture of Others." *New York Times* (23 May 2004).

Special Military Court. "Chief Military Prosecutor vs. Lieutenant Colonel Omri Borberg
    and First Sergeant Leonardo Correa [in Hebrew]" (15 July 2010).

Spyer, Patricia, and Mary Margaret Steedly, eds. *Images That Move.* Santa Fe, NM:
    School for Advanced Research Press, 2013.

Stahl, Roger. *Militainment, Inc.: War, Media, and Popular Culture.* New York: Rout-
    ledge, 2010.

———. *Through the Crosshairs: The Weapon's Eye in Public War Culture.* New Bruns-
    wick, NJ: Rutgers University Press, 2018.

Stamatopoulou-Robbins, Sophia. *Waste Siege: The Life of Infrastructure in Palestine.*
    Stanford, CA: Stanford University Press, 2019.

Steele, Jonathan. "The Tragedy of Jenin." *The Guardian* (2 August 2002). https://www.
    theguardian.com/world/2002/aug/02/israel2

Stein, Rebecca L. "'Fake News!': The View from Israel's Occupation." *OpenDemocracy*

(12 February 2018). https://www.opendemocracy.net/en/north-africa-west-asia/fake-news-view-from-israel-s-occupation/

———. "GoPro Occupation: Networked Cameras, Israeli Military Rule, and the Digital Promise." *Current Anthropology* 58, no. 15 (February 2017): S56–S64.

———. "Impossible Witness: Israeli Visuality, Palestinian Testimony and the Gaza War." *Journal for Cultural Research* 16, no. 2–3 (2012): 135–153.

———. "Inside Israel's Twitter War Room." *Middle East Report* (24 November 2012). http://www.merip.org/mero/mero112412

———. *Itineraries in Conflict: Israelis, Palestinians, and the Political Lives of Tourism.* Durham, NC: Duke University Press, 2008.

———. "The Other Wall: Facebook and Israel." *London Review of Books* (blog) (19 April 2011). https://www.lrb.co.uk/blog/2011/april/the-other-wall

———. "Souvenirs of Conquest: Israeli Occupations as Tourist Events." *International Journal of Middle East Studies* 40, no. 4 (2008): 669a.

———. "StateTube: Anthropological Reflections on Social Media and the Israeli State." *Anthropological Quarterly* 85, no. 3 (2012): 893–916.

———. "Travelling Zion: Hiking and Settler-Nationalism in Pre-1948 Palestine." *Interventions* 11, no. 3 (2009): 334–351.

Stein, Rebecca L., and Adi Kuntsman. "Selfie Militarism." *London Review of Books* (blog) (23 May 2014). https://www.lrb.co.uk/blog/2014/may/selfie-militarism

Stoler, Laura Ann. *Along the Archival Grain: Epistemic Anxieties and Colonial Common Sense.* Princeton, NJ: Princeton University Press, 2009.

Strassler, Karen. *Demanding Images: Democracy, Mediation, and the Image-Event in Indonesia.* Durham, NC: Duke University Press, 2020.

———. *Refracted Visions: Popular Photography and National Modernity in Java.* Durham, NC: Duke University Press, 2010.

Struk, Janina. *Private Pictures: Soldiers' Inside View of War.* London and New York: Routledge, 2011.

Swed, Ori, and John Sibley Butler. "Military Capital in the Israeli Hi-Tech Industry." *Armed Forces & Society* (2013): 1–19.

Talmon, Miriam, and Yaron Peleg, eds. *Israeli Cinema: Identities in Motion.* Austin: University of Texas, 2011.

Tamari, Salim, and Rema Hammami. "Anatomy of Another Rebellion." *Middle East Report* (Winter 2000). https://merip.org/2000/12/anatomy-of-another-rebellion/

Tausig, Shuki. "Persistent Commitment [in Hebrew]." *The Seventh Eye* (17 April 2012). https://www.the7eye.org.il/30525

Tawil-Souri, Helga. "Digital Occupation: Gaza's High-Tech Enclosure." *Journal of Palestine Studies* 41, no. 2 (2012): 27–43.

Tawil-Souri, Helga, and Miriyam Aouragh. "Intifada 3.0? Cyber Colonialism and Palestinian Resistance." *Arab Studies Journal* (Spring 2014): 102–133.

Tazna, Shlomo. "Government Committee: Muhamad a Dora Is Alive at the End of the Video [in Hebrew]." *Israel Hayom* (19 May 2013). http://www.israelhayom.co.il/article/89189

Tchaikovsky, Allen. "An Expert's Opinion [in Hebrew]." Israel Police, Digital Evidence Lab (14 December 2010). https://www.btselem.org/heb/legal_documents/20101214_nilin_shooting_difs_report.pdf

Tepper, Greg. "IDF Officer Seen Head-Butting Palestinian Youth in B'Tselem Video." *Times of Israel* (26 July 2012). https://www.timesofisrael.com/idf-officer-seen-head-butting-palestinian-youth-in-btselem-video/?fb_comment_id=10150934123041574_22142647

Thrall, Nathan. *The Only Language They Understand: Forcing Compromise in Israel and Palestine.* New York: Metropolitan Books, 2017.

Tobin, Jonathan S. "Was Nakba Shooting Another al-Dura Libel?" (21 May 2014). *Commentary.* https://www.commentarymagazine.com/jonathan-tobin/was-nakba-shooting-another-al-dura-libel-israel-palestinians/

Tofighian, Nadi. "Watching the Astonishment of the Native: Early Audio-Visual Technology and Colonial Discourse." *Early Popular Visual Culture* 15, no. 1 (2017): 26–43.

Tucher, Andie. "I Believe in Faking": The Dilemma of Photographic Realism at the Dawn of Photojournalism." *Photography and Culture* 10, no. 3 (2017): 195–214.

Tufekci, Zeynep. *Twitter and Tear Gas: The Power and Fragility of Networked Protest.* New Haven, CT, and London: Yale University Press, 2017.

"UN Calls for Probe into Shooting of Palestinian Youths." *Haaretz.com* (20 May 2014). https://www.haaretz.com/un-probe-shooting-of-palestinian-youths-1.5249007

United Nations. *Report of the International Fact-Finding Mission to Investigate Violations of International Law, Including International Humanitarian and Human Rights Law, Resulting from the Israeli Attacks on the Flotilla of Ships Carrying Humanitarian Assistance* (27 September 2010). https://www2.ohchr.org/english/bodies/hrcouncil/docs/15session/A.HRC.15.21_en.pdf

United Nations Conference on Trade and Development. *Report on UNCTAD Assistance to the Palestinian People: Developments in the Economy of the Occupied Palestinian Territory.* United Nations (2017). https://unctad.org/en/PublicationsLibrary/tdb64d4_embargoed_en.pdf

Urquhart, Conal. "Army Fury at Hebron Soldiers' Brutality Exhibition." *The Guardian* (24 June 2004). https://www.theguardian.com/world/2004/jun/24/israel

Virilio, Paul. *War and Cinema: The Logistics of Perception,* translated by Patrick Camiller. London and New York: Verso, 1989.

"Virtual Existence." *Jerusalem Post* (25 January 2007). https://www.jpost.com/magazine/features/virtual-existence

Wall, Melissa. *Citizen Journalism: Practices, Propaganda, Pedagogy.* Disruptions: Studies in Digital Journalism. Abingdon, Oxon; New York: Routledge, 2019.

Weimann, Gabi. "The Media's Stance Towards the IDF." In *The IDF and the Press During Hostilities: The Army and Society Forum* (pp. 119–138), edited by Baruch Nevo and Yael Shur, Israel Democracy Institute, Jerusalem (4 June 2002). Jerusalem: The Old City Press, 2003.

Weiss, Erica. *Conscientious Objectors in Israel: Citizenship, Sacrifice, Trials of Fealty.* Philadelphia: University of Pennsylvania Press, 2014.

———. "Struggling with Complicity: Anti-Militarist Activism in Israel." *Current Anthropology* 90, no. 19 (2019): 173–182.

Weiss, Hadas. "Homeowners in Israel: The Social Costs of Middle-Class Debt." *Cultural Anthropology* 29, no. 1 (2014): 128–149.

———. "Immigration and West Bank Settlement Normalization." *PoLAR: Political and Legal Anthropology Review* 34, no. 1 (2011): 112–130.

Weizman, Eyal. *Forensic Architecture: Violence at the Threshold of Detectability.* New York: Zone Books, 2018.

———. *Hollow Land: Israel's Architecture of Occupation.* London: Verso, 2007.

———. "Lawfare in Gaza: Legislative Attack." *OpenDemocracy* (1 March 2009). https://www.opendemocracy.net/en/legislative-attack/

"Western Wall Area Cleared." *Jerusalem Post* (12 June 1967).

Wessels, Joshka. *Documenting Syria: Film-Making, Video Activism and Revolution.* Library of Modern Middle East Studies. London: I. B. Tauris, 2019.

"West Bank: The Villagers Hemmed In." *The Economist* (4 September 2008). https://www.economist.com/middle-east-and-africa/2008/09/04/the-villagers-hemmed-in

Whitty, Noel. "Soldier Photography of Detainee Abuse in Iraq: Digital Technology, Human Rights and the Death of Baha Mousa." *Human Rights Law Review* 10, no. 4 (2010): 689–714.

WhoProfits. *"Big Brother" in Jerusalem's Old City: Israel's Militarized Visual Surveillance*

System in Occupied East Jerusalem (November 2018). https://whoprofits.org/wp-content/uploads/2018/11/surveil-final.pdf

Wigoder, Meir. "The Blocked Gaze: A User's Guide to Photographing the Separation Barrier-Wall." *Public Culture* 22, no. 2 (2010): 293–308.

Wolfe, Patrick. "Settler Colonialism and the Elimination of the Native." *Journal of Genocide Research* 8, no. 4 (2006): 387–409.

Wolfsfeld, Gadi. "The News Media and the Second Intifada: Some Initial Lessons." *Harvard International Journal of Press/Politics* 6, no. 4 (2001): 113–118.

Wolfsfeld, Gadi, Paul Frosh, and Maurice T. Awabdy. "Covering Death in Conflicts: Coverage of the Second Intifada on Israel and Palestinian Television." *Journal of Peace Research* 45, no. 3 (2008): 401–417.

Wright, Fiona. *The Israeli Radical Left: An Ethics of Complicity.* Philadelphia: University of Pennsylvania Press, 2018.

"Ya'alon Says Troops in Nakba Day Killings Were in Danger, Acted as Needed." *Times of Israel* (20 May 2014). https://www.timesofisrael.com/yaalon-says-troops-in-nakba-day-killings-were-in-danger-acted-as-needed/

Yemini, Ben-Dror. "The Blue-Eyed Poster Girl of Palestinian Propaganda. *Ynetnews.com* (27 December 2017). https://www.ynetnews.com/articles/0,7340,L-5062038,00.html

Yesh Din. *Mock Enforcement: The Failure to Enforce Law on Israeli Citizens in the West Bank.* Yesh Din: Volunteers for Human Rights (May 2015). http://files.yesh-din.org/userfiles/Yesh%20Din_Akifat%20Hok_%20English.pdf

Yesh Din, *Physicians for Human Rights, and Breaking the Silence. A Life Exposed: Military Invasions of Palestinian Homes in the West Bank* (November 2020). https://life-exposed.com/wp-content/uploads/2020/11/Exposed_Life_EN_FINAL.pdf

Yifrach, Yehuda. "Lieutenant Colonel Shalom Eisner and the Video War [in Hebrew]." *Room 404* (19 April 2012). http://room404.net/?p=51466

Yosef, Raz. *Beyond Flesh: Queer Masculinities and Nationalism in Israeli Cinema.* New Brunswick, NJ: Rutgers University Press, 2004.

Zawawi, Zahraa, Eric Corijn, and Bas Van Heur. "Public Spaces in the Occupied Palestinian Territories." *GeoJournal* 78, no. 4 (2013): 743–758.

Zeiger, Asher, and Hillary Zaken. "Officer Blasts Top Brass: Too Concerned with Looking Good for the Cameras." *Times of Israel* (18 April 2012). https://www.timesofisrael.com/shalom-eisner-blasts-top-brass-for-handling-of-incident/

Ziccardi, Giovanni. *Resistance, Liberation Technology and Human Rights in the Digital Age.* Dordrecht: Springer, 2013.

Zilber, Dudi. *Military Photographer: 40 Years of Bamahane Photography, the Exhibition* [in Hebrew]. Tel Aviv: Ministry of Defense Publishing, 1988.

Ziv, Itay. "Severe Images: The Brigade Commander's Incident Is Mainly Photogenic [in Hebrew]." *NRG* (2012). https://www.makorrishon.co.il/nrg/online/47/ART2/359/138.html

Ziv, Oren. "IDF Falsely Arrested Photographers During Palestinian Protest, Court Rules." +972 *Magazine* (23 August 2015). https://www.972mag.com/idf-falsely-arrested-photographers-during-palestinian-protest-court-rules/110928/

Zonshein, David. "Going to War with Cameras [in Hebrew]." *Haaretz.com* (27 May 2014).

Zonszein, Mairav. "Violence Is a Cruel Reminder of a Reality That Is Neither Calm nor Stable." +972 *Magazine* (30 April 2013). https://www.972mag.com/violence-is-a-cruel-reminder-of-a-reality-that-is-neither-calm-nor-stable/

Zureik, Elia. "Colonialism as Surveillance." In *Israel's Colonial Project in Palestine: Brutal Pursuit* (pp. 95–134). Abingdon, Oxon; New York: Routledge, 2016.

Zureik, Elia, David Lyon, and Yasmeen Abu-Laban. *Surveillance and Control in Israel/Palestine: Population, Territory and Power*. Abingdon, Oxon; New York: Routledge, 2010.

Index

Note: page numbers in italics refer to figures.

Stanford Studies in Middle Eastern
and Islamic Societies and Cultures

Joel Beinin and Laleh Khalili, editors

EDITORIAL BOARD
Asef Bayat, Marilyn Booth, Laurie Brand, Timothy Mitchell,
Jillian Schwedler, Rebecca L. Stein, Max Weiss